Reading Hemingway's *Men Without Women*

D1602106

READING HEMINGWAY SERIES

ROBERT W. LEWIS, EDITOR

Reading Hemingway's *Men Without Women*

GLOSSARY AND COMMENTARY

Joseph M. Flora

The Kent State University Press

KENT, OHIO

© 2008 by The Kent State University Press, Kent, Ohio 44242
All rights reserved
Library of Congress Catalog Card Number 2008014201
ISBN 978-0-87338-943-3
Manufactured in the United States of America

Library of Congress Cataloging-in-Publication Data
Flora, Joseph M.
    Reading Hemingway's Men without women : glossary and commentary / Joseph M. Flora.
        p.   cm. — (Reading Hemingway series)
    Includes bibliographical references and index.
    ISBN 978-0-87338-943-3 (pbk. : alk. paper) ∞
    1. Hemingway, Ernest, 1899–1961. Men without women.   I. Title.
    PS3515.E37M44 2008
    813'.52—dc22   2008014201

British Library Cataloging-in-Publication data are available.

12 11 10 09 08   5 4 3 2 1

I.M.

James Arthur Flora (1945–2003)

CONTENTS

PREFACE AND ACKNOWLEDGMENTS

When *Men Without Women* appeared in bookstores in October 1927, Ernest Hemingway was riding the fame that *The Sun Also Rises* had just secured him. Wishing to build on that foundation, Maxwell Perkins, his Scribners editor, had encouraged a second collection of short stories. Perkins believed that short stories, especially when collected, helped keep the public aware of an author and helped prepare the way for the novel in progress. Perkins knew, of course, that Hemingway had been writing and publishing stories—an important part of the young writer's efforts to secure an adequate income. He also knew how good Hemingway could be in that genre. It had been, after all, Hemingway's stories that brought Perkins to champion Hemingway's genius. The introduction had come through F. Scott Fitzgerald, who had been awed by the force of Hemingway's eighteen vignettes that William Bird's Three Mountain Press had published in 1924 as *in our time* in a run of 170 copies. (The next year those vignettes became interchapters for the sixteen short stories of Hemingway's first commercially published book; it used the same title of its predecessor but with standard capitalization: *In Our Time*.) Fitzgerald admonished Perkins to do whatever was necessary to get Hemingway away from the publisher Boni and Liveright and under the more prestigious Scribners imprint. In one of the most craftily plotted schemes in twentieth-century publishing, Perkins and Hemingway maneuvered to fulfill the legalities of his contract with Boni and Liveright and then enter into agreement with Scribners, where he would remain. Boni and Liveright had first right of refusal on Hemingway's next book. So he quickly wrote *The Torrents of Spring*, a parody of Sherwood Anderson, their famous author. As Hemingway expected, Boni and Liveright balked, and Hemingway was free to go elsewhere. Scribners quickly published the novel in 1926.

Hemingway's good fortune in having Perkins as editor was soon manifest. The reviews of *Men Without Women* left no doubt that Ernest Hemingway ranked among the major talents of the era. This was a collection of stories that could not be ignored. If some of the reviews caused Hemingway distress, Perkins was greatly pleased by the response. "Not one harsh note in the critical chorus," he headlined an advertisement teeming with glowing quotes that he forwarded to the author. Charles Scribner could rest assured that Perkins had made a good decision. Hemingway had to be pleased by the brisk pace of sales, which far exceeded those of most story collections, and he was soon earning more from his writing than he had at any other time in his life.

But money could not be for Hemingway—nor for us—the ultimate measure of a book's worth. Let's look more closely at the publication of *Men Without Women*.

The first review that Hemingway saw was by Virginia Woolf in the *New York Herald Tribune Books*. Beginning with reflections on the difficult task presented reviewers, she admits that there is ample room for a reviewer to miss the mark. Hemingway scholars, who have pondered the text longer than Woolf or most reviewers could, concur that Woolf did miss the mark. She objected to the heightened masculinity of the book emphasized in its title ("ferocious virility," Cyril Connolly called it), disliked his characters and compared them unfavorably to those of Chekhov and Maupassant, and faulted his overreliance on dialogue. She had to grant Hemingway a place among the moderns but did not find him modern in ways she and her circle championed. But no reader of her review—to which the entire first page of the book section (and more) was given—could doubt Hemingway's importance. *Men Without Women* received the kind of attention that would go to a novel. And it is likely that the modernity for which Woolf faulted Hemingway was the kind many found compelling. Her review alone reveals that the author of *The Sun Also Rises* had won his place in the major leagues.

Edmund Wilson, equal to Woolf's authority for American readers, ably countered the criticism that naysayers had voiced. In a lengthy review in the *New Republic*, he judged Hemingway's characters, notably Nick Adams and Jake Barnes, as "highly civilized persons of rather complex temperament and extreme sensibility." He grasped that *Men Without Women* bore important relationships to *In Our Time*. Clearly, he had more than passing familiarity with Hemingway's earlier work and could speak with an authority that Woolf, Joseph Wood Krutch (the *Nation*), Lee Wilson Dodd (the *Saturday Review of Literature*), and Cyril Connolly (the *New Statesman*) could not match. But even these adverse voices had to bow toward the young writer. Krutch cited a "virtuosity not short of amazing" and called the stories "painfully good." Dodd admitted to being "amazed" and "admire[d] the lean virtuosity." Connolly judged Hemingway "easily the ablest of the wild band of Americans in Europe."

In the *Bookman*, Burton Rascoe chose to emphasize the great merits of "Fifty Grand" and "The Killers," while admiring the "clean and incisive style" of the totality. In the *American Mercury*, H. L. Mencken praised the same two stories as "things to be sincerely thankful for." This was a good deal from the Sage of Baltimore, who had not been won over by *The Sun Also Rises* nor by Hemingway's preference for the "fragmentary."

If attention from the luminaries matters, so does anonymous attention in the right place. How to put a price on the unsigned review in the 24 October issue of *Time*, which, like some of the other important reviews, carried a likeness of the author? Unlike Woolf's more general reflections, this reviewer gives attention to the whole book, though he is sometimes careless with details. Still, the review ends by declaring *Men Without Women* a worthy companion to the powerful *The Sun Also Rises*. It describes the stories as "clear and crisp and perfectly shaped as icicles, as sharp as splinters of glass. It is impossible to read them without realizing that seldom if ever before has a writer been able to cut so deeply into life with the 26 curved tools of the English alphabet."

Publication of *Men Without Women* announced that the young Hemingway would be making his mark in short fiction as much as in the novel. For him, the short story was a congenial genre for the modernist sensibility. Indeed, *In Our Time* had already revealed his discovery that short stories, when gathered for a book, lent themselves to the larger aims of the novel. In many ways, *Men Without Women* mirrors that earlier experiment in form. (Later, Hemingway would virtually embed several novels in the great "The Snows of Kilimanjaro"; the dying protagonist is a writer who remembers incidents of his life that he should have written about but didn't.) Hemingway wrote several novels that continue to compel readers—though the novels have never eclipsed the great stories. Harold Bloom wrote: "It could be argued persuasively that Hemingway is the best short-story writer in the English language from Joyce's *Dubliners* until the present" (3). *Men Without Women* would doubtless play an important role in any such argument. Looking back at the publication of that book, Kenneth Lynn judged: "If *Men Without Women* was not destined to become the most widely influential book of short stories ever published by a twentieth-century American author, that was only because it followed *In Our Time*" (366). *Benét's Reader's Encyclopedia of American Literature* declared: "Some of the finest examples of Hemingway's mastery of description, dialogue, and atmosphere appear in this volume" (Perkins, Perkins, and Leininger 702). Hemingway himself sensed no diminishment from *In Our Time*. He wrote Maxwell Perkins that it had taken him five years to write the stories of *In Our Time* and five years to write the stories for *Men Without Women* (*Letters* 273). That a study of *Men Without Women* takes its place in the Kent State University Press series dedicated to exegeses of Hemingway's chief works is entirely appropriate.

The aim of this book is not, of course, to have the final word on the meaning of the stories that compose *Men Without Women*. Rather, the study attempts to probe the events of each story as we encounter them. It seeks to explain historical references, to identify allusions, to see how form suggests meaning. To borrow Robert Lewis's metaphor, the study is intended as a tourist guide. Those who have traveled the route often will find much that is familiar, but more recent travelers may find material that will open the stories in new ways. My hope is that even travelers familiar with the Hemingway terrain will find unexpected rewards.

For the journey, I begin with a brief introduction to each story. For examination of the story itself, I have selected segments of text to focus attention on, for which I cite page and line numbers from the Finca Vigía edition of *The Complete Short Stories of Ernest Hemingway*.

The illustrations near the middle of the book provided me an opportunity to accent key thematic values, not just for the story that occasioned the choice but for the work as a whole.

From the start, *Men Without Women* seems intent on destabilizing the reader, placing that reader in unfamiliar territory. Literally and figuratively, the reader is "in another country." The first photograph depicts Madrid's Puerta del Sol, much as it would have looked when Hemingway first saw this square and recognized its emotional power as the Gate of the Sun and the heart of the Spanish capital. Immersion into Spain is integral to the experience of *Men Without Women*. For Hemingway, nothing was more revealing about the Spanish soul than the corrida. Two illustrations represent the bullfight, the central drama of "The Undefeated," the long story that Hemingway placed first. Hemingway often played the teacher, and one of his goals in the story was to educate Americans about the corrida. A matador is the chief player in that drama, but he works with a team. The crucial member of the matador's team is the picador, who from his horse "pics" the bull and prepares him for the mortal combat with the matador. Zurito is the extraordinary picador of "The Undefeated." The professional in the second photograph is meant to evoke that majestic figure. Following the picador, we see the matador at the climactic moment of the kill, the moment that, more than any other, tests his quality. It represents what might lead an *aficionado* (Hemingway's term for the knowledgeable and sympathetic spectator; see Hemingway's "An Explanatory Glossary" in *Death in the Afternoon*) to feel something akin to Henry James's announcement of his own death: "So here it is at last, the distinguished thing." Both illustrations show a man on trial in a public arena, to be judged rightly or wrongly by the multitude. Both accent the masculine emphasis that disturbed Virginia Woolf. The picador and matador in the pictures are in bright sunlight, a condition integral to the ideal corrida. I hope that the reader of this book will look back a second time and then imagine these figures in the darkness of a nocturnal corrida, the only assignment that Manuel, the bullfighter of "The Undefeated," can obtain.

The Manuel of "The Undefeated" owes much to Hemingway's appreciation for the young torero known as Maera, who died from pneumonia rather than in the bullring. His death provides the stark ending to the brief "Banal Story." As its title suggests, that narrative is about story as well as about history. Metafiction is a recurrent theme in *Men Without Women*. The reader who turns to the photographs of Maera that Hemingway selected to illustrate his *Death in the Afternoon* will be well rewarded.

Though several stories show us Americans in Europe, Hemingway calls none to our attention in the opening story. Eventually, however, the collection makes America important in the book's dynamic, even when it does not seem to do so. The American presence in Europe is clearly to the fore in "Hills Like White Elephants," with the railroad station near Casetas in the Ebro Valley of Spain giving Hemingway the setting for his story of two American travelers. Making adjustments to the setting as necessary to heighten meaning, he created one of the most haunting stories of the tension between the sexes in the twentieth century. Travel, speed, uncertain destinations, and uncertain relationships play across this and other stories of *Men Without Women*. Like T. S. Eliot's *The Waste Land* (the 1922 poem that is the essence of high modernism), *Men Without Women* has a pronounced international flavor. Not surprisingly, structural and thematic connections between Hemingway's book and Eliot's poem are numerous.

Men Without Women creates a literary landscape that highlights motion, transience, hotels, rented rooms, hospitals. Two Nick Adams stories in the book demand reflection on domestic structures; those structures help define the gender issues important to the book as a whole.

When only weeks old, Ernest Hemingway had been carried from the house in Oak Park, Illinois, where he had been born, to the shores of Walloon Lake in northern Michigan. The family built there a cottage that his mother named Windemere. Here Hemingway spent summers during his childhood and early manhood; here he would spend his honeymoon following his marriage to Hadley Richardson on 3 September 1921. By then the cottage had expanded from the one Ernest first entered. Primarily, the cottage represented the values that we associate with Dr. Clarence E. Hemingway, Ernest's father. In time, Grace Hall Hemingway, Ernest's mother, had to escape her husband's house and eventually insisted on building Grace Cottage on the other side of the lake, where she would sometimes retreat. Significantly, Nick's father is the one with whom Nick shares the cottage in "Ten Indians." The family cottage is an important structure in "The Doctor and the Doctor's Wife," but we never see Nick in the family cottage in that *In Our Time* story—even when his mother summons him to her room. When in *In Our Time* a Nick now in young manhood enters a cottage in "The Three-Day Blow," it is the cottage of his friend Bill, and it is sharply defined as a space for men without women.

In Charles M. Oliver's ever-useful *Ernest Hemingway A to Z* the reader can find a photograph (353) of Windemere as one would see it coming from the lake. That view shows the public face of a family. Illustrations #5 and #6 of this book take us inside that family cottage, views that invite reflection on the family dramas enacted there. A look inside the fictional Adams cottage is even rarer. In *Men Without Women*, "Ten Indians" provides a revealing visit inside.

Shown in photograph #7 is the Hemingway home in Oak Park, Illinois, 600 North Kenilworth Avenue at the corner of Iowa Street. A side view would highlight even more the massiveness of the house planned by Grace and built with funds from her inheritance upon the death of her father. To the left, we see a large music room, one befitting her successful career as a teacher of voice. The music room dwarfs the medical suite at the front of the house where her husband saw his patients. (In her later years, Grace sold the house, and subsequent owners removed the music room.) In the final story of *Men Without Women* Nick remembers a house very like this one, and the memory is painful. In no Hemingway story do we see Nick inside the family house. The domestic structures evoked in this book reflect a powerful dynamic of Hemingway's fiction.

The final photograph shows Lt. Ernest Hemingway back in Oak Park in 1918; it was in many ways a troubled homecoming. Like Nick Adams in "Now I Lay Me," the final story of *Men Without Women*, Hemingway would ponder the heritage of the house that his mother had built and what he had learned as an ambulance driver from the crucible of duty on the Italian front in the Great War (World War I). Tellingly, the photograph shows him outside Oak Park High School, where he first gained praise for his fledgling fiction. The reader might recall the rural schoolhouse that the Garner family and Nick Adams pass on their journey home after their "swell" Fourth of July in Petoskey in "Ten Indians." (Constance Cappel Montgomery provided a glimpse of this school in her *Hemingway in Michigan*.) Nick never attended this school, but its presence in the story accents the education that Nick receives before the day ends. His lesson is painful. Each of the Nick Adams stories in the book furthers his education, and the training is sometimes harsh.

The photograph of Hemingway beside his high school should also remind us that he had come close to death from an Austrian trench mortar. Recuperation would be lengthy, as would the recuperation from the end of his romance with the American nurse Agnes von Kurowsky, who had helped care for him in a Milan hospital. That recuperation helped shape "Now I Lay Me." The first story having established the bullfight as an arena to study death, the last story further explores the arena of war. War and its aftermath are also dominant motifs of the book as a whole—as is the possibility for recuperation.

My own journey with Hemingway's stories began when I was an undergraduate. In freshman English we read "The Short Happy Life of Francis Macomber" in *The Quarto of Modern Literature*; everything in the story seemed important, and I cared greatly. The next year in a sophomore elective, I revisited Macomber and encountered for the first time "My Old Man" and "In Another Country." The textbook was *Ten Modern Masters: An Anthology of the Short Story*. The instructor did not have to labor to convince me that Hemingway was a master. And so he has seemed ever since. In time I would have the privilege of exploring his stories and novels with bright college students and with adults in post-baccalaureate settings. Hemingway was always among the most teachable of writers. Increasingly, he became one of my chief subjects for study. His stories contain secrets—secrets inviting rereading and providing unexpected rewards. In part, this study has been a search for secrets I missed in earlier readings.

My debts are many. The first "critics" to aid my understanding would be those early teachers. In graduate school, I discovered the first great wave of Hemingway scholarship. Those voices are now stilled, but their words on the page continue to merit attention. Meanwhile, other critical voices have been eager to share their findings. The pace of discovery has quickened considerably in the past decades as previously unpublished Hemingway material has appeared. Hemingway could still seem very wonderful, but in ways few readers in his lifetime imagined. There is more than a little truth in the proclamation of Nancy R. Comley and Robert Scholes: "The Hemingway you were taught about in high school is dead. *Viva el nuevo Hemingway*" (146). The Hemingway Society added immeasurably to the excitement of my Hemingway explorations. Many people I knew only in print became colleagues and often friends.

For encouragement, support, and suggestions on this project I must salute especially Robert W. Lewis, general editor for this series, and two readers who generously gave of their time by giving my efforts the benefit of their vast experience. Thank you, Larry Grimes; thank you, Bickford Sylvester. Barbara Sylvester also gave the manuscript the benefit of her trained eye. A special tip of the hat also to the late Paul Smith and the late Jim Hinkle for inspiration, encouragement, and knowledge.

It was a privilege to have the ever-generous Michael Reynolds as a close neighbor while he taught at North Carolina State University and also to have Linda Wagner-Martin join the faculty of my department. Linda often shared Hemingway news and books, and inevitably we would talk Hemingway together with graduate students. Reynolds Price, at Duke University, only eight miles away, has stood steadfastly as a Hemingway enthusiast. He calls himself perhaps Hemingway's greatest admirer.

Farther from home base, I would have frequent opportunity to talk Hemingway with John Fenstermaker, Allen Josephs, and Linda Miller. Although I might mention virtually the entire membership of the Hemingway Society, I would be remiss did I not thank, and praise, Susan F. Beegel, H. R. Stoneback, Jim Meredith, Jack Benson, Bert Bender, Earl Rovit, Gerry Brenner, Scott Donaldson, Paul Montgomery, and Jack Bryer.

Skilled with a camera as well as a text, Allen Josephs understood the moments I wanted to accent with illustration and shared his slides. In Spain, José Ortiz Sánchez located photographs of Madrid's Puerta del Sol. For the photograph shared here I thank the Museo Municipal de Madrid. For the photograph of the Hemingway house in Oak Park and for the photographs of Windemere interiors, I am indebted to the Marceline Hemingway Sanford Collection and to the Ernest Hemingway Foundation of Oak Park as well as to Gwenda Connor, administrative director of the foundation. A tip of the hat to Barbara Ballinger, who on short notice led me to the Windemere archives. I thank also Neal Morris at the University of North Carolina at Chapel Hill for his professional skill in getting the illustrations into digital format.

At the University of North Carolina, chair of the English department James Thompson furthered the project by granting me a research leave. Information, kindnesses, and encouragement have come from Susan Marston, Boone Turchi, Helen Brantley, Frank C. Wilson, Rebecca Christenberry, and indubitably Christine Flora.

The enthusiasm of the Kent State University Press for the Reading Hemingway Series has been constant. Joanna Hildebrand Craig, former assistant director and editor-in-chief, became an active participant in the Hemingway Society. Mary D. Young, managing editor, has demonstrated support no less vigorous. Able guides they have been. I was fortunate to have Sonia Fülöp as my copyeditor. She asked the right questions, reflecting no doubt her familiarity with matters Hemingway gained by her copyediting of H. R. Stoneback's *Reading Hemingway's* The Sun Also Rises. Working with the practiced hands at the Press has been a pleasure. I thank them all.

JOSEPH M. FLORA
Chapel Hill, North Carolina

SERIES NOTE

The following commentaries are keyed to the page and line numbers of *The Complete Short Stories of Ernest Hemingway*, the Finca Vigía Edition, Charles Scribner's Sons. The stories that comprise *Men Without Women* begin on page 183 and conclude on page 282 of this edition. Line numbers begin with the first line of each page.

The commentaries can be read in tandem with *Men Without Women*, story by story, or all together after a complete reading of the whole text. The guide is like other reference works that may be consulted variously by different readers. We believe this *Reading Hemingway* book will greatly increase one's pleasure in and understanding of *Men Without Women* one of Hemingway's finest works.

Reading *Men Without Women*

THE UNDEFEATED

As the first story in the book, "The Undefeated" bears special importance. As lead story, it accents Hemingway's acclaim following the 1926 publication of *The Sun Also Rises,* his first major novel. But justification for the position of the story far exceeds any commercial promotion. The placement is important to the thematic development of the collection. With the female presence more distanced in "The Undefeated" than in any of the thirteen stories of the book, the story merits priority as a story about men without women. It is certainly about the identity of one's self through profession. And while the narrative passionately studies the art of bullfighting, it speaks also to the art of writing—a concern that keeps surfacing throughout the book. The lead story alerts readers to search not only for victors but also for the company of the vanquished.

In *The Sun Also Rises,* bullfighting involved valor (and death) in the bright sun of a Spanish afternoon. In "The Undefeated," the bullfighting (and the majority of the narrative) takes place at night. Darkness also pervades the final story of *Men Without Women,* "Now I Lay Me."

The Sun Also Rises led many readers to a fascination with the culture of the bullfight. "The Undefeated" gave Hemingway opportunity to instruct readers in a more detailed way on the intricacies of the bullfight and the dynamics of the bullfighting world. He had begun that instruction in a report for the *Toronto Star Weekly* published on 20 October 1923 as "Bullfighting a Tragedy" (*Dateline* 340–46). He followed it more ambitiously in the interchapters of *In Our Time.* Those short pieces, chapters 9–14, anticipate the fuller treatment in "The Undefeated" of such motifs as the crowd's behavior, thrown cushions, death from goring, and the cutting off of the pigtail. The reader of *Men Without Women* who has also read *In Our Time* will have added pleasure.

"The Undefeated" is among Hemingway's longest short stories and might even be considered a companion piece to "Big Two-Hearted River," the longest piece of *In Our Time,* as well as its concluding story, which thus prepares the reader for numerous linkages to *Men Without Women.* The two stories have common subjects and themes. Both depend on age-old traditions and rituals (fishing in "Big Two-Hearted River" and the bullfight in "The Undefeated"). Both stories emphasize craft, knowing what to do and how to do it. In both stories the central act involves coping with violence (past and present) to define the protagonist's personal worth. Both stories protest that man is not made for defeat. Both stories exclude female presence or influence.

183:1–4 Manuel Garcia . . . through the door. The opening sentence of the story not only places the story in Spain, giving first and last names to two Spaniards, but also dissuades the reader from expectations of an autobiographical story. Readers had, of course, been tempted to view Jake Barnes of *The Sun Also Rises* as an embodiment of the author; from publication, the novel was viewed as a roman à clef. Several stories from *In Our Time* had close links to Hemingway's life, and these linkages interested readers. And though several stories in *Men Without Women* would also cause readers to think of Hemingway the person, the lead story does not.

Named first, Manuel Garcia dominates the story, first to last. Not many of the first readers of *Men Without Women* would have been aware of the historical reference of the name. But five years later, in *Death in the Afternoon*, Hemingway would write at length about this matador: "He had a complete knowledge of the bulls and a valor that was so absolute and such a solid part of him that it made everything easy that he understood; and he understood it all. Also he was very proud. He was the proudest man I have ever seen" (78). "The Undefeated" echoes much of Garcia's story. Hemingway had used other aspects of Garcia's career in chapters 13 and 14 of *In Our Time*. There he is called Maera, as the historical Manuel Garcia was known. As the first words of the story, the full name accents Hemingway's fascination with this matador. "Maera" derives from *madera* (wood), the essential core.

Following her study of the manuscript versions of *Death in the Afternoon*, Susan F. Beegel makes a strong case that the Manuel of "The Undefeated" may owe even more to Manuel Garcia, El Espartero, who was gored to death in Madrid in 1894 (see her essay "The Death of El Espartero"). Concurrent with the young Hemingway's first corrida was born the instinct to explore its history.

The opening paragraph creates a special aura about the fictional embodiment. Emmanuel—"God with us"—is the name given by Isaiah (7.14) for the messiah. The verb *climbed* suggests a strenuous effort, as if Manuel has struggled up to some Golgotha. At this point, the reader does not know what is in the suitcase Manuel puts down, but it suggests a heavy burden. And Manuel is given special insight here: he feels that someone is in the room, though no one has answered his knock. The image here suggests Holman Hunt's painting *The Light of the World*. Hemingway was very familiar with that work from his childhood: his mother had presented a copy of it to her church as a memorial to her father. In 1933 Hemingway evoked the painting once again in his story with the same title as the painting.

The name Miguel Retana carries no similar fame in the history of bullfighting. Hemingway accents an important difference between the two men by placing "Don" before the second name. The title for a gentleman, the designation here carries a gentle barb. Retana represents the dark commercial side of bullfighting. In *For Whom the Bell Tolls,* Hemingway places a Retana in chapter 14, where Pilar describes her life with the matador Finito. During an evening of festivities, the former manager of the matador Rafael el Gallo recounts a story of Rafael's perfidy. An unidentified Retana is a listener at the table; Pilar assumes knowledge of the man whose interest has been piqued. Hemingway likely wishes the name to evoke memories of "The Undefeated" and a person who is cognizant of the machinations of the profession.

183:5–12 **"Retana" . . . Manuel said.** The first line of the story implies command. Its repetition adds to the sense of urgency as Manuel now bangs at the door. Retana, having heard that Manuel has been released from the hospital, knows who is outside the door. Retana's "Who's there?" poses a question he need not have asked. Manuel's voice is one Retana knows well; Manuel has answered Retana with the informal "Manolo." Retana knows as well the answer to his next question: he knows why Manuel has come. Manuel's simple answer makes primary in the collection a cri de coeur that pervades much of Hemingway's writing as well as a final agony of his own life.

183:13–17 **the door clicked . . . bull-fight posters.** Presumably Retana, without rising, has unlocked an electrically controlled door; there is no indication of another presence. When Manuel enters the room, Retana is already behind his desk at the far side of the room. The body language reveals Retana's determination not to let any but business concerns prevail. There is no bodily contact. In every sense, Retana seems a "little man." He borrows power from the stuffed bull's head that is directly behind him. The bull's head dominates the wall of photographs and posters. The bull personifies the threat of death that is basic to the human condition. Because the taxidermist is from Madrid, we may assume that we are in the Spanish capital, where audiences in the ring were especially demanding.

183:18–21 **little man sat looking . . . the desk.** Narrative repetition underscores the degradation of this exchange for Manuel. Retana uses silence and his gaze to discomfort Manuel as much as possible. When he breaks the silence, his declaration sets the value of Manuel's life very low: "I thought they'd killed you." For him, Manuel would be a statistic. His photograph is not mounted on Retana's wall. Identifying a character by a trait is a favorite narrative device of Stephen Crane, useful for creating an aura of a harsh naturalistic world, as in "The Blue Hotel." The reader knows Retana's name. Bypassing it for "the little man," Hemingway gains a heightened sense of the harsh commercial world, at the same time demeaning Retana's lack of moral fiber. Knocking on wood, Manuel acknowledges the role of luck in his fate—a concept with accompanying rituals in most sports and one that would become an increasingly insistent motif in Hemingway's work: that Frederic Henry loses his St. Anthony's medal in *A Farewell to Arms* is ominous; early in *The Old Man and the Sea*, Santiago says to Manolin, "If you were my boy I'd take you out and gamble. . . . But you are your father's and your mother's and you are in a lucky boat" (13).

183:22–27 **"How many corridas"** . . . **looked at Manuel.** The clipped dialogue furthers the sense that this is a conversation no one enjoys having; exchange of information is minimal, factual. *Corrida* is short for *corrida de toros*. When Manuel answers that he has had only one bullfight, the "little man" never seemed smaller. Sometimes "one" is enough. (As a "great banderillero" with Belmonte, Manuel Garcia fought ninety to a hundred times in a season; see Hemingway, *Death* 77). In another kind of arena, the obtuse might ask a soldier if he had been in only one battle. It all depends on the battle, on the bullfight. Retana had read about the "one" Manuel had been in—one that came near to costing Manuel his life. His continued gaze seems less in amazement at Manuel's survival than for interest in any further use he might have for Manuel. Bullfighting always carries the threat of serious injury or even death, and no matador can expect to retire without a trip to the infirmary.

183:28–184:8 **Manuel looked up . . . stuffed bull's head.** Retana's gaze is countered by Manuel's looking at the stuffed bull's head. Not only has Manuel seen this bull many times before; this bull has haunted his thoughts: nine years ago the bull killed his brother. Although Manuel cannot read the brass plate, the narrator permits the reader to do so. The bull's name, Mariposa, means "butterfly," an ironic name for so fierce a beast. The bullfighting public of Madrid would recognize the name as "a series of passes with cape" over the matador's shoulders. The matador faces the bull, "zigg-zagging slowly backwards, drawing the bull on with a wave of first one side of the cape, then the other." The series requires great knowledge of bulls in order to be executed properly. Doubtless, the bull Mariposa had earlier been identified as a brave one. He had "accepted" nine *varas* (lances) for seven *caballos* (horses)— the language of the inscription suggesting a transaction, one that resulted in the death of the bull as well as of the apprentice bullfighter (*novillero*). Antonio Garcia died on 27 April 1909. This date places present time at 1918—pairing the ritualistic killing in the arena with the horror of the Great War. What Hemingway hints at here, he makes explicit in *Death in the Afternoon*: "The only place where you could see life and death, *i.e.*, violent death now that the wars were over, was in the bull ring" (2). It is the narrator who shares the inscription. Manuel "could not read it"— perhaps because the distance from his side of the desk is too great, but the line may indicate that his knowledge of the written word is minimal. Manuel's judgment is wrong: the purpose of the inscription is not in memory of his brother but in memory of the bull.

184:9–14 **"The lot"** . . . **"your cap."** Manuel's study of Mariposa leads Retana to soften his stance, granting that Mariposa was a worthy opponent, unlike the sorry bulls that the Duke of Veragua has just sent him. The great matador requires a brave and strong bull. In *Death in the Afternoon,* Hemingway reflects at length on the crucial role of the *ganadería* (the bull ranch) in the enterprise.

Retana has finally become interested in talking with Manuel, as is reflected in his "leaning back" and inviting Manuel to sit down and remove his cap. The invitation has come tardily.

184:15–29 **Manuel sat . . . watched him smoking.** Cap removed, Retana can better view the matador. The "one" corrida of the past year has "changed" Manuel's face. Retana notes that Manuel doesn't "look well," but the narrator sees more. Retana notes that Manuel's *coleta* (his pigtail—the mark of the matador) is pinned forward on his head so as not to show under the cap. Manuel the matador seeks another fight so that he might sport that *coleta* less strangely. But from the narrator's perspective, the strange look of Manuel marks him for death—as many years later in *A Moveable Feast* Hemingway would describe the poet Ernest Walsh as a man "marked for death" (123).

Manuel clarifies that he is just out of the hospital. How serious his wound has been is emphasized not only by his paleness but also by the rumor Retana has heard about the loss of a leg. The leg is the usual spot for wounds in bullfighting; the wound also links Manuel with Nick Adams, who in *In Our Time* in "The Battler" has been tossed from a boxcar and lands on his knee and who in "Cross-Country Snow" cannot do a telemark while skiing. In *Men Without Women* in "In Another Country," we learn unmistakably that Nick had been hit in battle on the Italian front of the Great War. The sympathy for Manuel that Retana has held at bay surfaces with his deeper look at the now capless bullfighter. Although he offers Manuel a cigarette, he does not join him in the ritual. (In "Big Two-Hearted River," the last story of *In Our Time,* Nick Adams smokes a cigarette as he recovers from the shock of seeing the burned country near Seney, Michigan.) Watching Manuel smoke, Retana begins to chart his own plan. Tellingly, he has remained on his side of the desk.

184:30–39 **"Why don't you"** . . . **"Tomorrow night."** Before making his own offer, Retana suggests the alternative that Manuel "get a job" and "go to work." Retana has been dealing with matadors for many years, and he knows that the practical advice will not be heeded. Manuel defines himself by his profession: to work is to be a bullfighter. Though Manuel may laugh at Retana's glib response, "Yes, while you're in there," he disregards the warning in the response. Just released from the hospital as he is, his visit to Retana carries a good deal of hubris. Nevertheless, wounded bullfighters were usually eager to return to the arena. Manuel is not unusual.

Sphinx-like, Retana continues to study Manuel before offering to put him in a nocturnal. There is no balancing pause from Manuel—and he quickly asks, "When?" That Retana can promise the following night suggests a callousness to match Manuel's hubris.

184:40–185:10 **"I don't like" . . . "or leave it," Retana said.** Having set aside medical wisdom that would mandate against returning to the ring immediately following his release from the hospital, Manuel pauses over the superstitious (or supra-rational) consideration: substituting brings bad luck. The rational mind would question Manuel's cause-effect assumptions. Salvador may not have been in good condition for the fight; possibly he was past his prime. Arguing for a fight in a week (when he presumably would feel stronger), Manuel appears to wish to convince himself as much as Retana: "I've got a lot of stuff." Retana turns to the practical concerns of managing his business, but his statements emphasize the importance of audience to the bullfight. It matters only if the audience is present—unlike Nick's fishing in "Big Two-Hearted River." Like the heroes of ancient epics and sagas, the bullfighter puts his life at risk for a people. "The Undefeated" gives a great deal of attention to the worth of the audience but never minimizes its importance. For Retana, it's all about money. Manuel would not draw, though in an earlier time he would have: "They don't know who you are any more." Manuel touts the youth of the current favorites: Litri, Rubito (The Blond One), and La Torre (The Tower), all "kids." In the nocturnal, Manuel will work with "young" Hernandez and face two *novillos* (underaged or overaged bulls). These are names of current bullfighters. Since time present in the story is 1918, Hemingway can quietly parallel their forays into their craft in the very period when he was making his own. Manuel's assignment with the young makes clear his standing in his profession—and his desperation. In *Death in the Afternoon,* Hemingway explains: "Novillada is a bullfight in which bulls which are under aged, or over aged, for a formal bullfight, that is, under four years and over five, or defective in vision or horn, are fought by bullfighters who have either never taken or renounced the title of matador de toros" (426). The majority of the deaths in the bullring come in the *novilladas.* The assignment will come late in the schedule—following the "Charlots," the Charlie Chaplin comic routines. When Manuel inquires whose *novillos* he will face, Retana makes clear that the stock will be inferior; the question helps define the nature of the *novillada.* Manuel knows well their makeup, but he again sets aside the rational and repeats his conviction that substituting brings bad luck. He makes the ploy in the fading hope that Retana will give him a better assignment.

185:11–29 **He leaned forward . . . in his pocket.** Retana's body language leaves no doubt that Manuel has but one possibility for a fight. Retana is not desperate to get Manuel. He wants to make a saving by replacing Larita, but he knows he can get others cheaply too. He tells himself, realizing how weak Manuel is, that he would like to help him. He would better "help" Manuel by refusing to give him a fight until he is stronger. The negotiation over the amount that Manuel will be paid qualifies considerably the amount of compassion Retana feels for "Manolo," the familiar form of the name he uses to his own advantage in the negotiation. The negotiation exemplifies Hemingway's statement in *Death in the Afternoon* about finances and the present-day *novillada,* which came about "through the desire to present a regular bullfight at less than formal prices due to the bulls being bargains and the men, due to a desire to present themselves and make a name, or to the fact that they have failed as formal matadors, are less exigent in their demands for money than the full matadors" (426–27). The fifty pesetas that Retana advances Manuel is all that Manuel's participation ends up costing him. The bullfight represented many things to Hemingway—a heightened test of manhood; confrontation of one's mortality; art of the highest order, comparable to tragedy—but he emphasized that the bullfight is also a business.

185:30–186:16 **"What about"** . . . **until it clicked.** Salary settled, Manuel inquires about the support team—the cuadrilla made up of bullfighters, picadors (who on their horses stab the bull, weakening it but also enraging it), and banderilleros (bullfighters who help run the bull with the cape and place the decorated barbed darts into the bull's neck or shoulder muscles). These are matters Manuel more reasonably would have addressed before agreeing on that salary. Manuel knows well what the "boys" who work nights for Retana are like—and Retana refuses to fund the "one good pic" that Manuel insists that he needs. (Hemingway has shortened *picador,* giving it a more informal flavor; *pic* is not a term that a Spaniard would say or write. But for an English-speaking audience, Hemingway has good precedent on his side. Chaucer's monk in *The Canterbury Tales* is a "prikasour," a hunter on horseback: "Of prikyng [pricking or spurring a horse] and of hunting for the hare / Was all his lust" (lines 190–91, General Prologue). "The Undefeated" uses *pic* as a verb as well as a noun. In *Death in the Afternoon,* Hemingway calls the ill-paid picador "the roughest and most constantly exposed to danger of death" of civil professions (436). To have any chance of success, Manuel realizes that he needs a good picador. Retana's desire to "help" Manuel has completely dissipated; Manuel will have to settle for Retana's team or fund that one picador who will give him "an even break." As Manuel makes his exit, Retana stays behind his desk. His last words bespeak the harsh realities of Manuel's situation: "Shut the door." When Manuel does so, and the door clicks, his fate is sealed.

186:17–23 **He went down . . . into a café.** Manuel's descent into the bright afternoon sun contrasts with the darkness of Retana's office. But the brightness is "hot" and threatening. He walks toward the Puerta del Sol, the Gate of the Sun, a landmark in the middle of Madrid and Spain. In *Death and the Sun*, Edward Lewine writes: "Madrid may be a young city with little indigenous culture in comparison to a place like Sevilla, but all of Spain is in Madrid, in its museums, its churches, its royal places, in its restaurants, and even in its people. A grand mix of immigrants from across the country" (124). Although the Puerta is walking distance from the ring, it is not a short walk (signaled in the story by the many people he passes and the intersecting streets that interrupt the available shade). Manuel is carrying a suitcase. Probably he walked from the hospital to the ring. This man needs rest.

Certainly, no one met him upon his release, and he sees no one he knows on this walk. Manuel is not only without a woman; he is very much alone. But he has a destination, a café, one he knows.

186:24–35 **quiet in the café . . . Manuel said.** The quietness of the café suits Manuel's need; he seeks its quietest place in a small room at the back. That none of the men in the café speak to Manuel would confirm Retana's judgment about his appeal on the program. The waiter recognizes Manuel but is unimpressed by his appearance following an absence of some length. He remembers, however, what Manuel desires—"a shot of the ordinary" with his coffee and milk—and he is quite willing to share what he knows about Zurito's whereabouts. It is significant that Manuel asks about Zurito before he places his order. Time is short for him to find his "one good pic." Hemingway models his fictional picador on the splendid matador Antonio de la Haba, called Zurito, and on Antonio's father and brother. "Zurito was the son of the last and one of the greatest of the old-time picadors" (*Death* 254). Old Zurito brought up the other son to be a picador, one who "has a perfect style, great courage, is a splendid horseman and would be the best picador in Spain but for one thing. He is too light to be able to punish the bulls" (*Death* 258). Old Zurito's family is not lucky, but Hemingway admires it greatly, as is reflected by the extended treatment he gives it in *Death in the Afternoon*.

186:36–187:38 **waiter came back . . . not interested in him.** When the waiter returns, he is accompanied by a coffee boy, a waiter in training. The boy says nothing while serving Manuel, but his presence is useful for the youth-age drama so important to the story. His apprenticeship in a café frequented by bullfighters accents the cultural importance of bullfighting in Spain. (In "The Capital of the World," a story first published in 1936, Hemingway made such boys central.) The boy is struck by Manuel's pale face. Winking at the boy as they note Manuel's pigtail, the waiter reveals his estimation of the failed bullfighter and then somewhat callously asks if Manuel will be fighting in the Charlie Chaplins (comic preludes not to be taken seriously), an assumption that embarrasses the boy. The waiter here is not the ideal of his profession. Manuel lets the implication pass as he tersely responds that he is in the "ordinary."

The waiter can brush off the sting Manuel must feel by stating that he understood that Chaves and Hernandez would be fighting in the main draw. Manuel must explain that Chaves "got *cogida.*" Being "tossed" by the bull is the occupational hazard, and the bullfighter knows that at some time he will "catch" the horn. The waiter seizes the news about Chaves and calls to his colleague in the next room. The waiter who quickly appears at Manuel's table may or may not be "Looie." The staff of the café wants more details. The circumstances of that billing have not concerned Manuel, but the waiter realizes that Manuel will be a substitute—the reminder of the ominous superstition. Manuel welcomes the comfort of his café au lait and brandy. They will not, of course, provide him with the nourishment he needs; his battered spirit welcomes a second shot of brandy.

As the coffee boy takes his departure, the waiters become more overbearing and a prelude to the study of the crowd that attends the bullfights the following evening. Retana, we recall, had asked Manuel what was being said at "the Café" about the duke's recent shipment of bulls. Manuel becomes a magnet for the waiters of the café, whose number reaches three but seems ever larger as Hemingway plays with identification labels. Initially called "a waiter," the first waiter eventually is called "the original waiter." Looie becomes the "other waiter" and then, after "a tall waiter" enters, "the short waiter." These self-proclaimed experts further question Manuel and share with each other their opinions of bullfighting in Madrid. The waiters understand a good deal about bulls and about Retana, but not as much as they think. The reader knows, of course, that neither Manuel nor Retana had brought up the subject of Chaves. Retana always has his sight on the next fight; Manuel is no stranger to the risks of the ring. He has recently been "hurt badly" himself. If the waiters know this, they have already forgotten it.

The tall waiter confirms quite accurately what the reader has recently witnessed: Retana wields tremendous power in the bullfighting business. He accents the sense of foreboding: "If you aren't in with him, you might just as well go out and shoot yourself." The tall waiter exudes assurance as he names fighters whom Retana has helped: Villalta, Marcial Lalanda, Nacional. The short waiter quickly agrees—minimizing along with the tall waiter the considerable merit of these matadors. In *Death in the Afternoon* Hemingway declares that competent aficionados are few (473). Callously, the waiters conduct their assessments in front of Manuel's table. Their words confirm Retana's assessment of Manuel's drawing power: "They were not interested in him."

187:39–188:2 **"bunch of camels" . . . the three . . . went out.** The tall waiter still leading, the three waiters mock the three matadors in the outer room as "camels." When the short waiter labels Nacional II "a giraffe," the tall waiter seizes the moment to emphasize Retana's power. (Height is not an advantage to the bullfighter.) Manuel can take no pleasure from the observations of these "experts." While they talk, he drinks the brandy that the careless waiter had "slopped over" into his saucer, a toast of sorts to bullfighters. As Manuel orders his third drink, he accents his disgust at the waiters, who ignore him while they make fun of other matadors of merit. The concentration of threes is pronounced: three waiters, three named matadors, three brandies.

188:3–10 **still asleep . . . went to sleep.** Brandy and sleep are boons to Manuel. Surely he needs the sleep, not, as he realizes, more of the hot afternoon sun. Wise to the ways of the world, he first secures his suitcase. His need for a good picador remains paramount in his thinking: he will wait for Zurito where he is.

188:11–17 **When he awoke . . . black Cordoba hat.** This paragraph contrasts with the opening scene of the story. Manuel is again across a table from someone, but the table does not impose the separation that the "big desk" represents. In place of the "little" Retana is a "big" man—Zurito, his heavy brown face like that of an Indian marks him as a man of the earth, not a tomb-like office. Waving the waiter away, Zurito shows a compassion for Manuel that no person in the story has yet shown him. Zurito is willing to wait for Manuel. In reading his papers, Retana had indicated that he wished Manuel gone; Zurito reads with different purpose— passing time while Manuel sleeps. The boon of good sleep he does not take lightly. That Zurito moves his lips as he reads further marks him as a man of the earth. His hat marks his origins in Cordoba, in southern Spain. The historical Zurito is from Cordoba: "dark and rather thin; his face was sad in repose; serious and with a deep sense of honor" (*Death* 254).

188:18–29 **Manuel sat up . . . folding the paper.** For the first time, the language of friendship enters the narrative. In addition to personal greeting, there is gentle humor when Manuel says he has been sleeping. There is honesty: Manuel admits things are not going well with him, as Zurito can clearly see in Manuel's "white face." Putting away his paper, Zurito lets us know that the bullfighter will receive his full attention. (Retana reads his papers when he wishes to dismiss Manuel.)

188:30–36 **"I got a favor" . . . two men at the table.** That Manuel has a better relationship with Zurito than he has with Retana is clear. He addresses Zurito with a nickname, Manos, short for *manosduros* (strong hands), the extended nickname. Those skilled hands are precisely what Manuel needs, as Zurito instinctively knows as he puts his hands on the table. Whereas the nonsmoking Retana offered Manuel a cigarette, Zurito suggests the communion of a drink together. The waiter who serves them senses the strength of their friendship.

188:37–189:6 **"What's the matter" . . . "any right to ask you."** Manuel requests that Zurito pic two bulls for him, the preparatory task for any bullfighter entering the ring. (Manuel will, as it happens, engage only one bull the next evening.) Using the more intimate form of Manuel's name, Zurito makes the asking of the favor as easy as he can, but he is quick in his refusal and firm and polite ("I'm sorry"). Zurito cannot have been surprised by Manuel's request. Manuel's resignation to the refusal does more to gain his end than argument—the tactic that he had taken with Retana—would have. Because Zurito cares for Manuel, he can't just walk away. In this dialogue of trust, Zurito can ask if the assignment is in a nocturnal; he is not surprised by the answer. Attempting to make his refusal seem reasonable, he cites his own age. Extending the conversation only increases the compassion he feels toward Manuel. He is appalled at the pathetic stipend Retana is paying, one that on the level of reason would put the issue beyond discussion. There would be no financial inducement for Zurito to sign on. In *Death in the Afternoon* Hemingway reports that matadors are the only bullfighters who make much money and that often even good picadors and banderilleros are poorly paid (201). Zurito, however, can command a good fee. Much more than reason or financial gain lies at the base of this conversation.

189:7–17 **"What do you keep on"** . . . **"going good lately."** Zurito's question is mainly rhetorical. Zurito understands more about the passion for bullfighting than he acknowledges. Still using the informal "Manolo," he argues that Manuel should cut off his *coleta,* signifying his retirement, a retirement that Manuel could justify with his age. (We do not know either Manuel's or Zurito's precise age. A matador who is still in the arena at forty-five would count himself very fortunate.) But Manuel wants to go out a winner; "an even break" might permit him to do that. The extended conversation increases the ominous sense that colors Manuel's plan. We respect Zurito's knowledge of bullfighting and bullfighters. Manuel "ought to get out and stay out." So reason would dictate. Given the result of Manuel's previous fight, Zurito does not seem convinced that he has "been going good lately." The reader has no way of knowing. It may be, of course, that bad luck broke the positive rhythm that Manuel avows.

189:18–37 **at his face** . . . **"I tell you."** Manuel's face is one of the recurring motifs of the story. Retana, the coffee boy, and now Zurito sense its message. Trying to prove that he was "going good" before he got hurt, Manuel cites the high praise in the press for his faena (the pass with the cape before the kill). Zurito says nothing in response to Manuel's defense. He again cites age as sufficient reason for a graceful exit. He prefers not to focus on performance, though he is finally pushed to declare that he knows the quality of Manuel's work well. Saying so is painful, and he avoids Manuel's eyes as he again urges retirement. Manuel would note the avoidance, for even as Zurito studies his face, he studies Zurito's. Pauses are important to the debate in progress. Finally, Zurito ceases his argument for retirement, stopped by Manuel's chorus that he is "going good."

189:38–190:8 **his hands on the table . . . "we'll eat."** Zurito has kept his hands on the table throughout the exchange. He is not a man to deceive. The body language here contrasts markedly with that of Retana behind the big desk. Leaning across the table, Zurito proposes a compact. He will pic for Manuel on the understanding that unless Manuel does very well, he will retire and cut the *coleta*. Zurito does not expect that Manuel will triumph, but the matador is all confidence, having secured Zurito's services. Zurito knows that only the night in the ring will settle the difference. He calls the waiter, letting us know that he is paying the bill. There is no mention of money for Zurito for his picing. Zurito's price has been, in fact, Manuel's agreement about the *coleta*. Zurito fully expects an outcome whereby Manuel will have to "cut the coleta," vowing that he will cut it off for him. But finally he simply marvels at Manuel's passion and lets Manuel's optimism conclude the exchange: "You won't have a chance." Manuel's euphoria is reminiscent of Nick's illusion about the Marge business at the end of "The Three-Day Blow" in *In Our Time*.

As the scene at the Puerta del Sol ends, Manuel's happiness is palpable. In limited space, Hemingway tells us much. Zurito is the one who calls the waiter and will likely tend to the reckoning. Then Zurito offers an invitation quite extraordinary in all of Hemingway's fiction. (Later in *Men Without Women,* Nick, in the story "Ten Indians," will be invited to have supper at the Garners' house, but he declines the invitation.) We sense immense compassion and affection as Zurito invites Manuel to "come on up to the house." Thrice Manuel will hear the words *come on.* The final time has the ring of benediction: "Come on up to the house and we'll eat."

When Manuel left Retana's office, he felt relief at having achieved a limited success, an agreement that was exploitive and probably foolhardy. But when Manuel prepares to leave the café at Puerta del Sol, he is "happy" because he has been able to convince "the best picador living" to pic for him. Because the story from the start has carried the tone of tragedy and its requisite sense of inevitability, the reader will read hubris in Manuel's euphoria: "It was all simple now." The scene does not end with those words, however, but with Zurito's invitation to go to his house. The placement makes clear the depths of Zurito's compassion and his understanding. The invitation carries overtones of the Eucharist, a last supper.

190:9–15 **Manuel stood . . . going on and on.** The printed text uses white space to convey the day's wait from Zurito's generosity to the nocturnal. From the noon sun of the preceding day, the story moves quickly to its greatest darkness. Manuel and Zurito stand side by side in the dark waiting for the Charlie Chaplins to end, waiting for their encounter with the bull. The reader is not told what Manuel is feeling; the narrator implies the intensity of the emotion by reporting that Manuel likes the smell of the horse stables (*patio de caballos*). The noise of the crowd anticipates their important role in events.

190:16–26 **"You ever seen"** . . . **in the patio.** Zurito knows that the tension in Manuel is keen, so he breaks the silence. It is not surprising that Manuel does not know the performers in the ring. For him, bullfighting is always of the utmost seriousness. It bespeaks tragedy, not comedy. The "fellows" to whom Zurito refers are short, like the tramp Charlie Chaplin portrayed, in marked contrast to himself, "big and looming." When the door opens, giving Manuel the view of the ring, he gets his look at the three Chaplin figures as they receive the applause of the crowd. Now that their act is over, Manuel feels the shift toward the moment of his own testing in the great arena, strikingly visible "in the hard light of the arc-lights." When the electric light goes on in the stable, the dark, essentially private wait ends.

190:27–191:9 **"I'll climb"** . . . **had gone through.** Zurito swings into action, heading toward the horse and instructing Manuel to gather the members of the cuadrilla, "the kids" on his team who have been watching the Chaplins from the runway between the *barrera* (a red fence around the sanded ring where the fight occurs) and the seats. The cuadrilla is composed of four picadors and four banderilleros who help run the bull with the capes and plant banderillas (harpoon-like instruments that catch under the skin) on the bull's withers. As the mules remove the dead bull from the Chaplins, Hernandez (identified in the café as a matador for the evening) appears and introduces himself; he exudes confidence. Calling him "a good-looking lad," the narrator reminds us that for a bullfighter, Manuel is "old." In close succession, the narrator identifies Hernandez as "the boy." The adjectives *cheerful* and *happy* describe him, suggesting emotions that Manuel cannot share. Hernandez speaks "cheerfully" as he comments on the size of the bulls. He has gained confidence from two previous nocturnals and the following he has acquired. He "grins" about the "beautiful" horses that the picadors are wrangling over because he knows that in the nocturnals there are no "beautiful" horses for this event. The mules return for the dead bull, signaling readiness for the procession (*paseo*) that will start the nocturnal.

191:10–22 **Manuel and Hernandez . . . in the dark.** A formal moment with the participants in place reflects the dignity of the bullfight. The comments of the picadors at the rear in the darkest part of the corral remind us of the compromises that Retana makes with that dignity, a grimly humorous accompaniment to their realization of decline: Retana "knows we'll be happier if we don't get a good look at these skins." The dark here is metaphorical as well as literal.

191:23–31 **Zurito said nothing . . . did not hear them.** Zurito knows a good horse just as Manuel knows a good picador. The narrator takes us into Zurito's mind, and Zurito's thought that the horse he had chosen "was all he needed" recalls Manuel's earlier "I've got to have one good pic." The corrida not only pits man against the un-tamed beast, but it also brings the domesticated animal against that untamed beast. The picador manages the domestic beast to stand against the untamed—bravery against bravery. This paragraph makes clear that Manuel has the picador he needs and his "fair chance." The paragraph crystallizes Zurito as the consummate profes-sional. He has discovered the quality of this horse, though that quality is not obvious to the others. His mind is focused on the fight ahead. He does not waste words, and he does not hear the other picadors. The reader mindful of Dr. Adams in "Indian Camp," the opening story of *In Our Time,* has a useful dramatic foil to Zurito. Dr. Adams tells Nick that he does not hear the screams of the woman on whom he oper-ates; he must focus on the medical challenge before him. At the same time, the doc-tor has failed to hear the silence of the woman's husband—also his patient, though he does not know it. Zurito, by contrast, comprehends the entire scene.

191:32–192:1 **The two matadors . . . "We'll go."** Waiting, Manuel thinks about the three *peónes* (helpers) behind them. Thinking of their age, he is also contemplating the future of bullfighting and, by implication, his own age. Like Hernandez, they are from Madrid and about nineteen. Their age doubtless causes him to remem-ber his brother. Of the three, Manuel is drawn to the gypsy—"serious, aloof, dark-faced," qualities that make us think of Zurito. Having ascertained the gypsy's name, Manuel gives him the first assignment. The narrator takes us briefly inside Fuentes's mind; we know that he is thinking about what he will do. The senior matador, Manuel, gives the signal for the formal entrance of the cuadrilla into the arena.

192:2–12 **Heads up, swinging . . . swept the sand smooth.** The bullfight is also color-ful spectacle. The procession, in prescribed costume that allows for personal style, marches across the arena to bow before the box of the president. The president is not necessarily an elected political figure, but the official charged with the conduct of the bullfight. His decisions determine if a bull is judged good enough to be in the corrida, and what honors, if any, will be bestowed. While the crowd cheers Hernan-dez, Manuel cannot miss their lack of affection for him.

The narrator wishes to create a detailed sense of what goes into a bullfight. He continues instructing readers, the majority of whom have never seen a bullfight, about its patterns and vocabulary. The heavy mantles for the procession, readers learn, must be replaced by lighter capes for the fight.

192:13–20 **Manuel drank . . . like Joselito and Belmonte.** The news that Retana has appointed a deputy to act as Manuel's sword handler and manager keeps him a looming presence. When Hernandez, who has been talking to his own manager, comes over, Manuel has the good grace to compliment him on his reception. Man-uel also receives a compliment—but only as the result of his question to his handler.

When the handler compares Manuel's entrance to those of the legendary Joselito (1895–1920) and Juan Belmonte (1892–1962), Manuel cannot evince the happiness that Hernandez shows. It remains to be seen if the handler (or anyone) might compare Manuel to the leading matadors of the golden age of bullfighting.

192:21–37 **Zurito rode by . . . with his left hand.** The pause before the appearance of the bull creates good drama. Zurito's apprehension as he rides in the strange "arc-light" helps create the sense of inevitability in the tragedy unfolding. The *toril* is the bull pen where the opponent that Zurito must pic is held. The exchange between Manuel and Zurito helps build the duration that creates tension and defines the picador's task: to weaken the bull with his jabs. "Cut him down to size" carries the precise verb. The long sentence describing Zurito makes specific the earlier description of him as an "equestrian statue," creating an impressive frozen moment. The slight movement of the horse's ears and Zurito's patting of the horse prepares the reader for the climactic moment when the energy of the bull will be released. The moment anticipates the scene in "The Short Happy Life of Francis Macomber," where in Hemingway's African story, the lion waits in the brush, "tightening into an absolute concentration for a rush" (16).

192:38–43 **red door of the *toril* . . . the dark pen.** The color red bespeaks the blood ritual about to unfold. The long-awaited moment when Manuel's antagonist appears has arrived, and the antagonist's power is fierce: "he came out in a rush." Because it is a nocturnal, the dark-light contrast contributes to the sense of a formal tragedy. In a narrative wherein point of view shifts frequently, the narrator takes the reader inside the mind of the bull. He was "glad" to be released.

192:44–193:2 **In the first row . . . "with plenty of gas—"** The event and the recording of an event are different matters. That a substitute bullfight critic is assigned this evening enhances the sense of tragedy and misfortune that overlays the story. The verb *scribbled* hints at more than penmanship. The critic can provide name, color, and number. But his "90 miles an hour" fails to measure up to the narrator's "he came out in a rush." Accounts of the corrida are not carried as sports news. Accounts are in a separate section of the paper, befitting the special place that the art has in Spanish culture. The fictional story aims to present bullfighting with an authenticity that a reporter or critic could not match. In *Death in the Afternoon,* Hemingway deals harshly with bullfight critics: they are, he charges, often paid to advance the career of a particular matador and have an influence far beyond what they deserve. A common name for a bull, *campagnero* means "bell-ringer," evoking a tolling church bell. We may also hear *campaña,* which means "military campaign" or "countryside." The bull brings to the heart of the city the elemental force of the country.

193:3–9 **Manuel, leaning . . . into the wood blindly.** The narrator contrasts the critic's seeing with Manuel's. Even before Manuel actually engages the bull directly, he is in the fight, directing it. The gypsy proves adept as he begins to tease the beast with his cape. When the bull charges him, his speed is made palpable as the gypsy vaults over the *barrera*. The narrator reminds us that the color of the fence is red, and the force with which the bull twice strikes it with his horns affirms the bull's power and the ease with which he in anger can seek blood.

193:10–13 **critic . . . lit a cigarette . . . "terrain of the bull-fighters."** The lighting of the cigarette reveals how jaded an observer the critic is. In contrast to the specificity of the gypsy's work with the bull in the preceding paragraph, he summarizes the action.

193:14–33 **Manuel stepped out . . . facing the bull.** The gypsy having completed his task, Manuel engages the bull, "swinging the cape just ahead of the horns." With each swing, the crowd shouts—identifying with the close encounter with the deadly horns. On the fifth swing, Manuel takes the bull even closer, the long sentence about the fifth swing capturing its grace. The movement leaves the bull facing Zurito "on the white horse." The image of Zurito on the white horse is an integral part of both paragraphs—linking the importance of the picador to the matador. After Manuel's sound performance, Zurito's skill is now necessary to weaken the bull.

Hemingway thought of the bullfight, a three-part drama (*tercios*), in terms of the classical tragedy, the first act leading to the picing of the bull on horseback. The preliminaries have taken us to that moment. (In the second act, the banderilleros, members of the team on foot, further weaken the bull by planting dowels with sharp points into his withers. In the climactic third act, the matador, on foot and alone, confronts the bull and is responsible for a clean killing.)

193:34–37 **second-string critic, drawing . . . "*tercio* of the cavalry."** Accenting the satire with his repetition of "second-string" and the cigarette, the narrator contrasts the majesty of his description of Manuel's efforts with the pedestrian prose of the critic. The critic does pay Manuel a compliment when he calls the fifth swing "very Belmontistic." All in all, Manuel's first efforts make a good beginning to his "return." In the veronica, the matador stands still and passes the cape before the charging bull; the *recorte* is "any pass with the cape in which it is snatched away from the bull or turned sharply from him; or quick movement which cuts the bull's charge; turning the bull on himself sharply with the consequent twist on his legs and spinal column" (*Death* 442).

193:38–194:20 **Zurito sat his horse . . . facing Zurito.** In a single sentence (long by the standards of the story) the narrator makes a single action of Zurito's picing the bull and lifting the horse into the air so that the horse passes over the bull but feels the bull's tail brushing his chest as the bull charges the cape that Hernandez now offers him. Although Hernandez successfully directs the bull toward the other picador, that picador cannot duplicate Zurito's picing. His lance only slides along the bull's back, and the horse is lifted and gored; the picador must be carried away and put on his feet. The death of a horse never provides pleasure in the arena, but the acceptance of the possibility is a condition of the corrida. The superior picador experiences this result less frequently—as the contrast here illustrates. Taking us into Manuel's consciousness, the narrator emphasizes the difference between the two picadors. Relieved that the fallen picador is okay, Manuel reflects on his good fortune in having Zurito on the team. He is comforted to see Zurito across the sand, "his horse rigid, waiting." With confidence he calls to the bull. The Spanish word *tomar* means "to take." One might translate the word as "Come on!" Getting the attention of the bull, Manuel performs an adept movement and brings the bull again opposite Zurito.

194:21–25 **"accepted a pair of *varas*"** . . . **"notably the *suerte*—"** The newspaper critic attempts literary flair as he describes the death of the horse: the bull accepting the *varas* for the death of one rosinante. The *vara* is the pic used in bullfighting. In his glossary to *Death in the Afternoon*, Hemingway has an illustration marking the degree of penetration possible with the *vara*. Rosinante is the name of Don Quixote's horse. The critic knows that the horse was an old nag. He aims for further humor when he writes that the bull "was clearly no horse-lover." He condescends to Zurito even as he praises his work: The "veteran Zurito resurrected some of his old stuff." A *suerte* is action taken according to the rules; the word also conveys luck, fate.

194:26–43 **"*Olé! Olé!*"** . . . **"a wonder,"** Manuel said. The man sitting beside the critic can appreciate what Manuel has just done much more than the critic can. Cheers and a slap on the back capture his approval, and the roar of the crowd also suggests that the nocturnal has given far more than a nocturnal usually does. It's a fine moment when the critic is jolted from his satisfied prose. Zurito again demonstrates his skill as a picador, and the precision of the narrator's sentences describing them contrasts with the critic's clever prose. Hernandez again proves the promising matador as he takes the bull out into the open arena under the bright light, where the crowd appropriately cheers. Zurito takes satisfaction in a job well done and characteristically pats the horse. Matadors, picador, horse have worked together. Zurito's picing merits Manuel's "It was a wonder."

194:44–195:8 **"I got him"** . . . **"at him now,"** Zurito said. Zurito's words cause the reader to ponder the weakened bull and his own skill. Twice Zurito says, "I got him that time." Twice he says, "Look at him now." The repetition accents the aging picador's ability to continue to perform superbly. But the repetition also cautions that we should not take our eyes from the worthy opponent. The bull counts as one of the undefeated of this story and of others in *Men Without Women*. Although he falls to his knees, he quickly gets up. As we look with Zurito and Manuel, we see the shine of the red blood flowing against the black of the bull's shoulder. Red, black, and white (here caught in the sand) are the emphasized colors of the story. Manuel pays tribute to his opponent: a good bull. Zurito's agreement is caught in his wish for "another shot."

195:9–33 **"I got to go" . . . That was Zurito.** Manuel, eager to perform with similar distinction, rushes to get into place. The *monos* (low-ranked workers, literally "monkeys") lead another horse forward—but not as Zurito would—toward the bull. Zurito has his horse under control and is able to move him toward the bull. His scowl results from the whacking of the horse by *monos*. Again the other picador fails to execute properly, and the bull is able to get beneath the horse. Such fare is what might be expected at a nocturnal.

The narrator presents the resulting chaos by going into Zurito's consciousness. A paragraph depicts what Zurito sees. The catalog comes in a series of fragments of energy through participles that seem to be poetry. The colors red and black are prominent. The paragraph begins with the frenzied *monos* and the inept picador ("swearing and flopping his arms") and concludes with the valiant Manuel spreading his cape before the lunging bull. After Manuel completes his veronica, the narrator takes the reader into Manuel's consciousness. Facing the bull, he sees the bull's head going down, readying for a charge. Close to the bull, he remains keenly aware of Zurito's location.

195:34–196:6 **Manuel flopped . . . no applause.** Manuel gets close to the bull's thinking as he resumes his cape work, ever mindful of the degree of danger. The sense of the close interaction between man and bull is interrupted by a one-sentence paragraph from the objective narrator: "The edge of the cape was wet with blood where it had swept along the bull's back as he went by." After Manuel completes the last of the veronicas and fixes the bull, the audience fails to show appreciation for what Manuel has achieved. Fixing the bull concludes the *tercio de varas*, the "act" of the pics.

196:7–22 **Manuel walked . . . "third of the palings."** Trumpets announce the start of the *tercio de banderillas*. *Monos* cover the dead horses with canvas and sprinkle sawdust around them. Manuel is thirsty from his strenuous effort, as his perspiration reveals. The critic also drinks, but a warm champagne—a fitting accompaniment to the half-hearted effort of his writing. Bored, he notes that the second third, the placing of the banderillas by men on foot (the word *palings* here means "pointed sticks"), is about to begin. In preparation for the *tercio de banderillas*,

Fuentes is ready with the banderillas, the sharp tools he will soon plant in the bull's withers; the narrator calls them "red sticks" to emphasize their purpose. In *Death in the Afternoon,* Hemingway describes this act of the corrida as the least complicated, best executed under five minutes lest the bull become "discomposed" (97).

196:23–39 **Alone in the center . . . from the crowd.** The bull remains a commanding presence, a being worthy to hold the center of the ring. The narrator makes every action he takes, from standing to catching the light on the steel points, important. Fuentes provides good theater as he "arrogantly" walks toward the bull, "unfixing" him. Doubtless, the crowd does not see the bull catch the light on the steel points of the banderillas, but the narrator does. That a single sentence describes the bull's charge, "his tail up," emphasizes his bravery, his potency, and the danger Fuentes faces. Fuentes meets the challenge with a skill that suggests the dancer as he "leaning forward drove the points into the bull's shoulder, leaning far in over the bull's horns and pivoting on the two upright sticks, his legs tight together, his body curving to one side to let the bull pass." The grace of his performance earns the crowd's "wild" approval—an approbation Manuel cannot equal. In *Death in the Afternoon* Hemingway describes the placing of the banderillas as the most picturesque part of the bullfight and that most pleasing to neophyte spectators. When he first began going to the fights, this act of the bullfight was the part that he did not like: the banderillas "seemed to make such a great and cruel change in the bull. He became an altogether different animal when the *banderillas* were in and I resented the loss of the free, wild quality he brought with him into the ring, the quality that reaches its greatest expression when he faces the picadors. When the *banderillas* are in he is done for. They are the sentencing" (98).

196:40–45 **bull was hooking wildly . . . new banderillas.** The narrator is also a fisherman, as he reveals in comparing the bull's jump to that of a trout that has just been hooked. The planting of the banderillas has let Manuel observe that the bull leads with his right horn. Hence, he sends the *peón* in with instructions for Fuentes to lead the next set of banderillas to the right.

197:1–14 **A heavy hand . . . make him manageable.** Zurito has also been watching the bull and Manuel carefully. He knows that a word of encouragement is in order, especially following the silence of the crowd during Manuel's last maneuvers. He echoes Manuel's earlier declaration (to him as well as earlier to Retana) that he is "going good." The last time that Manuel was "going good," he ended up in the hospital. Shaking his head now, Manuel will await the next and final third. And so the narrator again takes us into the drama of the waiting as Manuel assesses the corrida to the present moment. The area of doubt is substantial: he carries "a heavy sense of apprehension" as he plans his faena with the red cloth.

197:15–25 **was walking . . . wild about it.** As Fuentes proceeds with the new set of banderillas, he epitomizes flair. He walks "heel-and-toe, insultingly." He has the attention of the bull as well as the crowd. Staying close to the mind-set of the bull, the narrator accents the similarities between the opponents. Man and bull challenge each other. Through their cheers, the crowd becomes part of the sinking of the banderillas into the bull's shoulder muscles.

197:26–198:10 **"That kid" . . . He smiled.** With Retana's man and Zurito, we again watch Fuentes perform. A star is in the making. Fuentes gets "too damn close," Zurito says, but Fuentes is able to keep clear of the right horn as the bull is distracted by the capes the *peónes* had flopped over the *barrera* and crashes into the wood. Happy, Fuentes can point to his torn vest—a gesture pleasing to the crowd. Because the narrator has again gone into the bull's consciousness (the bull was sure that he could get Fuentes), the gypsy's moment is further heightened for the reader. Mentioned twice in the account of the second placing of the banderillas, Retana's man keeps us mindful that a bullfight is always business. Fuentes is having the triumph that Manuel has envisioned for himself.

198:11–26 **Somebody else . . . president must be.** As the arena is set for Manuel's third act, "nobody was paying any attention." Fuentes having demonstrated skill and style, the placing of the final pair of banderillas by another is less noteworthy, and the narrator omits detail. Manuel sweats because he is a man still weak from his recent injury and has already expended a great deal of energy. Sweat also confirms fear, apprehension. When Retana's man passes him the baton and the leather sword case, the narrative signals are not propitious. The narrator emphasizes the red of the muleta and the red hilt of the sword. As the sword is removed, the scabbard falls limp. The question of what Manuel will now be able to accomplish with the sword is paramount. Zurito loyally offers encouragement: Fuentes indeed has the bull in "good" shape for the encounter. As the trumpet sounds commencement for the third and final *tercio,* Manuel looks up at the "dark boxes, where the president must be." But perhaps not. The image is worthy of Thomas Hardy. At the end of *Tess of the D'Urbervilles,* we read that "the President of the Immortals, in Æschylean phrase, had ended his sport with Tess" (354). The final sport with Manuel is about to commence.

198:27–37 **substitute bull-fight critic . . . looking at nothing.** The critic has no great expectations for the third act. The narrator takes us into the critic's consciousness to emphasize his failings as craftsman and as human being. Dismissing the bullfighters of the nocturnals as "kids and bums," he makes plans to compromise on his story. Departing for his date at Maxim's, he glances at Manuel in the ring but misses completely the significance of the moment. The narrator, however, gives Manuel full dignity. His stance exemplifies the human condition as an existential Christ figure "standing very much alone in the ring, gesturing with his hat in a salute toward a box he could not see high up in the dark plaza." His adversary the bull also stands, "quiet, looking at nothing"—just as Manuel may be.

Readers who are existentialists will see *nada* here, the emptiness that grips the older waiter in "A Clean, Well-Lighted Place," the story that would become one of the great jewels of *Winner Take Nothing*. Readers capable of mysticism will sense other possibilities. Victim of his hubris, Manuel cannot see through the darkness above to any transcendent vision. The "looking" here unites man and bull, both now in an eternal realm as they replay a timeless act.

198:38‑44 **"I dedicate" . . . toward the bull.** As Manuel recites the formula of dedication, he as well as the reader must be aware of the irony—at least as we use the audience at the nocturnal as gauge. A single sentence captures Manuel's bow in the dark and his dignified steps toward the bull. Whether the president (or God) is present or not, what matters here is Manuel and how he will acquit himself.

198:45–199:14 **Manuel walked . . . white face.** Hemingway's use of repetition here is atypical, the first sentence of the paragraph duplicating the predicate phrase of the previous sentence. The repetition stresses the determined solemnity of that walking, furthered in additional repetition of the verb *walked* and then by the participle *walking*. The rhythm here is highly stylized, and the dependence on a grammatical series about what Manuel thinks and what he sees accents the drama—as drumbeats might as opponents once marched toward each other in battle. Each of the two paragraphs focusing on Manuel's walk toward the bull ends with full attention on the bull, and the second one is in the bull's consciousness. Manuel walks and the bull stands, its mind focusing on "getting this little one with the white face."

199:15–22 **Standing still . . . watched Manuel steadily.** Focus now switches to the muleta, the matador's instrument to challenge the bull into motion. Three times this paragraph notes its red color as it accents Manuel's intense seeing. The narrator's seeing also draws attention to itself. He describes the muleta as being "like the jib of a boat." When Manuel notices the splintered points of the bull's horns, the narrator notes that one of them is "sharp as a porcupine quill." (Like the earlier use of the trout simile, these would be natural to Nick Adams and to Hemingway—though this story holds no overt signals that the narrator is American.)

199:23–32 **He's on the defensive . . . legs tightened.** As the bull keeps his eyes on Manuel, Manuel attempts to think with the bull. He needs to bring the bull's head down so that he can get the sword above the horns. As Manuel widens the muleta and calls to the bull, the narrator freezes the moment for the bull in a one-sentence paragraph: "The bull looked at him." Like Fuentes, Manuel leans back "insultingly" and shakes the now widespread muleta. Thoroughly aroused, the bull focuses on the muleta, its color now described as "bright scarlet under the arc-light." *Scarlet* carries connotations beyond blood red—sin, guilt, atonement.

199:33–44 **Here he comes . . . Yuh!** The bull now moves toward Manuel, but at a speed that contrasts with Manuel's measured walk toward the bull. We hear the motion in the "Whoosh!" and sense the bull's resolve as he goes into the air with his charge as the muleta claims a kind of victory for Manuel: it passes over his broad back from head to tail. But the bull is now "like a cat" and ready to spring again. When he calls to the bull, he again notes the bull's legs tightening. The bull is ready to charge once more. "Yuh!" is the battle cry Manuel raises.

199:45–200:8 **He swung . . . across the arena at Manuel.** Completing a *pase natural,* an uncomplicated pass of the cape, Manuel proceeds to the more dangerous *pase de pecho,* wherein the muleta is drawn close to the chest (*pecho*). Alliteration emphasizes just how dangerous the maneuver can be: "The hot, black bull body touched his chest as it passed." Manuel's weakened condition from his last fight is doubtless a factor in his close call. Zurito, concerned, quickly sends Fuentes toward Manuel with a cape in case he is needed.

200:9–23 **Manuel was facing . . . "Watch the *faena.*"** But Manuel is able to continue with the bull, and he has the bull's head lowered. Retana's man recognizes that the *pase de pecho* was the kind of movement that Belmonte liked to perform, and Manuel may have been playing on his model. Zurito is not concerned with the crowd's nonresponse to Manuel's effort. He is willing to overlook a good deal about the glib responses to Manuel's effort (the "Where did the boss dig this fellow up?" carries the metaphor of death), but when Retana's man declares that Manuel is about to return to the hospital, Zurito fiercely insists that he knock on wood, and after Retana's man knocks, he tells him to watch the faena (that means *all* the cape work) in the final third of the bullfight.

200:24–32 **Out in the center . . . dark plaza.** In his next efforts, Manuel is able to pull the bull to his knees. His success produces praise (aimed at appeasing Zurito?) from Retana's man and applause from the dark plaza. But it is Zurito's seeing that matters: courageous though Manuel may be, he is not a great bullfighter, and Zurito's words so declaring carry authority. The great bullfighter knows his limitations, and Manuel does not. Physically, Manuel is too weak for this conflict but thinks that he can will himself to excellence. The ultimate test of the great bullfighter is whether he knows how to kill well, and Zurito knows that "finishing" has been Manuel's most difficult challenge. Manuel can do impressive work with the cape, but he does not do well with the sword.

200:33–45 **The bull . . . that kind of thing.** Because Zurito sees Manuel's weak-nesses, he orders two lads to be ready with their capes for diversionary maneuvers, and Hernandez and Fuentes also stand ready. But Manuel wants his moment with the bull. With the team, we see Manuel "white and sweating," but we are also privy to his thoughts, to his fierce determination to take the bull himself.

201:1–14 **The bull was standing . . . would be gone.** The bull has been considerably weakened, "all lead," Manuel judges. He concludes everything is in readiness for the kill. After taking us into Manuel's mind, the narrator moves outward to summarize and to praise Manuel the professional: "He knew all about bulls. He did not have to think about them. He just did the right thing." Manuel's artistry resembles Hemingway's view of his own art of writing. There is something profoundly instinctual about the writing if one has been a keen observer. "If he thought about it, he would be gone."

201:15–30 **Now, facing . . . on the bull.** The narrator quickly takes us back into Manuel's mind at the moment before he thrusts his sword into the bull behind the horns. The catalog in Manuel's mind simultaneously accents his control, his orders to himself. Those orders are focused at the front of his mind ("his only thought") in the words *Corto y derecho,* which the narrator quickly translates as "short and straight." The words in the catalog that may puzzle are "lance himself short and straight." As he "launches" himself on the bull, he makes a "lance" with his body to form, together with the extended sword as the tip, a great man-sized spear (lance). The cultural allusion is to the knight on horseback with his "lance" or spear, driv-ing self and spear forward into his equally armed opponent. It's a very quick, direct move. The passage uses a comparison that makes vivid the challenge of the action Manuel is about to take. He must "put the sword" in "a little spot about as big as a five-peseta piece straight in back of the neck." A five-peseta piece is a small coin about the size of a nickel with a hole in the middle. Before seeking that spot, Manuel makes the sign of the cross—an act of prayer. A single-sentence paragraph heightens the moment of the putting, and the meaning of "lance himself" becomes clear: "*Corto y derecho* he launched himself on the bull."

201:31–45 **There was a shock . . . under his armpit.** The climactic moment that was to have made the man and bull one, as it does for Villalta in chapter 7 of *In Our Time,* does not occur. Manuel finds the bull over him. He has hit hard bone rather than achieving the consummation he had sought. His "good luck" comes in his kicking, which has kept the bull from getting a clean thrust at him—the consummation that the bull sought. But Manuel is quickly back on his feet, "undefeated," as is the bull.

202:1–13 **"Get him out" . . . and charged.** The bull smells blood, however, and the flow will increase as the *tercio* moves toward conclusion. Manuel orders Fuentes to get the bull away from the dead horse. Since the bull's splintered horn carries some canvas with it, the crowd has a moment of comedy. Hernandez again shows his promise as he runs behind the bull and lifts the end of the canvas "neatly" off the horn.

With the bull again positioned for a defensive stand, as Manuel approaches him for a second attempt at a kill, the key word describing the bull is *seemingly*. The bull is seemingly incapable of a charge. A charge is necessary for Manuel to redeem his performance. The ideal is for bull and matador to meet each other.

202:14–21 **Again there was the shock . . . the capes.** When Manuel again strikes bone, the bull responds impressively. This round is clearly his (if the first was a draw). Manuel cannot kick this time. All the energy in the paragraph emanates from the bull, who pumps and finally "hits Manuel in the small of the back," driving his face into the sand. The bull rips through one of Manuel's sleeves, tossing him clear while Fuentes and Hernandez distract the bull with their capes.

202:22–29 **Manuel got up . . . after the action.** Like Nick Adams at the start of "The Battler," the middle story of *In Our Time,* but the last to be written for the book, Manuel gets up. Given the punishment he has just received, his energy is extraordinary. The severity of this second shock is reflected in Manuel's inspection of the sword point and his rush to get a replacement. The severity is further heightened when Retana's man tells Manuel to wipe the blood from his face. As the cuadrilla steps aside after the bull again stands defensively, Manuel looks in vain for Zurito and the assurance he represents.

202:30–45 **Manuel walked . . . handkerchief in his pocket.** Manuel's third attempt with the sword again shows his resolve and the steadfastness of his opponent. The bull will not charge; Manuel must. This time the shock with the sword is so great that the sword, now bent, flies into the air. The sword has the bull's blood on it, but the handkerchief that Manuel puts in his pocket has his blood on it as well as the bull's.

202:46–203:8 **There was the bull . . . sword jumped.** The bull is difficult in every way. "All bone," seemingly, he is now positioned where Manuel does not choose. And when Manuel "chops" the muleta back and forth in front of the bull, the bull does not move. So Manuel again must attack under difficult circumstances, and the sword buckles when he again strikes bone—shooting high and into the crowd. Ironically, this disastrous thrust had been begun with Manuel's thought that he would "show them."

203:9–19 **cushions thrown down . . . as he ran.** Manuel's bravery evokes the crowd's mockery. The cushions come "out of the dark," out of ignorance; the crowd does not comprehend the merit of this "bloody face." The scene echoes the scorn heaped upon

Jesus at his Crucifixion. Rather than being offered vinegar, Manuel is hit with "an empty champagne-bottle," perhaps the one the substitute critic left. But Manuel is admirable as he takes their scorn, "watching the dark, where the things were coming from." He is rewarded when someone throws his sword back into the ring. Picking it up and straightening it, he gestures to the crowd ("the public of Madrid, the most intelligent and generous of the world," Manuel had earlier recited) and says, "Thank you"; Manuel will proceed not for the crowd ("the dirty bastards") but for himself. Audiences in the larger cities tend to be more severe than those in the provinces. Manuel's treatment is not unusual. Nevertheless, the great bullfighter must perform above the insults of the crowd. Manuel allows the abuse to affect his concentration.

203:20–28 **There was the bull . . . gone.** Repetition of "There was the bull" turns Manuel from the crowd back to the challenge that brought him to the ring—from "bastards" he turns to "bastard"—the real opponent. Still the bull will not attack, and Manuel takes another course—and he jams the sharp peak of the muleta into the bull's muzzle. The crowd's complicity in the untoward conclusion is substantial when Manuel trips on one of the cushions, and the bull jams his horn into Manuel's side—a wound suggesting late moments of the Crucifixion. Instinctively he holds onto the bull's horns and is tossed into the air. When the fallen Manuel looks and the bull is gone, the reader concludes that the cuadrilla led the bull away.

203:29–36 **coughing . . . toward the bull.** A man may be broken yet undefeated, as Manuel proves here. Feeling "gone," Manuel is in a sense separated from his own body. He pays it no mind as he calls for muleta and sword. Hernandez, however, sees the wounded body and so urges Manuel to repair to the infirmary. But had Manuel done so, responsibility for killing the bull would have fallen to Hernandez. So in a fierce surge of energy, Manuel twists from Hernandez's grasp and rushes toward the bull.

203:37–45 **There was the bull . . . in the air.** Grammar again marks the bull as the reality that Manuel must confront. "There was the bull," yet another paragraph begins. Now as weakened as the bull, Manuel succeeds in the consummation he has been seeking. This time the sword goes in "all the way" and Manuel is "on top of the bull." The intensity described is heightened by the naming of the "hot blood" on Manuel's knuckles. The bull "lurches" then slowly goes down over on his side, then "suddenly four feet in the air." The death depicted here is likened to the intensity of sex: "He felt the sword go in all the way . . . and he was on top of the bull."

203:46–204:8 **gestured at the crowd . . . pushed him up.** But there is no romantic note of triumph. Manuel gestures to the crowd, following the prescribed format—though he likely wishes to give a very different kind of gesture. What it is that

Manuel wishes to say is not specified, and, indeed, he is so weakened that only coughing marks his efforts. The passage is fiercely naturalistic in its details about the dead bull and Manuel's state of mind and body.

204:9–16 **They carried him . . . very busy.** Manuel's fate continues to parallel the bull's. The bull must be removed from the ring, and so must Manuel. There is no urgency about removing the bull, but there is about removing Manuel. The two actions do intersect, for the mules that block the gates are there to get the bull. Both are objects. In the infirmary, Manuel remains the passive figure as he is placed on the table and his shirt cut away. "Everybody was very busy." But Manuel is still alive, and attention to his physical sensations begins to play against the details of objectification.

204:17–32 **electric light . . . going to die.** Those sensations show how much Manuel is fading. When the lights over the operating table cause him to shut his eyes, he relies on sound. The footsteps on the stairs stop when Retana enters the room. The distant sound of the crowd in the arena announces the next encounter with a bull. The world will go on without him, and so will the bullfights. Smiles from Retana, the doctor, and one of the assistants in white are incongruous, suggesting nightmare. When Manuel himself speaks, when Retana speaks, when Zurito speaks, Manuel cannot hear them—he only sees their lips move. The series of short sentences and the pronounced repetition indicate a kind of inevitability. Three sentences in a row begin with Zurito's name; Manuel's vision switches back and forth rapidly from Zurito to Retana. When the assistant gives Zurito a pair of scissors, Manuel's mind is filled with protest: "To hell with this operating-table."

204:33–42 **Zurito . . . "That was all."** More important to Manuel than the presence or absence of the priest is his *coleta*. When Zurito holds up the scissors, Manuel recalls the compact he made. A surge of energy enables him to sit up. His hearing is also restored, and he regains his voice. "You couldn't do a thing like that, Manos" is the first sentence he has spoken in the infirmary. His "couldn't" (rather than "wouldn't") seems accurate. The action and words of the man near death strike the right chord in Zurito: "I won't do it." Assured, Manuel repeats the claim made when he secured Zurito's services: he was "going good" but didn't "have any luck." In "Today Is Friday," the story based on the Crucifixion that Hemingway wrote in Madrid one year after the publication of "The Undefeated," the first soldier says of the dead Nazarene, "Oh, he ain't lucky. But he looked pretty good to me in there today" (273:9). And so we might say of Manuel in his determined encounter with the bull.

204:43–45 **lay back . . . face.** After the great surge and the securing of Zurito's promise, Manuel can lie back, indeed must. Three repetitons of the word *very* and the adjective *tired* mark the surrender. The preparation for surgery is given from Manuel's point of view rather than as an objective description. The medical staff place "something" over his face; then the "thing" is removed.

205:1–9 "I was going good" . . . awkwardly, watching. The closing scene mirrors aspects of the opening scene. The reader is pointedly reminded of Manuel's exchange with Retana. Retana heard then, as he hears now, the much weakened Manuel declare that he "was going good," that he was "going great." The little man has paid his respects, as it were, but has no intention of remaining for any death watch. He shrugs his shoulders, as if to say, "I told you so." But Zurito will remain. Appropriately, the last speech of the story belongs to him: "You were going great." Zurito's answer may be double edged, but he recognizes the sense in which Manuel is one of "the undefeated." Though Manuel may have ranted against the crowd in the arena, it is his judgment that counts here. He killed his bull. Manuel's consciousness has disappeared in the final paragraph. The medical procedure is now described from an objective perspective: "The doctor's assistant put the cone over Manuel's face and he inhaled deeply." The moment of death is difficult (awkward) for those who care, for those who "watch." In the story that is Zurito. If Hemingway has succeeded, the reader watches with him.

The narrative ends with conspicuous silence, a rhetorical device Hemingway often favored. It requires the participation of the reader. In a sense, it tests the reader. What are the possibilities here?

Manuel has, we know, survived other gorings. Will he survive this one? Historians of the corrida confirm that although a matador can, during the course of a career, expect to end up in the infirmary, often a wounded matador will be back on the program in a couple of months. Several years may go by before there is another death. Thanks to improved medicine, notably the entrance of penicillin into health care, the rate has decreased. The antibiotic would, however, have been approved too late to help Manuel. Odds are also against Manuel because he has scarcely recovered from his previous goring. Were Manuel to "survive" the wound of this nocturnal, he would certainly be finished as an active matador. Competition for assignments is keen; many wait in vain to achieve the opportunities that permit a secure life as a professional torero. Manuel made a bargain with Zurito, and although Zurito does not cut the *coleta,* he would not pic for Manuel again. Even if we posit a reading in which Manuel survives this goring, one way or another, Manuel has retired from bullfighting.

But "The Undefeated" has provided readers with ample evidence that Manuel expires. The story teems with elements of classical tragedy: a protagonist of a certain nobility and a certain hubris and a testing of his fiber. There are numerous signals that an admirable warrior has aimed high, but death rather than public triumph results. This is, of course, the most satisfying conclusion. Manuel dies as a matador in a contest with a worthy opponent, convinced that he was "going good." This is the ending that the title supports. We, of course, know that Manuel was once again not good with the sword. We know that his judgment that the only thing he needed was "one good pic" was far off the mark. He had the pic, but not the necessary skill.

In *The Tragic Art of Ernest Hemingway* Wirt Williams insists that "The Undefeated" is "authentic" tragedy (90). As we have seen, like a classic tragedian Hemingway has surrounded Manuel's attempt to prevail with signals of inevitable failure and signals of death. Furthermore, Manuel has an abundant supply of hubris that Aristotle identified as a key element in the tragic protagonist. Manuel's final line of the story highlights that hubris: "Wasn't I going good, Manos?"

But that last speech also separates Manuel from the tragic protagonists that move us most profoundly—an Oedipus, a Hamlet, a Lear. Manuel has learned nothing from his final corrida; the operative word of his last utterance is the first-person pronoun. Manuel has been led to no discovery about himself or his place in the universe, that transcending moment that marks the conclusion of classical tragedy. In Aristotelian terms, the audience is led to pity Manuel but not to experience any purgation of fear or terror. Instead, with Zurito, we realize Manuel's limitations even as we admire what is heroic about him. He dies a good human being with a fierce dedication to his art. Yet he is at the same time uncertain of his merit. He requires Zurito's approval, a sure sign that he has not faced his hubris and died acting accordingly. For "authentic" tragedy in Hemingway, we must look elsewhere.

That said, Williams was not wrong to discover the aura of the tragic in "The Undefeated." Manuel's final sentence evokes considerable pity and terror—those staples of tragedy—from the reader who has identified with him. It invites reflection from that reader who has strongly identified with a profession—a political figure, an artist, a bullfighter, a writer. Validation from others inevitably matters and often none more than the final judgment. A president worries about approval ratings and about his place in history. The professor rejoices in the named chair for its symbolic value as much as for accompanying tangible benefits. The baseball legend wants that place in the Hall of Fame. The writer may scorn the vanity of all prizes but almost always welcomes the Pulitzer or the Nobel if it comes along.

The public rewards do not, however, completely remove the gnaw of doubt. "A writer must face eternity, or the lack of it, each day," Hemingway declared when he received the Nobel Prize, looking back over a life given to writing. Each bull, each story, presents a challenge—an opportunity for a superb kill or a disaster. And the professional in any forum runs the risk of not recognizing when he or she is no longer "going good." Manuel is not alone in his hubris.

As the dying Hamlet is fortunate in having Horatio at his side, Manuel is blessed to have Zurito at his. Zurito watches over the dying Manuel with understanding of both the man and the man's art. Like Horatio, he alone could "truly deliver" the story of a noble heart.

IN ANOTHER COUNTRY

Coming upon "In Another Country," a reader of *Men Without Women* has just completed a story both literally and figuratively in another country. Foreign locales and foreign spaces challenge readers throughout the book. American readers constantly find the values of their native culture challenged. From the Spain of "The Undefeated," "In Another Country" takes the reader to an Italy under the burden of the prolonged Great War, later to be designated World War I. American readers of 1927, unless they had been combatants in the war, tended to romanticize it as America's heroic rescue of the allies. Most Americans were focusing on a new era of prosperity, the Jazz Age. Hemingway's story brings attention back to the realities of war "in our time." "The Undefeated" and "In Another Country" give prominence to the two arenas for violent death that Hemingway would sometimes link.

If there are no women in "The Undefeated," "In Another Country" gives dramatic force to the title *Men Without Women*. The reader gets to glimpse a few of the women in Milan, but the woman who matters most is a wife about whom we hear but whom we do not see. The reality of women and wives—and how men relate to them—could scarcely be more important to the story.

Hemingway likely came by his title through his reading of T. S. Eliot's poetry. Eliot had taken as epigraph for his 1915 poem "A Portrait of a Lady" these lines from Christopher Marlowe's *The Jew of Malta*: "Thou has committed—/ Fornication: but that was in another country, / And besides, the wench is dead." Although the epigraph corresponds to realities that Hemingway would foreground in 1929 in *A Farewell to Arms,* the story scarcely requires the unnamed narrator to be seen as the "thou" of the epigraph and Frederic Henry, as the critic Julian Smith proposed. In the context of Hemingway's story, "another country" is the reality beyond passion, the "unnamed bourne from which no traveler returns" (Shakespeare, *Hamlet* 3.1.79–80), the country that is to the fore at the end of the story. Among the very best stories in Hemingway's entire canon, "In Another Country" explores territory of his deepest concerns.

206:1–8 **In the fall . . . from the mountains.** The opening paragraph is as admired as any in Hemingway's work. F. Scott Fitzgerald famously noted its power and beauty, a sentiment since repeated by many. Its admirers include Ralph Ellison and Andre Dubus. Its rhythm and its imagery make it poetry as much as prose. The opening sentence recalls the eternal sadness that Matthew Arnold evoked in "Dover Beach," a world bereft of earlier certitudes. The sentence is surely "the one true sentence" that Hemingway in *A Moveable Feast* described as requisite to making a paragraph or story flow (12). "In the fall"—the opening words of the story—link hauntingly to the story's title. The "fall" seems also the mythical fall from innocence as well as autumnal Milan. The condition of war becomes the destiny of the race: "In the fall the war was always there." There is no antecedent for the "we" of the first sentence, and only gradually does that "we" get defined. (The definition will not, however, lead the narrator to reveal his name.) "Going to war" is no longer the lot of this "we," a group experiencing a separate peace. And although the world is cold and dark, the narrator resists despair. Electric lights provide comfort, as they do in several Hemingway stories, and the narrator enjoys looking at the shop windows. Outside the windows there are reminders of death that link the war to the tradition of the hunt—a tradition that combines competition among hunters and the basic search for food. The narrator does not mention any items in the shop windows; rather he calls attention to the foxes, deer, and small birds hanging outside the shops—fallen game. Four times he mentions the wind that comes down from the mountain, making the cold fall of the second sentence emphatic in the last sentence of the paragraph.

Reading sequentially, we also note that the beginning of "In Another Country" follows the ending of "The Undefeated" in accenting exit from an arena of testing and death.

206:9–20 **We were all . . . so much difference.** The tone of this story could not, however, be more different from that of the previous story. In place of the dramatic immediacy that marks "The Undefeated," we have meditation, summary. We have a narrator who is precise, exacting; he is in careful control of what he chooses to tell. The paragraph takes us to the hospital—the institution, the concept even, much on our minds throughout "The Undefeated" and in much of Hemingway's work. Both stories deal with the wounded. The second paragraph emphasizes journey, distances, noting that two of several possible routes to the hospital to which the narrator and others journey every afternoon are along the canal and are longer. Time is what the narrator and his companions seem to have in abundance. Always, however, the routes take the walkers to a "choice of three bridges." It is necessary to cross the canal to enter the hospital. The narrator takes pleasure in shapes and proportion. Wounded out of the war, he keeps a sense of aesthetic beauty. He reports that the hospital is not only "very old" but also "very beautiful." The world still has pleasures, a truth captured in the image of the woman selling roasted chestnuts, which are warm afterwards in his pocket. The paragraph takes the reader finally through the gates of the hospital and into the reality that links the first two stories so pointedly. "There were usually funerals starting from the courtyard." The last sentence inches us closer to the narrator. We not only ponder his purpose for the trip to the hospital but also catch a whiff of a sardonic view. The narrator mocks the machines, which can make little difference to the wounded men who will be using them. Bodies can be healed sometimes, but minds and spirits present a markedly different challenge. World War I heralded the arrival of mechanized warfare. Readers of *Men Without Women* confront the aftermath of such warfare, the realities that nations tend to push aside once wars have ended. Hemingway will not let his readers wallow in images of the heroic. Wars are not ended with truces.

206:21–207:2 **The doctor came . . . "like a champion."** A doctor's son, Hemingway provides a gallery of doctors in his fiction. This doctor practices a bedside manner that exudes optimism. It provides an ironic contrast to the narrative tone that the narrator has created. In a clever joke, Hemingway contrasts the distance created by language between the doctor and the patient. In Italy, certainly at the time of the story, *football* to the doctor means "soccer." The American narrator plays a very different game. The doctor's "You are a fortunate young man" expresses a partial truth at best—as many wounded in war know. The doctor treats the narrator like a child as he promises that his patient will play "better than ever." But the narrative stance creates a persona who is decidedly not a child. Lurching, the machine counters its promise. Hemingway's fiction teems with wounds as well as with doctors. Hemingway protagonists frequently have knee or leg problems. At the opening of "The Battler," Nick checks his knee after his fall from the train (97). In "Cross-Country Snow," also in *In Our Time*, Nick cannot telemark because of his knee (144). In *A Farewell to Arms* Frederic Henry undergoes surgery because of knee/leg wounds and later "practices not limping" (140). For Harry in "The Snows of Kilimanjaro," a scratch on the knee leads to gangrene and death. The narrator here underplays his injury. That his knee does not bend and that "the leg drop[s] straight from the knee to the ankle without a calf" indicates that he has been in a cast for an extended period and that the calf muscle has atrophied. Medical practice then (if not today) would have dictated immobilization of the knee.

207:3–7 **In the next machine . . . greatest fencer in Italy.** Against the younger narrator and his companions the story early on juxtaposes an Italian major. Older, contemplative, and also wounded, the major judges the doctor's manner sardonically. His wink at the narrator initiates the link between the narrator and the major that will structure the story. The pattern of teacher/student (tutor/tyro) is one that Hemingway favors. The ability to find humor in a problematic universe is a trait that usually marks strong Hemingway characters. The major knows well the severity of the major's wound: "Will I too play football, captain-doctor?" He expects no miracles, as the mocking question reveals. The major's roots are aristocratic, as his sport and his formality suggest. "Captain-doctor" is European formality. His sport, fencing, bespeaks the background of nobility. His use of "football" in his question to the doctor rather than "fencing" heightens the sardonic tone. Having described his malfunctioning knee, the narrator now describes the major's hand. It is the opposite of the large, strong hands of Zurito, the noble picador of "The Undefeated." The narrator compares it to a baby's hand. Between two leather straps, it bounces up and down and flaps "stiff fingers" when the doctor examines it. It is no longer under the major's control. The war has exacted a great price from him. But he retains the distinction of having been "the greatest fencer in Italy."

207:8–17 **The doctor . . . said the major.** Responding to the tone, the doctor opts to answer the major's question with "evidence" rather than with words. The major inspects "very carefully" the photograph of a small hand that, after taking the treatment with the machines, has become "a little larger." Not much impressed, he is not willing to note improvement in the "before" and "after" photographs but chooses indirection, asking if the photograph is of a "wound." Politely, he can only observe, "Very interesting," as he returns the photographs. The doctor, the great exuder of confidence, trying to get behind the major's indirection, asks if the major has "confidence." Confidence or the lack of it is central to the story. Some readers may be put in mind of Herman Melville's *The Confidence Man*, the smiling hypocrite who pedals false hope, including remedies for incurable diseases. The only Melville novel in the Key West inventory is *Typee* (Reynolds, *Hemingway's Reading* 158), but Hemingway's comments about Melville in *Green Hills of Africa* indicate that he had read other Melville works as well. Of early American writers, he singles Melville out as exceptional in his ability to chronicle "how things, actual things, can be" (20). Hemingway's commentary on American writing in *Green Hills of Africa* cautioning that reading the critics can cause a writer to lose confidence would signal his continued interest in the theme of confidence. For the writer, as for the bullfighter Manuel in "The Undefeated," the importance of confidence cannot be minimized. The major of "In Another Country" recognizes, to a degree that Manuel does not, that the confidence must be based on realities.

207:18–34 **three boys . . . any more.** Following the brief history of the major, the narrator succinctly describes the companions who accompany him on his daily visits to the hospital. We notice immediately the use of the noun *boys* and that the narrator counts himself a "boy"; the companions are about his age. Throughout time, Hemingway reminds us, the brunt of war has fallen on the very young. His three companions from Milan had to set aside career aspirations when the service to their country so demanded. They each had professional goals: one to be a lawyer, one to be a painter, one to be a career soldier. The narrator does not mention his own career aspiration, though by story's end, it seems clear that he wishes to be a writer. As the four young men make their daily journeys to the machines, there is more than a little doubt that their aspirations will all be realized. The major's reaction to the doctor's optimism about the machines becomes emblematic. The machines, the occasion for the gathering of these wounded men, are essentially unimportant in themselves. The routines of the comings and goings have greater significance. Following the sessions with the machines, the young men often gather at the Café Cova. As is his wont, Hemingway names actual places, but the name of the café could hardly be more appropriate. *Cova* means brooding or hatching or a brooding place. The word is well-suited to this scene with its overtones of disappointment and meditation. It is appropriate to this company of the young men, a brood of young animals not yet adult, futures beckoning. The conversation of the young men doubtless reflects their doubts and their hopes. Significantly, the café is next to the Teatro alla Scala. Mentioning Milan's historic opera house, the narrator heightens the sense of the world of art, beauty, and civilization that the war has placed in peril, a world now more uncertain for the lives of these young men. To what extent will they be able to find meaning and pleasure in the treasures of their culture?

If Italy is engaged in a war against the Central Powers, it also is in a war against itself, uncertain of its goals. The four young men are threatened when they walk through the communist quarter, resented as "officers"—young but also privileged. *A basso gli ufficiali!* translates as "Down with the officers!"

We know about the narrator's leg wound, but nothing specific about the wounds of the three youths from Milan. The narrator lets one vivid injury reflect the psychological angst of the group. Strategically it comes at the end of the paragraph of journey as he describes the fifth "boy" who sometimes walks with them. This Italian may also be described as privileged (he comes from an old family and had attended a military academy), but that counts for little now. Injured within an hour of going to the front, he must now wear a black silk handkerchief across his face because he has no nose and his face is being rebuilt. But the rebuilding makes no complete transformation such as the doctor has predicted for the narrator. Because the narrator writes removed in time from the events, he can report that the doctors never got the nose right, that the young man later emigrated to South America to work in a bank. A victim of the war, he cannot fit into the Old World culture—literally, he is in another country. The nose injury carries considerable weight. Identification of the nose with the male sexual organ and syphilis was common throughout Europe. In his essay "Why Doth the Poxe Soe Much Affect to Undermine the Nose?" John Donne found poetic justice in the fact that the nose would quickly reflect the disease contracted by the corresponding organ. He reports that the Roman emperor Heliogabalus chose his lovers not in the bath but through observation of the nose. In Laurence Sterne's *Tristram Shandy,* Shandy reports that during the course of his breach birth, Dr. Slop mistook the baby's hip for his head and flattened his "nose."

Tristram's father lamented thereafter the impaired "nose" and the baby's truncated name; through the servant's error, at the hasty christening *Trismegistus* became *Tristram*. Donne and Sterne use the nose analogy for comic purposes. Hemingway here does not. The war has taken something from these young men that can never be restored.

Although the fifth boy was in the war only briefly, the experience has been life altering and created profound uncertainty. The American narrator wounded and recovering in another country shares a good deal of that uncertainty. The three companions from Milan have seen a good deal more of the war, having served, it is probable, from the war's beginning in 1914. They deal not only with rehabilitation but with the scorn and misunderstanding of many of the citizens whom they served. The narrator captures the note of eternal sadness in the final sentence of the paragraph, one that is among Hemingway's most beautiful: "We only knew then that there was always the war, but that we were not going to it any more."

207:35–208:2 **We all had . . . did not understand.** The medals common to the four young officers were intended to reward them by marking their bravery and to inspire others. But the medals are as suspect as the machines in the hospital. Their bestowal depends a good deal on chance. The noseless soldier, who has paid as great a price as any of the young officers, does not have a medal simply because he had been at the front so short a time. The officer intending to be a lawyer has three medals but is little cheered. Having served as a lieutenant in the Arditi, "he had lived a very long time with death and was a little detached." The Arditi were elite assault troops, their designation coming from the Italian verb *ardire*, meaning "to dare." By definition the Arditi were the brave. The concept now means little to the lieutenant.

His condition mirrors that of his companions: "We were all a little detached." The word *detached* plays against the word *confidence* highlighted by the doctor as he promotes his dubious assurances. There is no community of the brave here; they are bound together by the circumstance of their afternoon meetings at the hospital. But it is an important bond, separating them from the men and women who go about their ordinary lives even in wartime. The long sentence that ends the paragraph begins with an introductory clause that describes the walks of the young officers through the hostile section of town; it ends with the force of the periodic sentence: "we felt held together by there being something that had happened that they, the people who disliked us, did not understand." (The impact of the sentence comes at the end with "did not understand." The dependent clause is indeed periodic.) "In Another Country" means to instruct its readers on what that "something" is.

208:3–8 **understood the Cova . . . still patriotic.** The concept of understanding provides a neat link to the interior of the Café Cova. The young soldiers see it as a haven with a pleasant atmosphere where they can relax and read the illustrated papers in the racks if they so choose. But there is no indication that they do turn to the papers and reports on the war. The narrator gives more attention to the girls who are "always" at the tables than to the papers. The "girls" at the Cova are the first women to make an appearance in *Men Without Women*. What the narrator—and his companions, no doubt—understand is that the goodwill of the girls does not genuinely reflect their feelings. The narrator's humor is sardonic when he pronounces the café girls "the most patriotic people in Italy." At the time of the writing of the story, Mussolini is in power. In theory he has abolished the brothels, but cafés are accepted as fronts for easy assignations, a fact reflected in the narrator's wry observation from his later vantage in time: "and I believe they are still patriotic." Easy patriotism is ever suspect in Hemingway. Chapter nineteen of *A Farewell to Arms* mocks the super patriot Ettore, who makes mention of the "patriotic" girls at the cova (121).

208:9–33 **The boys . . . a hawk either.** The focus at the Cova for these wounded soldiers is their talk with each other about the experiences that separate them from all noncombatants. Deep into the story Hemingway slowly edges the story to its central concern: the narrator's own uncertainties. As the Cova is the comfortable place where the soldiers can share with each other, the narrator has found that comfortable place in the story for movement into a confessional mode. He "confesses" to his comrades (and now to the reader) that his medals are a result of his being an American and having been wounded, not for any act of heroism. His circumstances resemble those of the noseless soldier much more than those of the three Milanese; both may be said to have suffered an "industrial accident." The narrator will have a closer bond with the noseless boy because neither knows how he would have "turned out" had he had extended service in battle. Hemingway gives us a "we" within a "we." Although he is not ashamed of his medals and ribbons, the narrator finds an emptiness in the "beautiful language" of the citations. Replete with such words as *fratellanza* (brotherhood) and *abnegazione* (sacrifice), the language belongs to the politicians and to the girls at the Cova. (Hemingway's own citation for the Silver Medal of Valor contains both the words *fratellanza* and *abnegazione* [Lewis 224].) The narrator knows that these words have little to do with experience at the front. The passage anticipates Frederic Henry's scorn of patriotic abstractions in *A Farewell to Arms* (185). Combatants are little concerned with the grander concepts of patriotic celebration. The ultimate challenge of war is proving one's courage to oneself.

The three soldiers from Milan have done that. The narrator finds a vivid metaphor to describe these three. They are "hunting-hawks." Having faced death many times, they have a vision that is hawk-like, fixed a great distance into another country beyond death's thrall. Unlike the narrator, they do not lie on their beds at night afraid to die or in apprehension about how they will react when they are again sent to battle.

The narrator recognizes a great gulf fixed between himself and the hawks. "After the cocktail hour," he imagines himself having done what they have done to get their medals. But after the cocktail hour, the narrator must confront himself—as does the Tiresias-like narrator of T. S. Eliot's *The Waste Land*, who after the "violet hour" makes his way homeward (ll. 218–21). Just as Eliot is subtly evoked in the story's title, he may be lingering in the starkest confessional moment of the story. *The Waste Land*, like the bulk of Eliot's poetry, is also confessional as it portrays isolation, uncertainty, fear of death. Numerous images are common to both writers. Hemingway's narrator, as reluctant a confessor as Eliot's Prufrock, now describes himself "walking home at night through the empty streets with the cold wind and the shops closed, trying to keep near the street lights." More important, the description echoes the opening paragraph, and now the narrator's vulnerability is palpable: "I was very much afraid to die, and often lay in bed at night by myself, afraid to die and wondering how I would be when I went back to the front again." It is appropriate to the isolation the narrator feels that he never names his Cova associates—or the major or the doctor. He has made no lasting friendships.

Although the narrator would not ever make this confession to his Cova associates, he can now make it to us—an act of strength and courage. Through this fictional moment, Ernest Hemingway also makes a confession: "I was not a hawk, although I might seem a hawk to those who had never hunted." Dismissing Hemingway as a writer of machismo will never do.

208:34–41 **The major . . . in my mind.** From the intense confessional moment, the narrator quickly turns the direct spotlight from himself back to the major, who had not been part of the Cova gatherings. The narrative ceases to have the flavor of the personal essay and becomes a sustained dramatic scene. The transition comes smoothly. From the "either" that ends the preceding paragraph, the narrator quickly implies another "either." The major "did not believe in bravery." Because the major is not a hawk, during the hospital sessions with the machines, the narrator is able to establish a comfortable relationship with him. With the major, he does not have to deal with the significance of his medals. His skepticism about the machines having impressed the narrator, the major quickly becomes "teacher" to the young American. The major detects and checks intellectual smugness in his pupil, who, having found Italian easy, says that he "could not take a great interest in it." The lieutenant must unlearn his notion of easy. The major begins to teach the necessity of training, of discipline. A great fencer knows all about discipline, about practice. Humbled, the narrator no longer accepts the "easy" but checks his grammar before speaking.

208:42–209:6 **came very regularly . . . his fingers in them.** The major holds himself to the high standard that he exacts from his pupil. He exemplifies the disciplined life. Although the narrator is "sure" that the major does not believe in the machines, he is impressed that the major is willing to be part of the medical experiment and never misses a session. He is shocked, therefore, when the tutor of ultimate self-control explodes and denounces the machines as "nonsense" and attacks the narrator as "a stupid impossible disgrace." It may seem a strange moment in the narrative for the narrator to report that the major is physically small. But obviously something has happened to the major to produce this outburst. Finally, any human being may be rendered small and helpless against overwhelming forces, as the narrator provides an image that freezes desperation. The major sits "straight up in his chair" and looks "straight ahead at the wall," his right hand in the machine, the straps thumping his fingers up and down. He looks into a void, much as in "Bartleby, the Scrivener" Herman Melville's Bartleby looks at a wall, and as Hemingway's Ole Andreson does in "The Killers" (221).

209:7–28 **"What will"** . . . **"damned thing off."** Distraught though he may be, the major gains a kind of control by grasping his role as teacher. Asking the narrator what he will do when the war is over, he challenges him to "speak grammatically." (The question is one that the major must also face.) The major's next question takes us closer to what it is he wishes to convey to the young American. Although the American is now, apparently like all his Cova companions, a man without a woman, he does hope to marry. The major's adamant dictum that "a man must not marry" reasonably perplexes the American. "If he is to lose everything, he should not place himself in a position to lose that," the major declares as he sets up a striking challenge: "He should find things that he cannot lose." War is all about losing things, seemingly more than winning things. The men who gather at the hospital have all experienced loss. "Angrily and bitterly" the major instructs that "losing" a marriage is the ultimate loss and will not brook argument. The narrator emphasizes again the image of the desolate man looking "straight ahead" at the wall. Those who read on the biographical level will know that Hemingway wrote "In Another Country" during the tumultuous time when his marriage to his first wife was ending; suicide was one of the options he considered.

209:29–43 **He went back . . . out the door.** Seeking to regain his composure, the major now instructs the narrator with actions more than with words. Even in times of extremity, order and routine are useful. He goes to the next room for the light treatment and the massage. His anger now subsiding, he can ask the doctor for permission to use the telephone, and he shuts the door as he conducts his necessary business—business that very possibly deals with the details of his wife's funeral. When he returns to the room, he is "wearing his cape and had his cap on." (The image anticipates the efforts of Frederic Henry in *A Farewell to Arms* to reclaim his life after his wounding and recalls the much published picture of young Hemingway wearing cape and cap and his theatrical posing in Oak Park after the war.) The major apologizes to the narrator for his rudeness, explaining that his wife has died.

Though his regular visits to the hospital keep him mindful of death and dying, owing to his sessions with the major, he feels the profundity of the major's grief, feeling "sick" for him. In "Indian Camp" a young Nick Adams had asked his father if dying is "hard." Clearly, the dying can be very hard on those who loved the deceased. The major—who had exemplified Old World dignity and self-control—declares through tears, "I am utterly unable to resign myself." His departure that day from the hospital constitutes one of the most emotional scenes of the book. Though the tears are abundant, the major strives to achieve a stoic dignity. "Looking at nothing," he carries himself "straight and soldierly" as he walks past the machines and out the door.

209:44–210:10 **The doctor told me . . . out of the window.** In a story that has so much to say about war, the death that is immediate to action is of a civilian, a woman, and the cause is pneumonia. The influenza pandemic of 1918–19 killed more people than the Great War. The major had waited until he had been "invalided out of the war" before marrying his young bride, his delay probably the result of his wish not to make her a widow. (The wrenching of the beloved during war becomes a prominent Hemingway theme.) Likely, the major ponders that earlier decision. It is significant that after he observes the three-day rituals of death, he returns to the hospital for the sessions in the machines, but the grammar lessons with the narrator have ended. He ignores the three photographs placed during his absence in front of his machine. The photographs portray hands with wounds like the major's now healed. The reader is reminded that the major has lost his profession as well as his wife. The narrator ends his story with a frozen moment in which the major at first seems the epitome of negation as he looks out the window, staring, it seems, at nothing.

But the major may be looking through nothing, into another country, much like the hunting hawks. After the three days' absence, we may detect something of resurrection, certainly of recovery. Perhaps no reader has experienced "resurrection" at the ending more intently than did the fiction writer Andre Dubus. Dubus had taught the story many times during his eighteen years on the faculty at Bradford College. Two years following his retirement, on the night of 23 July 1986, trying to help two disabled motorists, he was hit by a car and both legs were badly crushed. When he left the hospital two months later, his left leg had been amputated below the knee. In the hospital, he thought often of Hemingway's "The Gambler, the Nun, and the Radio," the powerful hospital story that Hemingway would write for *Winner Take Nothing.* Dubus would never be free from physical pain until his death in 1999. Dubus also lived with what he calls "spiritual pain." In 1988 on the advice of his priest, he began tutoring two teenage girls who were in state custody. They read "In Another Country," and Dubus discovered meanings he had missed before. (Hemingway frequently insisted that great stories reveal new secrets when they are reread.) Dubus told the girls, "The story is about healing too. . . . Look at [the major]. Three days after his wife has died, he is in motion. He is sad. He will not get over this. And he will get over this. His hand won't be cured, but someday he will meet another woman. And he will love her. Because he is alive" (58).

And though the final paragraph of the story focuses on the wife's death and the major who loved her, the story requires that we look back to the narrator who recounts their story. The narrator scarcely mentions himself in that final paragraph, save to link himself to the major as one skeptical of the possibility of healing. ("I always understood we were the first to use the machines.") He knows, as the major now knows, that death can strike suddenly and quickly. The major's plight at the end of the story would be mirrored at the end of *A Farewell to Arms*. Although both the major and Frederic Henry are wounded in battle, the women they love are the ones who die unexpectedly and suddenly. Story and novel end depicting bereft men. But despair is not the final note. Henry has survived, for he narrates his story. The major presents an example to the young narrator of "In Another Country." Order, discipline, ritual (even if he does not believe in them) carry him forward.

HILLS LIKE WHITE ELEPHANTS

Although *Men Without Women* accents the masculine perspective, Hemingway placed third in the collection a story that brings the feminine to the fore. In the literal sense, the story portrays a man with a woman. The story takes its title from the woman's statement; the story's force comes from the tension between the woman's way of seeing and the man's. The title of the collection suggests separation, but not necessarily physical separation, as the ultimate outcome. "Hills Like White Elephants" portrays a couple learning to be alone together.

The story comes somewhat eerily after a story in which a young American had been warned not to marry, advised that he should seek those things that cannot be lost. Although the American man of "Hills Like White Elephants" is not married, the depth of his commitment to another is a primary question of the story. He is a male counterpart to Brett Ashley of *The Sun Also Rises*. Brett is unable to commit to any man but makes a number of men agonize over her. The girl in the story is the female counterpart to Jake Barnes. Because of his war injury, even the possibility of physical union is denied him. He will be there when she needs help; as the novel ends, he and Brett have become expert at being alone together.

Notwithstanding Bernice Kert's declaration that neither the incident in "Hills Like White Elephants" nor the woman in it grew out of Hemingway's experience, the story carries haunting echoes of his marriage to Hadley and might well have alerted second wife Pauline to the author's desire for "a life without consequences." (James R. Mellow took the title for his 1992 biography of Hemingway from the narrator's declaration about Harold Krebs, the protagonist of "Soldier's Home" in *In Our Time*: "He did not want any consequences" [32].) As Michael Reynolds reveals in *Hemingway: The Paris Years*, during the summer of 1924 Hemingway was deeply unhappy because Hadley's period was late and he feared that he would again become a father. His pronounced unhappiness caused Hadley great distress. Reynolds wrote that Ernest had made her "feel like a worthless drag on his life. It was not a nice revelation, nor did the space between them immediately close" (219). By spring of 1925 Pauline Pfeiffer had made her entrance into the Hemingways' lives.

211:1–9 The hills across the valley . . . to Madrid. The Ebro Valley in Spain lies midway between Valencia and Barcelona, an area known for its lush scenery and the excellent fishing in the Ebro River. The opening sentence foregrounds landscape. Hills traditionally carry metaphoric meaning. They are like the female breast, providing variously nourishment, comfort, beauty. The sentence itself is soothing. The Ebro is a major Spanish river, reaching from its source in the Cantabrian Mountains to the Mediterranean. A 1925 sketch for the story places the action near the town of Casetas (Caseta on some maps) on the Madrid-Barcelona line. Casetas is about ten kilometers northwest of Zaragoza, between A-68 and the old national highway N-232. Both highways run parallel to the Ebro railroad, and the station is away from the center, a little northeast of the big road, A-68, and almost on the river, in the floodplain. Except for the distant mountains, the description in the story is quite accurate. The second sentence immediately highlights division, contrast. Associations of life and nourishment connected with a river give way to associations of mechanization and speed connected with the two lines of rails. The station carries connotations of waiting and departure; located between the two lines of rails, it accents the possibility of choice about direction. Because there are no trees and no shade in this middle ground, the station gathers the heat of the day, and this one is "very hot." The shadow of the building provides some relief from the stark imagery, as does the entrance to the bar. A curtain made of strings of bamboo beads provides color and interest as well as a practical function: the beads keep the flies somewhat at bay. Entrances (doors, gates) are traditional symbols of the vagina, the entrance to the womb.

Then we immediately meet the central characters. The man is identified as "the American," foreign to this culture. With him is "the girl"; in what sense she is "with him" is the point of the story. Calling her "girl" places her in the more vulnerable position. Pointedly, she is not called "wife" or "woman." They are both sitting "outside" the station and outside a culture. The oppressive heat adds to the challenge of a forty-minute wait. Forty minutes can be an eternity, or it can be a pleasant interval; much depends on circumstances. "Very hot" temperatures suggest a difficult wait and may imply more than thermometers. A literal junction has been described, but *junction* is the right word also for the transition, the new direction that the story will produce for the American and the girl. Time moves with a fierce inevitability in the opening paragraph and in the story. Those who want to take the train to Madrid have only two minutes to board. The girl in the story has to decide if she wants to be with this man, and at what price—and she does not have much time to make that choice.

211:10–16 "What should we drink?" . . . "Two big ones." That the first speech of the story is a question could hardly be more appropriate. Though alcohol will play an important part in this story, the drink also becomes metaphoric. Drinking is at once a way of making the forty-minute interval more pleasant and a way of checking the heat. Removing her hat, the girl signals her desire to relax, to cool off. That she initiates the first dialogue of the story suggests her vulnerability, her dependence. When he leaves her question unanswered, the girl makes the decision, anticipating a story in which she gets to make a crucial decision. Acquiescing with her choice of beer, the man orders the beers in Spanish, which sets him up as the one knowledgeable in that language. He is the one able to penetrate that particular boundary, symbolized by the bead curtain. Although we read it in English, the woman in the doorway likely speaks in Spanish. That the woman speaks from the doorway keeps the image of thresholds before us. That the man desires "big ones" suggests not only thirst but frustration. He would like some relief.

211:17–25 **woman brought . . . "doesn't prove anything."** The Spanish woman knows her job and performs it efficiently. She is curious about the "other" culture on the other side of the curtain—she looks at them as she completes her task. Until the end of the story the reader also "looks at the man and the girl" and like the woman will make a judgment. The Spanish woman's looking is juxtaposed against that of the girl, who is gazing at the line of hills. The hills in the hot sun are white, and the country is dry and brown—imagery that evokes finality, conclusion rather than vitality.

The girl responds imaginatively to what she sees. Her comparison is at first literal: the hills remind her of white elephants. White elephants are venerated in parts of Southeast Asia but elsewhere are typically seen as unwanted possessions or as objects that no longer have value to their owners but might to someone else; hence, white elephant sales. But a white elephant in nature may signify the rare, the special. For the man, the unwanted white elephant is the girl's pregnancy; for the girl the pregnancy is a prized possession. But she senses that aborting the pregnancy is her best chance of keeping the man.

The white elephant that the girl sees is, of course, in the distance. The man is not interested in feminine flights of fancy. Nor does he seem eager to make pleasant conversation to ease the wait. The girl recognizes her companion's mood. That she is not surprised by his tone indicates that she has experienced his testiness on other occasions. The conversation has little promise. His response is like an adolescent taunt. Proving something will become an important motif of the story, as the man tries to prove to (to convince) the girl that she should have an abortion. He wants "reasonable" decisions.

211:26–212:24 **The girl looked . . . "I guess so."** The girl has no wish to play his game. Looking at the bead curtain, she tries to refocus the conversation and so asks for a translation of the words on the bead curtain: "Anis del Toro." Her companion's response is minimal, telling her only that it is a drink. If his companion had a dictionary at hand, she would have discovered more. *Anís* is the Spanish botanical term for the anise plant. Anise is a plant with clusters of small yellowish-white flowers and licorice-flavored seed; aniseed is the licorice-flavored seed of the anise plant, used in medicine and as flavoring; anisette is an anise-flavored liqueur. In several senses, "Anis del Toro" is hypermasculine and threatening to the girl. The seed of the bull makes her potentially a modern Europa, the Phoenician princess abducted by Zeus in the form of a white bull. The seed of the bull can be bitter medicine for the girl of the story. When she asks to try it, she has no notion of its taste.

The man handles imperatives well. (The girl speaks only one imperative in the story, making even it a question.) And he gets results, as is betokened by the emergence of the Spanish woman. Again we are reminded of the curtain and the contrast of cultures. The Spanish woman wastes no words but gives the price, "four reales," thinking the man wishes the reckoning for the two beers. In the context of the "new drink" that the girl wishes, the implication is that there will be a price attached. A real is a Spanish coin. The Americans are getting good exchange for their money, though the initial total will climb during the forty-minute wait—especially the emotional price. The line "We want two Anis del Toro" is striking because the couple here is in agreement. The prelude has all been division: between the hills and the valley, between the station and the platform, between the man and "the girl." The girl will get her new drink. The Spanish woman continues to speak in minimalist speech when she asks if they want water with the strong drink. The reader senses that there are complexities involved with this new drink. The man translates into English for the girl but offers no advice. He nevertheless gives the girl a choice—as he does later in the story in dramatic terms. The choice requires some hesitation, and the girl is eager for his advice. She wants guidance, wants her choice to be good, but his enthusiasm is minimal, like his guidance on the small matter of water. The Spanish woman is a bit annoyed with the delay, but her repetition of the question is controlled, although not in the language of courtesy. It is telling that he makes the decision. No narrative statement tells us that the woman has departed and filled the order. The gulf between lines 9 and 10 is a significant omission accenting that the man and the girl have not said a word to each other in the interval. The tension is palpable. Once the drink arrives and the girl tastes it, she makes a judgment—again using a simile. Licorice has a strong taste; so the girl immediately puts the glass down. It is not much to her liking. She might wish for this drink to pass from her, as Jesus would have preferred that the impending crucifixion not be required. (In Luke 22.42 he prays that "this cup" pass from him.) Similarly, Hemingway's story uses the metaphor of drink to underscore moral choice and moral consequence.

Her second metaphor will elicit an even harsher response from the man, but she knows it is a good one. The taste of licorice is not one that allows for much nuance, not a taste one would want to characterize everything. The girl agrees, unhappily, that life moves inevitably toward the bitter. Mentioning absinthe, she underscores that the man has taken her toward increasingly strong drink. Absinthe, one of the most powerful of alcoholic drinks, is banned in the girl's homeland. Her implied accusation stings. He does not want the conversation to continue in this vein. But his command that she "cut it out" takes on a special edge when the story moves more directly to the unstated word of the story: *abortion*. The language of mundane discord contrasts with the language of metaphor.

The girl's line "having a fine time" reminds us of the philosophy of the Jazz Age. It is, of course, in this context that the entire story must be viewed. Nevertheless, the girl rightly reminds her companion that her response has not been untoward and lets us know how the words that caused him to command her to "cut it out" would have been spoken—reasonably, with a certain bemusement. Backing off, he now is ready to be more agreeable. Again, he speaks in the imperative. It will soon be crystal clear that his aim is indeed "a fine time" and that he has a plan to secure it. Taking him and the reader back to the story's prominent simile, the girl is ready to start again. By asking him if her statement was bright, she gives him the chance to give a more courtly response than he initially provided. His response is terse, a half measure to right his initial error. The emptiness of a life dedicated to the "fine time" is on her mind. That the girl is thinking of "new drinks" in a metaphorical way is clear. We know that she is indeed "bright." Noticeably missing in the wastelander's life she portrays is work. In America, none of the drinks they tried could be legally purchased; America is not the place for a "fine time." Begrudgingly ("I guess so") the man acquiesces to her description of their lives; all they do is "look at things and try new drinks." He does not mention work or career or family.

212:25–32 **The girl looked . . . the girl said.** Reflecting her disillusionment with the Jazz Age philosophy, the girl turns to the peace that she sees in the distant hills. Set aside as a paragraph, the isolated sentence underscores longing and distance. The hills suggest a promise that is beyond the couple's reach. We get pleasure in the visual world only through her angle. She is willing to see the hills for themselves in her conciliatory approach, but she seems unable to divorce them from any metaphorical value. She gives the hills "skin," an attribute of elephants (though "hide" might be more technically correct) and certainly of babies. Still unsuccessful in turning the conversation in the direction he wishes, he refrains from touching the offending simile—or the skin metaphor. He suggests another drink (not Anis del Toro); perhaps that was useful in getting the conversation where he wants it. Her optimism minimal, she agrees. It is implied that the Spanish woman received the new order and delivered it. Some minutes pass probably, but the scene may be safely omitted, the bead curtain reminding us of the inner and outer contrast. From the landscape, attention is back to drinking, what they "do." Accenting the positive, the man pronounces the beer "nice" and "cool." Perhaps with a note of sadness, the girl completes a trio of adjectives with *lovely* even as the text puts her identity as "girl" squarely before us.

212:33–45 **"It's really an awfully simple" . . . "made us unhappy."** The stage is now set for the man to press for resolution of the issue that has so divided the couple.

With the word *operation*, a new frankness enters the dialogue. To punctuate the shift in tone, the man gives for the first time a name for his companion. *Jig* is a nickname with a lengthy history. *Cassell's Dictionary of Slang* notes that in the eighteenth century it became "a joking, mocking name for a person" (798). It suggests a measurement (as in jigger) or a dance: to dance a jig. A criminal or wrongdoer who is caught might hear the words "All right, the jig is up." In this story teeming with the essence of Eliot's *The Waste Land*, we may also hear, "jug, jug," an indictment of a culture where the more spiritual meanings of sexuality have been compromised. *Cassell's Dictionary of Slang* cites *jig* as a term for sexual intercourse beginning in the seventeenth century and says that *jiggle* could mean sexual intercourse as far back as the mid-nineteenth century. That Jig feels that she has become little more than a sex object to the American man is not surprising. According to *The New Partridge Dictionary of Slang and Unconventional English*, the verb *jiggle* describes the walk of a woman "so as to accentuate the movement of the breasts" (1102). (In 1958 in the rock-and-roll song "Chantilly Lace," the Big Bopper celebrated "a pretty face" accompanied by "that jiggle in the walk" and "that giggle in her talk.")

The man's speech teases us with two *really*s. If the procedure that he wishes Jig to undergo is not "really" an operation, what is it? As to its being "an awfully simple" operation, the "awful" may hit the right note. Should the operation prove "simple," its psychological impact may not. In this speech he addresses her with a name for the first time. To some degree, the man's language is repulsive to Jig. She does not look at him, but at the ground by the table leg. What he has placed "on the table" pains her. Her looking is again to the fore. There is a great deal that he does not see. His certainty is beguiling. The idea of knowing becomes pronounced for the rest of the story. *Know* is heard as *no*, that other frequently used word. Denials mark the story. The "it" that is "really not anything" is never named—for to use the word *abortion* would evoke a violence, a denial of life. The unspecified "it" had been useful to Hemingway before. In the very early "Up in Michigan," first published in *Three Stories and Ten Poems* in 1923, Liz Coates loses her virginity to a rough lumberman who, somewhat like the man in "Hills Like White Elephants" asserts his will: "She was frightened but she wanted it. She had to have it but it frightened her" (62). In "Hills," the man's "It's just to let the air in" hides the magnitude of the decision and the action. The repetition of "know" echoes a scene from "The End of Something," the memorable story in *In Our Time* about the end of a romance between a younger couple. There Nick accuses Marge of "knowing" everything, but again the male is the manipulative partner. Jig's silence is conspicuous. In her heart she knows that the decision is more complicated than the man allows. For many, abortion is an unspeakable notion. But the man is determined that the conversation continue. Her silence is at least not protest. He casts himself as the great supporter willing not only to go with her but also to stay with her "all the time." The ending of the story casts doubt over the duration of the relationship and whether or not she has the abortion.

When he describes the procedure as "perfectly natural," we are reminded that the position of the Catholic Church (and hence most Spaniards) is that the process is *contra naturam,* against nature. Jig is able to look beyond the abortion. Her asking what they will "do" afterward (look at things and try new drinks?) is pivotal to the conclusion. Jig has a much longer view, feeling not only their apartness now but a more permanent apartness. She doubts his declaration that they will be "just like they were before." If the girl has read *The Sun Also Rises,* she might think of the novel's final line: "Isn't it pretty to think so?" Jig is "perfectly" reasonable in asking what makes him think so. The man's declaration that the pregnancy is "the only thing that bothers us," "the only thing that's made us unhappy," is self-deluding, simplistic; his "only" is suspect. The "thing"—certainly for her—is a child. She already knows that "look[ing] at things and try[ing] new drinks" does not mean happiness. The pursuit of happiness is, of course, a time-honored American goal. What happens, the story asks, when that pursuit conflicts with, or is complicated by, a new life? The man feels that the new life is a threat to his liberty. It's his right to life that concerns him.

213:1–27 The girl looked . . . "you feel that way." The story pauses slightly as the girl marks his claim by looking again at the bead curtain, the marker of a boundary. Looking and talking have been the focus of the story, but it dramatically shifts for a moment to the tactile. The girl "put her hand out"—but not to take the man's. Taking hold of two strings of beads, she is grasping for something to hold on to, perhaps the desperation of prayer. (Catholic prayers are regularly conducted with beads.) Jig turns his declaration into a melancholy question that can be read in several ways. A slight accent on "you" can reflect her different judgment. He, in contrast, speaks with certainty. He "knows." And the reader doubts. The girl is not afraid of the procedure, but of the consequences. The man may know several people (or few or none) who have had abortions, but he has given little thought to the effect of abortion on the psyche. The girl is anything but "girl" in her utterance. She is an ironist, given to the long view. Detecting her doubt, his "Well" provides a resting place, a signal that he is being reasonable. His message is quite the opposite of his words, as the girl surely recognizes. He ends by again casting himself as the authority ("I know") and echoes the haunting "perfectly simple." Accustomed to following his agenda, Jig puts the brunt of the decision on him. Her "really" asks him to look deeply into the situation, to be very certain. Jig's irony causes him to backtrack a bit. He doesn't "know" that it's best but offers a slightly more measured "I think." And he shifts the responsibility. He doesn't want her to have the abortion unless she "really" wants to, and he knows from her hesitation that she doesn't "really" want to. Not able to get what she wants, Jig grasps for what she can get. Her "you'll be happy" indicates that she knows that her own happiness will suffer, but she wants him to love her, perhaps hinting that she is not now sure that he loves her. His love is something that might be taken away. Significantly, the word *love* makes its first appearance in the narrative—and it comes from the woman. The unborn child, presumably a fruit of love, is never linked with the notion of love.

Sensing that he is winning, the man is quick to assure Jig that she need not doubt his love. His "You know" indicates that the division, the unhappiness, has grown profound. The pregnancy has made her doubt the reality of his love. Although Jig feels some reassurance at his words, she continues to hesitate—wanting a guarantee. The word *it* has special play in the sentence. The abortion is the thing that dare not speak its name. Her "it will be nice again" is general, as if she were talking about the weather—certainly the climate of their relationship. Hemingway takes us back to the controlling metaphor (the fourth mention of the "white elephants") and the poetry in her soul. The word *it* continues to be used in an ambiguous way and continues to give a staccato rhythm to the exchange. He can't think about "it"—which doesn't seem to be the same "it" found in "I'll love it." Because she "knows" how he gets when he worries, she is made to feel guilty as the cause of his worry. The American man is a master manipulator.

Not ever to worry—what magic could produce that state and allow the characters to remain human? No one is being "perfectly reasonable" here. But Jig's romantic instinct wants for the moment to believe that she can keep him from ever worrying. How he gets when he worries is obviously not pleasant, and she would prevent this unpleasantness if she could. He affirms again that he wouldn't have to worry about the operation, but his "perfectly simple" sounds like that world of magic. Aiming for release for him, she makes her decision. Her assertion that she does not care about herself makes clear that her decision does require sacrifice of what she wants. By uttering a second time that she doesn't care about herself, she gives him some cause for worry, for guilt. Jig is a complex person. The notion of the woman who is willing to sacrifice herself was much on Hemingway's mind. The heroine of *A Farewell to Arms* will make a similar declaration. Catherine is willing to give all for Frederic. More than any of Jig's other lines, this one has the man's attention. "I don't care about me" is an alarming sentence for a young woman. In Emily Brontë's *Wuthering Heights*, although Catherine Earnshaw tells Nelly Dean, "I *am* Heathcliff" (74), Nelly tells Mr. Lockwood, "Well, we *must* be for ourselves in the long run" (81). In the Gospels, Jesus speaks about a healthy concept of self. Loving one's neighbor as oneself implies concern for the self. In the traditional marriage covenant, two become as one—become a "we." Such is far from the reality here. Although the man makes an affirmative response, his alarm is also evident. His concept of their relationship is being severely questioned. Jig has not made his way easy. Jig the realist as opposed to Jig the romantic is speaking. There is no conviction in her "then everything will be fine." The man hears the ironist. Her irony disturbs him, but it also suggests an awareness that if she has the abortion, feeling as she does, the relationship is doomed. Jig's decision has become a no-win situation.

213:28–31 **The girl stood up . . . through the trees.** Usually the character is a male, but the action of standing up is oft repeated in Hemingway and marks a moment of resolution. Jig commands the scene, as essentially she commands the story. Her decision is the vital reality. She is the one who sees the natural world, who notes the fields of grain and the trees along the river. This is the scene that the story first invited us to see. Beyond the river are the mountains—beckoning like some Kilimanjaro. The shadow of cloud that moves across the field doubtless strikes Jig as telling. It's a destination she does not think they can reach. The grain, the trees, the river bespeak fecundity. Through the trees, she views the river, which looks like the river of life.

213:32–45 **"And we could" . . . "wait and see."** The girl interprets the scene for her companion and for the reader. She likens the moment to the expulsion from the Garden of Eden. Adam and Eve, the story says, could have had Eden forever, but by their own choice they have rejected it, lost it, made happiness "impossible." Seeing and not seeing, listening and not listening characterize the story. The man has heard the words but missed the import. When he counters that everything is still theirs for the taking, his verb *can* becomes the replacement for her "could." The stichomythia has great power—Adam and Eve arguing in their fallen world. Jig begins four speeches in a row with "No," echoing the earlier "know." His lines play against her knowledge that they can't have the whole world: "We can have everything," "We can have the whole world," "We can go everywhere." The program exudes a language of selfishness. He contradicts her at every point. To her "It isn't ours anymore," he asserts, "It's ours." He denies her finality that "once they take it away, you never get it back." We note the ominous "they" that will be useful to Hemingway soon in the ending of *A Farewell to Arms*. ("They threw you in and told you the rules and the first time they caught you off base they killed you" [338].) She breaks the pattern of the argument, emerging as the wise one: "We'll wait and see."

This passage also plays powerfully against the accounts of the temptations of Jesus as described in the Gospels of Matthew (4.8–9) and Luke (4.6–7). In both Gospels the devil shows Jesus, then at the start of his ministry, all the kingdoms of the world and tells him that he can have them all if he will fall down and worship him. In "Hills," the American man parallels the arch tempter. Jig, like Jesus, rejects the easy promise. Surveying the valley of the Ebro and the hills beyond, she demonstrates her dignity and her understanding of values her partner seems incapable of grasping. His words are hollow.

214:1–7 **"Come on back" . . . "maybe stop talking?"** From the bright sun and her penetrating view, the man beckons Jig into the shade, where she might view matters differently. He doesn't want her to "feel that way"—as long as she feels that way, he doesn't want her to have the abortion, he earlier said. For him, *feel* has suddenly become the operative verb, replacing earlier emphasis on knowing and thinking.

Instinctively, she rejects the notion of feeling and returns to his insistence on knowing things. The practiced arguer, he keeps pounding at his declaration, which she doesn't believe. Her interruption ("Nor that isn't good for me") shows how well she knows him. The sarcasm is evident in her "I know." She asks for another beer, not because she is thirsty but for some relief from his barrage. He may agree on the beer, but the nagging goes on. The pattern of the argument has many comic touches, not the least of which is the shift in gender roles. Her "I realize" is quick and dismissive. Not talking would for her be a relief.

214:8–21 **They sat down . . . "stop talking?"** Sitting down at the table gives a pause to the unpleasantness and indicates their readiness for the next beer. It is significant that the couple does not sit down and look at each other. He, however, wishing to pursue the argument, looks at her. She, by contrast, looks at the "dry side of the valley." Returning to the conversation, he instructs her in such a way as to make her at fault. She is not realizing what he has said. He makes himself into the magnanimous one, the one willing to make the sacrifice. The "perfectly willing to go through with it" has an ironic edge since perfection is what has been irrevocably lost. Great manipulator that he is, the man has used "perfectly" throughout the conversation. The word *it* gets no clear antecedent. Jig is a good listener. She hears that the unborn child (an "it") doesn't mean "anything" to him. Her modest proposal that "We could get along" doesn't offer an attractive agenda: getting along rings minimally. On one level, he pays her the supreme compliment: "I don't want any one else." Rather than selfishness, he offers adoration—a pregnancy takes her from him. So he switches the meaning of "it" once again as he strikes the now familiar refrain: "I know it's perfectly simple." When she agrees—"Yes, you know it's perfectly simple"—her voice, which would likely accent the "you," indicates that she has a different kind of knowledge. Righting this relationship would not be "perfectly simple." When he counters, "It's all right for you to say that," does his voice accent "right" or "you"? The first would be less aggressive, but the point is moot. He will give no ground, but Jig knows how to gain an advantage, and so she remains in the interrogative mood. When he responds with "I'd do anything for you," he pronounces the words of the traditional gallant. Often the promise proves hollow, and Jig is not taken in by the line. Her request that he stop talking is not the request that he had expected. Her repetition of "please" seven times accents her desperation. Writing "The Short Happy Life of Francis Macomber," Hemingway may have recalled Jig's line when he dramatizes Robert Wilson's barrage of words, crushing Margot. Only when she offers "please" is Wilson willing to stop (28).

214:22–26 **He did not . . . the girl said.** Stunned, he stops for a few moments. In contrast to Jig's looking from the platform across the fertile plain, the man looks at their bags against the wall, an impasse. The labels on the bags depict a history and reflect the life he wants—not a home but hotels, travel, adventure. And he wants that travel to be without consequences. The hotels where they "spent nights" takes the theme back to the sexual. The sexual energy will be spent, with nothing other than the spending as the reward. He does not pause for long, but his meaning is not caught in the precision of language. He does not say what he does not want her to do. His declaration that he doesn't "care anything about it" could mean that he doesn't care anything about her decision (though he clearly does) or that he doesn't care anything about the unborn child. For him, the pregnancy is not something of value. Threatening to scream, she uses a defense of last resort.

214:27–35 **The woman . . . "finish the beer."** The appearance of the Spanish woman saves them for the moment. Ever practical, as she puts the two beers on the felt pads, she notes that the train will arrive in five minutes: they cannot linger over the beer. We are told that the woman entered through the bamboo bead curtain, but not that the man pays the tab. There is a point in keeping the emphasis on the beads that Jig earlier fingered, beads that speak of division, desperation, and supplication. The impending arrival of the train keeps to the fore the importance of time to the story. It is running out for the couple's relationship, and it moves apace in the process of gestation. Jig needs to have a translation of the woman's caution (we are again reminded of Jig's dependency). The repetition emphasizes the inexorability of time and the passing of opportunity. It's time to drink up and pay up. By smiling in thanks at the woman, Jig affirms that she means to be pleasant. That the smile is "bright" punctuates her effort and her intelligence: she recognizes where the conversation with the man has led. Composed, she is ready to proceed with her new knowledge, and so she can now smile at him. Her smile is as enigmatic as that of the *Mona Lisa*. Uncomfortable, the man looks for something to "do" in the next five minutes. Since the train to Madrid travels on a different track, he finds reprieve at the difficult moment by announcing that he should carry the bags to the other tracks, from the side of the station that looks on the fertile valley. When Jig tells him to come back so that they can finish the beer together, we sense great finality—the end of something. The man is in no hurry for the final libation—even though the five minutes are already fleeting.

214:36–43 **the two heavy bags . . . "I feel fine."** The bags are heavy, about as much baggage as the man wants. The action of carrying the bags around the station is appropriate to the theme of division central to the story. Seeing no train yet, he counts on a little more time. Delaying his return to Jig, he enters the barroom, where he sees others waiting for the train, more relaxed than he. He orders and drinks an Anis, the drink that tastes like licorice, the drink that Jig made into a symbol of decay. He studies the people, all waiting "reasonably" for the train—people from a different culture. For them, the waiting at the station has not been a strain. The man breaks through the bead curtain, willing to negate whatever spiritual dimension Jig may have attached to the beads she had previously fondled. Jig retains her role of acceptance. Again she smiles at him enigmatically. When he asks her if she is feeling better, we may be reminded of his earlier "You know how I get." Are her feelings the issue here—or his? Her response implies that she is not the issue any longer; he is. Her "There's nothing wrong with me" lets us know that she does not view her pregnancy as a disease. The repetition also suggests an assurance, a wisdom beyond that any buzz from the drinks may have produced. The woman emerges as the stronger of the two, willing to accept consequences and able to accept limits. Tellingly, Hemingway gives her the last word. Whatever her decision about abortion, she has become the one who "knows"—but she does not need to flaunt her new strength.

THE KILLERS

For many years the Hemingway story one was most likely to find in anthologies, "The Killers" served as a prototype of the Hemingway story. That fame was enhanced further when a movie that owed its opening and some of its themes to the story advertised itself as *The Killers* and prompted the Hemingway connection in its advertising. Universal's 1946 adaptation starring Burt Lancaster and Ava Gardner eventually took its place among the classics of film noir. In 1964 Universal took another slant on the theme, this work an effective neo-noir that bore even less direct relation to the short story, though thematic links to the story remained. Ronald Reagan played the villain, his last role in Hollywood; Lee Marvin and Clu Gulagar made splendid hit men. In 1959 and 1960 Buick Electra Playhouse presented A. E. Hotchner's adaptation for television.

With the placement of "The Killers" in *Men Without Women* directly after "Hills Like White Elephants," Hemingway accents the waiting central to both stories. In that waiting, both stories depend on dialogue to advance the narrative. The issue in both stories is the ending of a life (the boxer Ole Andreson in "The Killers," and that of an embryo in "Hills Like White Elephants"). Both stories end with a conspicuous silence—there is no killing in the first story; the reader cannot be certain of Jig's decision about whether or not to abort. Ole believes his murder certain, and most readers have concluded that Jig will follow through with her declaration to "do it" even though her partner gives her a lot of space to reconsider that decision. The title of the Spanish story emphasizes metaphor; the title of the story that follows eschews metaphor for blunt reality.

215:1-5 **Henry's lunch-room . . . "want to eat."** The opening is lean, spare, which is drastically different from the longer, discursive opening he rejected. Physical action carries the terse opening paragraph. There is purpose, no hesitation, in the two men who enter. Changing the verb tense from past to present in the paragraph, we would have a virtual script for a movie. The name *Henry* invites readers to view the story as a variation of an O. Henry story; John V. Hagopian and Martin Dolch suggest specifically "The Ransom of Red Chief," citing the town by the name of Summit in both stories and the shared intention in both of "amusing" a captive. Paul

Smith suggests that the name *Henry's* for the lunchroom is itself a witty allusion: [O] Henry's (142). If "The Killers" is a prototypical Hemingway story, it may be contrasted with the prototypical O. Henry story, famous for the surprise at the end.

That we are in a lunchroom indicates a certain informality, suggests transience, haste—lunch more than dinner. (Why does Ole choose Henry's? Likely, he does so for food, not companionship, and moderate prices. Since this lunchroom was a saloon before Prohibition, there is a mirror in back of the counter permitting Ole or anyone sitting at the counter not only a close view of those working on the other side of it but a view of the rest of the room as well.)

Like the opening paragraph, the speech we first hear is direct, plain. George uses the language of efficiency. The minimalism is in keeping with the atmosphere of the lunchroom that was once a saloon. His question asking what the men want is more loaded than it first seems. The customer's response to George is a bit unexpected. Food, as it turns out, had not been his primary concern when he entered Henry's, but now he must give some thought to that matter. His question to his companion marks them as a team. The response, echoing his partner's questions, sets the tone for the story. It could go anywhere.

215:6–9 **Outside . . . they came in.** The narrator's words immediately following the balanced speeches of the two men let us know that there will be a very dark underside to the comedy of the opening dialogue. At five o'clock the emerging darkness outside is enough to trigger the arc light; the time is late autumn—a season of death. We suddenly realize that there is someone else at the counter. That the narrator immediately provides first and last names gives Nick special importance, especially for readers who recall his importance in *In Our Time*. Nick is watching, and the reader watches more intently with him. The appearance of the two men caught his attention and now their statements have as well. Nick's purpose in the lunchroom becomes of immediate interest. This is not terrain like any in which he is found in *In Our Time*. Subsequent events reveal that he is still quite young, but old enough to wander from the confines of the home of the doctor and the doctor's wife. Why is he present? What is he talking about? Does he seek advice about where he might go? What he might do? Perhaps he has been watching George, too— seeing George's job as a dead-end affair, a stepping stone at best. We can only guess. But he is not here because he is hungry. For the present, he is just an observer, perhaps "killing time" with his acquaintance, George.

215:10–216:4 **"I'll have a roast" . . . elbows on the table.** The ordering of the dinner showcases Hemingway's comic gifts—though the comedy being played becomes increasingly dark. The first man selects standard family fare. That the narrator cannot yet give us a name for this speaker (whereas he could immediately give one to George—and a full name to Nick Adams) is appropriate to the secrecy that surrounds the two customers. George's words are again minimal as he reports that the selection "isn't ready yet." In a higher-class establishment, we would expect a less blunt reply, something more positive for the customer. Although the first man is annoyed, the vehemence of his question marks him as an aggressive type: "What the hell do you put it on the card for?" It is not unreasonable for the item to be listed on the menu, as he implies. But he is also enjoying the game he is playing. *Hell* is a word natural to the vocabulary of the two men; they will utter it five times during their wait at Henry's, a forceful touch in Hemingway's creation of the story's atmosphere. George again relies on the language of efficiency. His explanation that the dinner will be ready at 6:00 has us as well as the men looking at the clock, aware of passing time—just as we were in "Hills Like White Elephants." Making a whole paragraph of the sentence showing George looking at the clock dramatizes the theme of time. George must turn from the man to look at the clock and then look back. The counting of minutes becomes crucial for building tension as the story proceeds. Probably the man has a watch, but it is perfectly reasonable for him to point out the discrepancy between George's statement and what the clock says. As many have noted, the situation prefigures absurdist drama. Why, one wonders, doesn't George or someone else move the hands on the clock? Is George the reasonable force he seemed to be? The first man again shows his impatience. He would like to get something to eat, and on rereading we are struck that his appetite could be real under the circumstances. Responding to the petulance of his customers, he lists the options but wastes no words. But the first speaker wishes to play verbal games instead, enjoying the unease that George has not been able to hide. He asks for items not on George's list. The exchange with George has all the marks of vaudeville, as Hemingway intends. It is not, however, the dinner that the men really wait for. Poor George.

Eventually, the second man, Al, orders ham and eggs. Were he a practicing Jew (his Jewish heritage is clarified later), he would not be ordering ham. That is a minor point that has struck many critics. A much more significant point is that if he were a true believer, he would not be in the business of killing. His companion, whose heritage is apparently Roman Catholic, is similarly far removed from what is most fundamental in that creed. The description of Al's clothes at this point in the story sends the reader back to see again the events that have already transpired, to imagine the expressions on George's face and Nick's face as the two enter. Al's derby hat and black overcoat, his silk muffler and gloves, are in keeping with the vaudeville tenor of the dialogue. The clothing is certainly unexpected in any neighborhood diner or lunchroom. Though Al's face is small, he is a large threat. The whiteness of his face removes him from the natural world; he is not much in the natural world. His tight lips suggest that he is selfish, not warm or passionate. He is also the "tight-lipped" one of the duo. His partner is more given to pleasure in the sound of his own voice.

The narrator still awaits the first speaker's name. His order is only slightly different (and would not be fare for an observant Jewish patron). Like Al, he is small—

but he knows how to compensate for his size. They are "dressed like twins"—in genuine vaudeville style. Both wear overcoats that are too tight. (The tightness, we later surmise, is a result of the large guns they conceal.) The portrait is comic in its stress on their "twinness": both men are leaning forward, elbows on the counter. Neither bows to etiquette, the conventions of society.

216:5–25 **"anything to drink?" . . . "bright boys," Max said.** Although the narrator does not so report (doing so might detract from the tension that overlays the dialogue), it becomes clear that George has passed the two orders back to the kitchen. While the food is being prepared, the two think about something to drink. Al's question implies that since there is no dinner available, there may not be drink either, which from his perspective is the case. The three items George lists are, of course, nonalcoholic. Henry's is not a speakeasy, and we may well infer that the story takes place during Prohibition. The brevity of the list supports the sense that the diner is modest. Silver beer is something like cream soda. *Bevo* sounds like a local name; its root (like that of *beverage*) is from a Middle English verb meaning "to drink." Ginger ale is the right ending of the series: in the climactic spot it teases with "ale"—as strong a drink as one can get in Henry's. Perhaps a nonalcoholic drink is all that a reasonable person would expect in a neighborhood diner even prior to Prohibition. But these recent arrivals demand special treatment.

The stichomythia is carefully patterned: Al and Max ask questions, and George provides answers. Suddenly, one question goes to Nick Adams. The reader may have all but forgotten Nick is present. He has had no lines, has apparently said nothing. George's unease has been to the fore, but a second reading of the story may have the reader imagining Nick's perspective as the two men take control of the diner with their sarcasm.

The drinking options cause Al's companion to join the sport of ridiculing the diner and the community. The killers are not local and would rather be elsewhere; they have no desire to be in so backward a town. Summit is a suburb of Chicago on the Des Plaines River. Its name rings ironically. The narrator's reference to Al's companion as *friend* is moot. That term also rings ironically. The two men are business partners and perhaps no more.

The companion is "friend" to the extent that he joins the game of adding to George's unease. When Al asks what people do at night in this "hot" town, he gives Max a satisfying moment and his best line: "They eat the dinner. . . . They all come here and eat the big dinner." He is pleased with his wit—and the ridicule of George as well. George prefers not to argue with the assessment of Summit. His assumption is not that the customer is always right, but rather these two are not to be trifled with. The game here is cat and mouse, George being the mouse.

Al continues to seek George's breaking point. Nick is studying George's responses as well as the taunts of the two men. Calling George "pretty" might evoke a strong reaction from George under other circumstances. "Boy" suggests immaturity and condescension, especially with *bright* as the accompanying adjective. (In the story "The Light of the World" in Hemingway's 1933 collection *Winner Take Nothing*, Nick observes that Tom reacts very differently when he encounters this insult in a real saloon.) George retains a submissive role, even as the narrator reminds us that both of these dark men are little men. Their behavior here is certainly little and belittling. The insult becomes precise when Al labels George "dumb." George's responses here prove to be rather smart. With George so neatly labeled, Al turns toward Nick, all but forgotten—surely inviting the reader's reflection on Nick's emotions during the banter with George. Al is accustomed to asking questions and getting answers. Asked his name, Nick also responds minimally, letting a last name suffice—a tougher stance than "Nick" would have been. It is useful for the reader to be reminded of the primal Adam, the innocent in a world he never made.

It's time for Nick to be similarly insulted. Al repeats the snide label twice, the second time as a question to Max. This is Al's first direct address of Max by name, granting permission now for the narrator to use it. The label *bright boys* stresses the convergence of Nick and George's fate. Both are young, naive. That the town is "full of bright boys" indeed makes it a Summit.

216:26–44 **two platters . . . went on eating.** The eating of the dinners follows the extended attention to the ordering of the dinners, then the wait during the cooking, a segment with its own humor. George does not remember which "twin" ordered which dish, the dishes being essentially the same, as the side dishes of fried potatoes accent. Mention of the wicket into the kitchen prepares us for a drama soon to take place there. The strange interlude while the order was being prepared more than justifies George's uncertainty about which dish goes to which man and provides Al with another opportunity to belittle George. Who speaks the line "Ham and eggs"? It might be George, offering the plate to whichever man wants it. More likely, Al is the speaker, adding further to George's befuddlement as Max reaches for the plate. (Giving one speaker two speeches in a row without some tag is a device that Hemingway sometimes found useful.) The testing of George gets more complicated. Although Al said that he ordered ham and eggs (he did), Max takes them, which leaves the bacon and eggs for Al. Neither man comments on the switched orders. Their expressions convey their sadistic pleasure as George's anxiety increases. Every word and every gesture of the two men ensure that George will not look away from these customers. He surely intuits that the men keep their gloves on for a purpose that does not bode well. His stare gives Max's sadistic belligerence further play. George's "nothing" to Max's question is prudent, for Max likes a fight, enjoys seeing George squirm: "You were looking at me," he accuses. Al remains part of the act. He does not for a moment think that George is joking: Max and Al are the jokers. Laughter can ease tension, and George attempts to oblige. He long ago decided that the best course is to give these two what they ask for, if he can. But in the killers' routine, laughter is not the desired response; it is fear, and the two men have been succeeding. They are the ones who get to laugh at the victims of the joke. Poor George cannot win: agreement is the wrong answer. "That's a good one," Max responds—as if George has told him a funny story. The reader may be less inclined to mock George's mental abilities. George is playing a new game about as well as might be expected. The impersonality of the work of the hired killers is underscored by their eating. They may not be getting the six o'clock dinner, but their appetites are hearty and the fare satisfactory, else they would have complained about it. "They went on eating." Paul Smith suggests that in writing this scene of multiple confusions Hemingway discovered the "ironic dislocation" that became essential to the story (139–40).

216:45–217:32 **"bright boy's name"** . . . **shut after them.** Their dinner completed, Al and Max reorder the scene in preparation for the real business of their visit. The reader is suddenly reminded of Nick's presence. Nick has been silent all this time—analyzing, no doubt mesmerized by, the two men and their manipulation of George. From the "thinker" George, attention shifts to another "bright boy." Asking Max the name of that "bright boy," Al may have forgotten that he had already asked the question, or he is testing Max, who had not remembered either; nor does either particularly care. "Bright boy" will do for address and is certainly more fun than "Nick." Al and Max don't know George's name either. Max might have said, "your friend," but he chooses instead "boy friend," the sexual innuendo obvious. Nick bristles, more inclined than George to protest being bullied. Nick had grown up with the understanding that the world is rational, can be explained. But the idea he will have to come to terms with is that the world does not make sense. Max's "There isn't any idea" has a level beyond glibness.

When Max orders Nick to the other side of the counter, we may surmise that this is the moment when the large guns under the too tight overcoats become visible. Or it may be that the tough, aggressive behavior of the two men is enough to cause Nick to join George on the other side of the counter. Risking more than he has before, George repeats Nick's question: "What's the idea?" But likely his tone is less assertive than Nick's a moment before. That the "idea" is not humorous is clear, and just as clearly this is George's business and Nick's—though they have been told otherwise in a telling phrase: "None of your damn business." Al's "damn" adds to the aura of the infernal, and a few moments later Max follows suit: "We know damn well where we are." George and Nick must wish that they were not where they are at this time.

Being thorough about their business, Al and Max want to know who is in the kitchen. In responding, George partakes of the unthinking racism of his time. The word *nigger* recurs in quick succession. That Hemingway was aware of the plight of the black person in his country should be no surprise. In "The Battler," the last of the stories to be written for inclusion in *In Our Time,* a black convict joins the catalog of memorable characters in the Hemingway canon; Bugs impinges dramatically on young Nick Adams's life, helping to shape Nick's understanding of life. With the introduction of Sam, the cook, into "The Killers," Hemingway again depicts a revealing reality of his time. Even the narrator twice uses the term, which is natural to George, Max, and Al, making race the telling feature of identification. The narrator turns only later to letting Sam's profession serve as identification marker.

Other repetitions occur. Twice, Al will order George to call Sam. (Interrogative and imperative—these are the operative grammatical moods for Max and Al.) Twice George asks "What's the idea?" the question Nick had asked only moments before. Al repeats his command in answer to the question.

Somewhat desperate, George risks even more. When he asks, "Where do you think you are?" he risks a great deal. Perhaps he hopes that Al and Max have made some mistake. How can they belong here? Max, less patient than Al, returns to the conversation, his "damn well" asserting that they don't make mistakes. Asking "Do we look silly?" Max uses speech that plays on the dark comedy of the scene. George and Nick may be surprised that Al is annoyed with Max. There is no need to argue with a "kid." He repeats his command that George bring the cook out. George may be wondering if Max and Al's appearance has something to do with the cook. Decently, he shows his concern for Sam by again risking a question, which again permits Al to amuse himself with homosexual innuendo. Summoned, Sam immediately does as he is told. He is puzzled by the request for his presence in the dining room; usually he is out of sight. Al and Max look him over, finding little threat in his appearance. Al chooses the hurtful epithet though he knows the cook's name. (Al and Max never use Nick's name either, though they have asked for it. To address someone by name implies recognition of personhood.) When Sam is addressed with the epithet, he knows that there is implied threat, knows the behavior that is expected—submission. The narrator's appositive is by definition unnecessary, but its use as the unthinking appositive suggests a more neutral use of that complex word—George's earlier use. Sam does not ask, "What's the idea?" but responds as he has been conditioned to respond: "Yes, sir." *Sir* enters the story for the first time; it is not a natural word for George, but it is a natural word for the African American of the time. Southern blacks knew that omitting it could be perilous to them, and northern blacks like Sam would likely use *Sir* to address a white intimidator. Al gets down from the stool because Max and Al are ready to move from preliminary diversion to execution of their strategy.

Although there is no mention of it, Al's gun may now be visible, though it is also possible that the aggressive speech and manner of the two men in black continue to be enough to intimidate a young man and a black man into obedience on the assumption that there are guns behind the threats. Nick knows that the "bright boy" of Al's order is himself. Al addresses Sam with the expected epithet. Al is the "little man" (like Retana of "The Undefeated") who can make an ultimatum stick. That narrator again supplies an appositive for Sam, this time his profession, "the cook." As Nick and Sam enter the kitchen, George's question about the duo's intention seems to get an ominous answer: "The door shut after them." The possibility of execution behind it is strong.

217:32–218:6 **man called Max . . . a group picture.** As attention returns to the scene in the outer diner, the narrator again teases with appellations. "Max" would suffice for designation, but "The man called Max" implies that such might not even be his name. It might be the name of someone in a vaudeville team—not much clue to identity. The narrator shares something of the uncertainty of George and Nick trying to pin matters down. That Max sits directly opposite George emphasizes the degree of control. In back of George is a mirror that allows Max to see what is behind him. This is the moment the narrator chooses to report that Henry's was formerly a saloon, now a lunch counter. But it is a lunch counter now incarnating the saloons of the Old West—scenes of shootouts and killings. Anticipation and waiting are often part of those scenarios; so it is in Henry's.

Max doesn't wish to be bored during the waiting. George will suit for further insult and amusement. Invited to say something, George replies with a quite natural question: "What's it all about?" Max is in no hurry as he enjoys George's anxiety. The food passageway to the kitchen having been propped open, Max is able to bring Al into the drama, delaying a bit longer an answer. Like the cat with the mouse, Max still delays—twice inviting "bright boy" to guess what "it's all about." All the while, Max's primary attention is focused on the mirror, which gives him a clear view of what is behind him. From the kitchen, Al is also concerned with a clear view. Accordingly, he instructs George and Max to alter their positions slightly. The narrator's "like a photographer arranging for a group picture" doesn't clarify what "it's all about"—but it is an ironic simile for his instructions. With the possibility for blood behind his purpose, the ketchup bottle as propping instrument is appropriate. It is not a group picture that is being arranged, but, it will soon be made clear, potentially a group slaughter. Hit men do not like to leaave witnesses.

218:7–27 **"Talk to me" . . . "a friend, bright boy."** Al's instructions have made it clear that something is going to happen. Silence best serves George and is the effective narrative preparation for Max's revelation. "I'll tell you" sets up an effective delay as the knowing Max can at last inform "bright boy." The announcement that they are going to kill "a Swede" is appropriate to the impersonality of the victim as far as Max and Al are concerned. Max's third sentence finally puts a face to the deed. Ole Andreson is the only character in the story other than Nick Adams to be given two names. The designation of "a Swede" invites comparison of "The Killers" to Stephen Crane's "The Blue Hotel," a harsh frontier story that results in the death of an unfortunate Swede. Blind chance plays an important role in both stories. Terrorized, George answers Max's questions promptly, minimally. Explaining the reason for this setting for the killing, Max ends by undercutting his own position as the knowing one. In asking the question about Ole's patterns, he admits the possibility that the evening's premise might be amiss, and George's "sometimes" presents an uncertainty in a story of uncertainties. The uncertain note for Max comes with a second "don't he?" as he asks the time Ole usually arrives. (The clock so strangely set is a fitting emblem for the uncertainty about events.) Max is irritated, his "knowing" now suspect. He wants George to "Talk about something else."

So he turns to the movies. The situation of the moment anticipates the gangster movie; Max and Al seem to have stepped from the screen of the 1930s and 1940s. The movies that Max has known have been silent films. He associates them with narrow escapes, adventure, entertainment. The waiting seems to have become burdensome for Max. Something seems wrong with this script. Max seeks to recapture his confidence at George's expense. "The movies are fine for a bright boy like you." Encountering Max's statement, the contemporary reader will likely delight in the memories of the contribution Hemingway's story made to the movies—perhaps recalling the 1946 film noir that replays some of these same lines in a lonely diner as two paid killers arrive to await the appearance of a Swede they mean to murder. Or the reader may juxtapose the crude Al and Max against the much more sophisticated killers who grab our attention in the 1946 neo-noir film. In either case, Hemingway's story was "fine" for the movies.

George refuses to follow Max's lead. He asks, instead, a real question. There must be a "reason" that Max and Al would want to kill Ole. In a reasonable world, he would have done something of great magnitude to compel them to murder. But it is not a "reasonable" world. Max and Al have never even met Ole. From the kitchen, Al shares in the pleasure of this frightening admission. He takes pleasure as well in their efficiency as a hit team. George pushes for some reason for the killers' determination to finish their task. The stark revelation that the men are paid killers gives George a harsh truth. Murder can be quite impersonal. The ironical words are *for a friend*. Friendship, to judge by their relationship to each other, is not a prized value for Al and Max.

218:28–35 **"Shut up," said Al ... "where you were."** From the kitchen, Al rebukes Max, sparring with him. Al's annoyance with his comrade is emphasized with a "goddam" as well as a "damn." Max's defense rings hollow, and after this spat with Al, the baiting of George ceases. Snidely, Al mocks Max's Jewish heritage and in doing so shows his obsession with homosexual innuendo. A "kosher convent" is a lame joke; *convent* derives from the Roman Catholic tradition and usually means "nunnery." The allusion to kashruth (observed by Orthodox Jews) reminds us that Al's meal was not kosher.

218:36–219:9 **George looked up . . . "not coming."** A one-sentence paragraph heightens the suspense of the story and plays nicely against its cinematic conception. The clock suggests that the hour at which Ole arrives fast approaches, and

Max guards against eventualities of other customers—instructing George on the routine he wants him to follow. George has more than Ole's arrival on his mind. He has absolutely no doubt that Max and Al will dispatch Ole and asks about his fate—and Sam and Nick's. Max's answer is perfect for maintaining suspense. He holds out some hope for George, better ensuring his cooperation if others come in. When George notes that the clock reads 6:15, he knows that Ole should arrive in five minutes. The killers are also primed for Ole's arrival. Anticlimatically, the door opens and a streetcar motorman enters. He is a regular customer, knows George, calls him by name. Henry's is a neighborhood establishment. The request is for *supper*, the common designation for the evening meal, a term more appropriate to Henry's than the *dinner* that Max and Al requested. George gives the excuse he has been instructed to give, though it is a strange way to run a diner. Sam's name is familiar to the motorman, or George would have said, "The cook's gone out." As George looks at the clock (cinema often gives glimpses of clocks at dramatic moments), we note that the time when Ole usually appears has arrived. Max has to praise George's performance, though he does so in condescending words. "Bright boy" remains. "Regular little gentleman" is common in adult praise of a small boy who has pleased. Al provides a contrast from the kitchen, affirming for George what the reality is. Max has, in fact, become fond of George, though his words leave George far from certain of Max's sincerity. Captors who get to know their hostages frequently come to "like" them. It is to George's advantage that Max has been talking to him, sitting right in front of him. A good half hour beyond Ole's expected arrival passes. George has good reason to observe that Ole isn't coming this evening.

219:10–21 **Two other people . . . "ten minutes," Max said.** Business is not brisk at Henry's, and this fact may have played a part in Ole's choice of Henry's as a favorite diner. George is experienced enough to make a ham-and-egg sandwich. It is a dramatic moment for him and the reader, enabling both to see the kitchen. Al's station and his sawed-off shotgun (the first specific mention of a weapon) confirm that the situation is dire. George and the reader see Sam and Nick tied back to back and ponder what this waiting has felt like to them. On the floor, in the corner, they have not heard what has been going on in the other room. Each has a towel stuffed in his mouth, but each can see Al and the shotgun. Although the derby hat gives a comical aspect to Al, neither Nick nor Sam nor George likely thinks about much other than the danger they are in. Pleased by George's efficiency, Max lightens the scene—at least for himself—and again plays the homosexual note. George would "make some girl a nice wife." George shows his philosophical side. His "Yes?" is bemused, for it puts the spotlight on him now that it seems clear that Ole is not coming. Will he have the chance to be a spouse? He shows a gentle irony as he calls Ole Max's "friend." Duration is crucial to the fictional technique of the story. George will have to wait a bit longer.

219:22–45 **Max watched . . . a vaudeville team.** The times are out of joint for Max and Al, too, as the clock continues to tick. It is now forty-five minutes past Ole's usual dinner hour. This is a dramatic moment for George as Max indicates to Al that they are wasting their time. Five minutes more—sometimes the lover's request, but here prolonged agony for George—and for Nick and Sam, who can hear Al; they now realize that their waiting is about to end. For Max and Al, the absurdity (and risk) of further waiting is manifest when another customer enters. The potential customer underscores the absurdity of a lunch counter that is open but without a cook. His question is couched in diction that conveys more of the situation than he realizes: "Why the hell don't you get another cook?" He is too annoyed to wait for answers, not sensing that George is at the moment in a kind of hell.

Max also sees the absurdity of a diner without a cook. He is ready to chart a new course of action. What do they do with George, Nick, and Sam? George has been in a difficult spot for some time, and he does not crumble now. He has been acting with grace under considerable pressure. As Al and Max confer, George wisely remains silent. His dialogue with the killers has ended. Al likes all ends tied up. It's "sloppy" to leave witnesses behind. Although his tone makes clear that he is also ready to leave, he criticizes Max's methods: "You talk too much." He is repeating a charge that he made earlier in the evening when he also accused Max of talking "silly." Max is more laid back than his partner. His notion of "amusement" is appropriate to the vaudeville routine that their costumes and speech have captured. Al won't let Max have the last word on the matter. When he leaves the kitchen, Sam and Nick do not know why. But they sense some relief as Al places the sawed-off shotgun under the waist of his overcoat, where it had been when he entered Henry's. The image of the bulge at the waist—the promise of death rather than life—will reappear in the opening scene of *A Farewell to Arms,* where the narrator Frederic Henry describes an autumnal scene in 1915 with troops marching by and "under their capes the two leather cartridge-boxes on the front of the belts, gray leather boxes heavy with the packs of clips of thin, long 6.5 mm. cartridges, bulged forward under the capes so that the men, passing on the road, marched as though they were six months gone with child" (4).

Max takes pleasure one last time in George's emotional swings of the evening. His final words, "bright boy," make an effective adieu. "Bright boy" has become Max's name for George; Al has maintained a more descriptive stance with the expression—lumping George, Nick, and Sam together as "bright boys." The appellation *bright boy* occurs twenty-four times in the story, seventeen of them from Max's lips. *Bright boys* occurs twice. For him, Nick and George do not matter as individuals. Max's advice to George to play the races is a metaphor appropriate to his view of life. George indeed counts himself "lucky" as the two men leave. In "Today Is Friday"—created in the same burst of creative activity as "The Killers"—the first soldier says of Jesus: "Oh, he ain't lucky" (273:9). The departure takes us back to the opening words of the story. The moment brings a kind of closure. If this were

George's story, it could well end here as the killers go into the ominous night, passing under the arclight and crossing the street. Their tight overcoats remind us that they have destruction to deal. They look like a vaudeville team still—but they are something very different.

219:45–220:25 **George went back . . . "go up there."** Al and Max gone from the diner, George enters the kitchen to see how Nick and Sam have endured the past hour. A two-sentence paragraph memorably captures Nick's reaction. The first sentence, "Nick stood up," echoes exactly the opening sentence of "The Battler" from *In Our Time*. There Nick has been tricked by the brakeman and thrown off the moving freight train on which he had hopped a ride. His instinct there is for anger, recovery, revenge. Here, as we read the companion sentence, we sense shock: "He had never had a towel in his mouth before." Following the lead of Cleanth Brooks and Robert Penn Warren in their influential textbook *Understanding Fiction* (317), multitudes of readers have seen the sentence as the pivotal sentence of the story, one that places Nick Adams as the central figure.

The image underscores Nick's innocence. What he has just experienced with Al and Max has been far more threatening than the danger he faced in "The Battler." His first words—"Say . . . . What the hell?"—are appropriate to his attempt to "swagger off" the ordeal, but they are also eerily appropriate to the infernal that Al and Max illustrate. There is nothing of the youthful in Sam's reaction to the towel in his mouth; he has probably endured humiliation often. He feels the corners of his mouth, the physical discomfort real. There is no swagger in him. After George explains the purpose of the visitors, Sam, even more determinedly, chooses noninvolvement. Nick, however, does not hesitate when George advises that he should warn Andreson. Explanations do not concern Sam; he wants only that the terrorizers indeed be gone. The simplicity of Nick's acquiescence to George's advice anticipates a life of engagement. Like many of his generation, he would respond promptly to the endangered Allies once his country entered the Great War. George understands that there is danger in attempting the rescue; he prefers that the decision be Nick's, that he feel no pressure from his friend. Sam's admonition of avoidance is insistent, but he is not surprised that he is ignored. With no expectation of changing Nick's mind, he generalizes that "Little boys always know what they want to do." The epithet *boy* returns with a new qualifier, one that suggests the innocence and naïveté of Nick's choice, an innocence paralleled in "In Another Country" by his decision to volunteer in the war. "I'll go up there" encapsulates Nick's heroic bent.

220:26–30 **the arc-light shone . . . came to the door.** The extended paragraph following another scene of stichomythic dialogue marks the transition to the final movement of the story, one that plays against the first—an arrival and a departure, an attempt at rescue rather than killing. The arc light recalls the image of the departing killers and the bare branches of the autumnal scene. Nick goes into the dark and all its uncertainty, following the streetcar tracks, grateful for the light of the arc light that points to the side street where Hirsch's rooming house lies. Nick, determined in his mission, does not hesitate at the door and immediately rings the bell. When a woman answers, we reflect that she is the first woman to appear in this story. The female presence—images of creation and nourishment (which the tight coats of the killers with their bulge of "pregnancy" parody)—has been strikingly absent.

220:31–43 **"Ole Andreson here?" . . . look at Nick.** There is nothing in Nick's appearance that would lead the woman to distrust him as he asks if Andreson is in, and she promptly leads him to Andreson's door. The sound of her knock, we later reflect, must have had a heart-quickening effect on the boxer, who has been expecting a knock at the door—the frightening knock of death. The allusion might be to *Macbeth* or to *The Waste Land*. The woman's "somebody to see you" could only heighten Andreson's anxiety. It is Nick who tells Andreson what he wants to know, and Nick—we gather—is someone he knows, probably from Henry's. The two fully named characters of the story now come together. Entering as invited, Nick sees Andreson lying on the bed with his clothes on. Perhaps he had prepared to go to dinner and then lacked the courage to proceed. The bed is too short for the prizefighter, a big man—in contrast to Al and Max, both little men. He is not only a man without a woman; he is a man who is very much alone. That his head is on two pillows suggests that he was expecting to see something, but he does not look at Nick. Nick is not the visitor he expected.

220:44–221:30 **"What was it?" . . . "Thanks for coming around."** Nick's exchange with Andreson is markedly different from earlier dialogue in the story. Andreson sets the tone by using past tense as he asks Nick, "What was it?" Andreson counts his life in the past tense. Nick's summary is as brief as possible, presenting the essentials, issuing the warning. No one is trying to impress anyone, and Nick thinks his account sounds silly. "You talk silly," Al had said to Max. Nick's words sound silly to him only because they reflect the irrational sequence of the evening and the absurdity of the world.

Andreson's response perplexes Nick. Andreson, looking at the wall, recognizes that he has no place to turn. His posture and attitude recall Herman Melville's "Bartleby, the Scrivener." A copyist in a Wall Street firm, Bartleby had concluded that his life has reached a dead end and so chose to cease struggling. When asked to perform a task, Bartleby would reply, "I would prefer not to." His response was baffling to his well-meaning employer, just as Nick is similarly baffled by Andreson's response to his news. Nick's response to danger and adversity is quite different.

Andreson does not seek information or companionship. Nick's information can be of no assistance to him. So he continues to look at the wall rather than at Nick.

Thanking Nick for coming, he is dismissing him. Once again the one-sentence paragraph not part of the stichomythia gives the reader a moment of pause and of silence. There is no new information, but emotional weight, as Nick looks at the "big man" lying on the bed, in essence already a corpse. Nick still wants to believe that Andreson has some choice. "No" is Andreson's insistent word, his Bartleby-like refrain as Nick continues to press for some positive course of action. The desperate one here is Nick, not the boxer. Andreson's grammar tells us something about the world that shaped him, which is not like Nick's. Son of a medical doctor, Nick has learned better grammar. That will help him as a writer (*In Our Time* creates a Nick Adams destined to be a writer), but it also accents that he has had a more protected youth than Ole Andreson had. As the boxer again rolls over toward the wall, Hemingway echoes "Indian Camp," the opening story of *In Our Time*, and Nick's question there: "Is dying hard, Daddy?" (70). Nick ponders the same question in this story—and now has a better answer. In the early story, he could see himself only faintly in the dead husband. Readers who know *In Our Time* know that Nick in chapter 6 of that work has his back against a wall—but can still look outward, make a "separate peace," an option not open to Andreson. Again, the single-sentence paragraph creates a powerful pause. Following the pause, Andreson defines the issue, a kind of confession to Nick. He waits for the moment of his choosing when he can do the difficult thing: he wants to face his executioners with dignity. Nick has difficulty comprehending Andreson's position. He believes in action, controlling the events of his life. Andreson's life has been a life of action and of complications. Harold Krebs of "Soldier's Home," a story in *In Our Time*, wants a life without consequences and at the end of the story plans to seek it by leaving town. Andreson would be able to tell him that "running around" won't work. We again read, like an insistent drumbeat, that he "looked at the wall." Still, Nick wonders if the boxer couldn't "fix it up some way?" His pun here (but not Hemingway's) is entirely unintentional. Andreson is certainly in a fix, but his certain death may be the result of a fixed fight. He has been involved in one fix too many. He is, in fact, convinced that his fate is just: "I got in wrong." Nick now feels his impotence, too. Returning to George is as positive an action as he can now project, and George will want to know the outcome of Nick's visit. The narrator once more gives Andreson the full dignity of both names. Not looking at Nick, he continues looking at the wall. The reader's empathy is increased by Ole's good manners as he again thanks Nick. His "So long" is likely to be among the last farewells that he will ever make. The words carry a weight beyond the informal farewell that they typically convey

221:31–46 **Nick went out . . . the woman said.** As Nick leaves the room of impasse, he takes a final look at Ole—an image that will likely haunt him for a long time. The narrator freezes an image, repeating information firmly in the reader's consciousness: Ole Andreson lies on his bed, facing the wall, with all his clothes on. The youth, an admirer of the boxer's skill, contemplates a fallen hero. The woman waits at the bottom of the stairs. She confirms sympathy for Ole, her voice kind, gentle, concerned. To her, he is "Mr. Andreson," a "nice man," a "gentle" man. Brooks and Warren liken her to the Porter at Hell Gate in Shakespeare's *Macbeth* (319). Except for "the way his face is," one cannot tell he is a fighter. The language of civility here is, of course, in marked contrast to the prevailing discourse. Nick passes beyond the woman's commonsense reading that Ole "don't feel well" (her grammar, like that of the other characters in the story, contrasts with Nick's). Nick has come to acknowledge the dignity of Andreson's decision to accept his fate. The feminine gentleness, rare indeed in *Men Without Women,* has one of its poignant moments. Just inside the door, the landlady and Nick are aware of the harsh world outside this realm. Mention of Andreson's face points to the price that his profession can exact. (Nick will eventually learn a great deal about the price of the writing profession.) Nick's good manners are in evidence as he bids the woman good night, even attaching a name to the farewell. That Nick wrongly assumes that the woman is the landlady, Mrs. Hirsch, adds a minor but telling note about a world in which assumptions appear at best tentative. That Mrs. Bell runs Mrs. Hirsch's boarding house recalls Henry's lunchroom, formerly a saloon with no Henry in sight, and a clock that is incorrect. The mistake also accounts for the echoing "good-night" and its dark finality.

222:1–26 **Nick walked . . . "not think about it."** The story ends where it began, back at Henry's lunch counter, with the three characters who were at Henry's before the killers arrived. A stark paragraph invites reflection on Nick's thought on this "good" night as he makes his return to Henry's. There is no new information. The darkness, the arc light, the car tracks are all familiar to us. But it is a lonely walk. If Nick sees anyone else on the streets, that does not register. Nick shows no fear. Henry's is called an *eating-house* for the first time—an appellation slightly off key for what was formerly a saloon. Nick is not returning to eat, but to report to George.

Once Nick arrives, minimalist George hastens to ask the essential question. Ensuing conversation is brief, clipped. Nick responds with the essential result of his visit, letting the facts carry the emotional weight. Although he had advised against Nick going to Andreson's, Sam opens the door when he hears Nick's voice. He wants only to see for himself that Nick is all right. He quickly asserts his philosophy of non-involvement and closes the door. Some critics have asked why no one phoned the police. Sam's response is part of the answer. Grateful for their own survival, George and Nick—both young—have thought only of getting the word to Andreson. And if they had gone to the police, what possible benefit to the boxer would that have been anyway? Alerting Andreson, George and Nick have concluded, is the practical course of action.

After Nick tells George of the boxer's reaction, George also has to confront the reality. In a single word, Nick reports Andreson's decision: the boxer will do "Nothing."

The single word—evoking the despair of nihilism—carries great weight, encapsulating Andreson's resignation. Having met Al and Max, George has no doubt that they will kill Andreson. Hemingway's favorite Shakespearean play was *King Lear*, commonly considered the darkest of the tragedies. The word *nothing* is also a climactic word in that play, companion to frequent repetition of "no" and "never."

Nick's response is different from that of his friend. George reaches for explanations. Twice the verb Nick uses in response to George's verdict is *guess*. From Summit, George is conscious of the underside of Chicago, the big city that makes the many suburbs possible—the reality that the suburbs have sought to escape. He thinks Andreson got "mixed up" in something there, which he soon makes specific: the boxer double-crossed someone. George also responds emotionally to Andreson's fate: "It's a hell of a thing." Those are the last words we hear from George. There is nothing glib about his use of the word *hell*; previously it had helped define the emotional terror that Max and Al had created. Now the word applies to the special hell of Ole Andreson's wait for the arrival of those killers. In Hemingway's story, as later in Jean-Paul Sartre's *No Exit*, "Hell—is other people" (47). In what appears an irrational world, George chooses to proceed as if there is meaning and so reaches for the towel and begins wiping the counter.

For Nick, the future is more uncertain. George almost seems trapped behind that counter in Summit. Nick determines that he will leave Summit. That departure will not, of course, take him from the reality of a violent world. Nick has identified emotionally with Andreson's plight to a profound degree. The "awful thing" for him is not that Andreson will be killed but rather Andreson's "waiting in the room and knowing he's going to get it." Nick's last words in the story are companion to George's last words. "It's too damned awful," Nick declares. On this evening George and Nick have learned a great deal about hell and damnation in the modern world.

In the famous last line of the story, George advises Nick that he "better not think about it." George will likely be a better master of that art, but Nick is one of Hemingway's characters for whom the burden of thinking—especially at night—remains heavy. Stopping the thinking machine has become Nick's primary problem, a problem that will resurface in coming years. Now his problem is trying not to think about Ole's dying; it will shortly become his fear of his own demise and possibly his own resignation before a malevolent world. He ends his statement by echoing his earlier "It's an awful thing." But we need not see the ending of the story as dark only. Nick alone has been spurred to action, a departure and a new beginning. Where he might go is already foretold to the reader of *Men Without Women*. He will make his way to Italy to the Great War, where killing can be as impersonal as it is for Max and Al. But that is not the final conclusion of the matter. Nick's aspirations as a writer also are important and entail leaving Summit. In this story accenting waiting, there is much waiting implied as the story ends.

CHE TI DICE LA PATRIA?

First published in the "Opinion" section of the *New Republic* on 18 May 1927 as "Italy 1927," Hemingway's account of his trip with good friend Guy Hickok to Italy in March 1927 became "Che Ti Dice la Patria?" in *Men Without Women*. A patriotic slogan of Gabriele D'Annunzio, writer and political leader of the late nineteenth and early twentieth centuries, the title signals that the setting is Italy and reminds readers of pre-Fascist times and present reality. Minor punctuation differences (chiefly additions) likely reflect suggestions from Scribners. The new title may be translated as "What is the country saying to you?" But one does not read the story in the way that one reads the article, as journalism cast as fiction. One reads the story as fiction cast as journalism. Readers of "Italy 1927" had every right to assume that the narrator of the magazine piece is the writer with the byline, Ernest Hemingway. Readers of the story must confront the narrator differently.

Hickok, eleven years older than Hemingway, was an experienced newspaperman on assignment for the *Brooklyn Daily Eagle*. For the *Eagle* he wrote his own accounts of the excursion to Italy, and Paul Montgomery suggests that Hemingway may have read them before writing his account. Readers may sample Hickok's narrative in Montgomery's "Hemingway and Guy Hickok in Italy: *The Brooklyn Eagle* Articles." Clearly, Hemingway's methods are very different, though both writers explore the impact of Fascism on Italy. Hemingway identifies his companion only as Guy in his account. Hickok calls his companion Ernest Hemingway. The narrator of "Che Ti Dice la Patria?" remains nameless.

In Hemingway's account, the journey lasts ten days. Michael Reynolds describes that journey in *Hemingway: The American Homecoming*: Hemingway and Hickok left Paris in Hickok's Ford coupé on 15 March; Hemingway arrived back in Paris on 26 March. (Hickok was stranded in Dijon while his Ford was being repaired.) The two entered Italy on 18 March, arriving back in France on 24 March (112–15). But Hemingway's "ten days" strikes the ear as right for the focus of his narrative. "Che Ti Dice la Patria?" is the most political short story in his oeuvre. Carlos Baker's description of the journey in his biography makes clear that the journey had many meanings for Hemingway (182–83). The lesson in artistic selection is vivid.

223:1–17 **The road of the pass . . . then the woods.** The story begins in early morning and ends as dark descends that same day. The precision of detail indicates that the narrator is a keen observer, a narrator to be trusted. Although the description of the setting accents the beauty of the natural world, it also carries an ominous note. Early though it may be, time is already a concern. The roads will become dusty, and the traveler has miles to go before he sleeps. A *we* without antecedents teases, especially in the context of *Men Without Women*. The word is unidentified until line 25. What kind of unit is the "we," the reader at first wonders. Does "we" signify a married couple? Lovers? Close friends? The wooded country explains the charcoal-burner industry, a sign of the honest efforts of the working class. Sunday, especially in rural Catholic Italy, evokes the norm of religious devotion, family cohesion—a day of rest. The third use of the word *pass* prepares the reader for a heightened sense of passage and a certain inevitability, as the travelers are "always dropping." The word *village* evokes the simple life, a setting where one might hope to find a "simple" meal. That the fields are brown and the vines thick (and the roads likely to be dusty) suggests that the season is advanced. The white houses and the men in Sunday clothes playing bowls evoke the normal, the traditional, the wholesome. (For an account of the ancient Italian game *bocce*, "bowls," see Lowerson, 139–41.) The pleasing image of the branches of pear trees candelabraed against the white walls of houses is checked when the narrator adds that because the trees have been sprayed, the houses are "stained" into a "metallic" color—the most ominous note of the setting. A distinct boundary separates the village from the affirming woods. The passenger rather than driver, the narrator has had opportunity to note carefully these and subsequent scenes encountered on the journey.

223:18–224:21 **In a village . . . "leans out on the turns."** The motion of the story pauses in the fourth paragraph in the unnamed village. The young man who approaches the car breaks the pattern of normal Sunday life in the village. He is on the move. His request for a ride to Spezia is reported, not heard in his own words. Succeeding dialogue suggests that the request was not spoken graciously. The narrator's response is factual but obvious; the young man can see that the two spaces in the coupé are occupied. The response sets the tone for the episode. That the car is old, a coupé, and a Ford emphasizes that the travelers are not wealthy and are probably American, in another country. The young man, still without any awareness that he asks a great deal, is direct and terse. He does not mind being "uncomfortable." The narrator turns to his companion for his input. The reader learns that the companion is male (here a man without a woman). A family name is withheld—as is the purpose behind the journey. Guy's statement that the young man will be uncomfortable plays on the obvious and suggests that he views the world with a certain amount of detachment. The young man's arrogance is apparent as he passes his parcel through the window with an imperative without grace notes. Assistance from two men who tie the young man's suitcase to the back of the car creates some degree of community complicity in the action. The gathered crowd knows that he is a Fascist but does not draw back from his handshake. The young man shows himself committed to a cause, accustomed to travel for it, accustomed to discomfort, to holding on tightly. He stands on the running board on the driver's side of the car, holding on with his right hand through the open window. He blocks Guy's view and leans outward on curves—thereby decreasing everyone's safety. The uninvited passenger again commands ("You can start") to the pleasure of the crowd before whom he grandstands. Guy's question to the narrator (he surely heard what the passenger said) is clearly rhetorical, a part of the story's dominant irony. The narrator calls the passenger "our guest." He and Guy share pleasure in the ironical mode—a team markedly different from Max and Al of "The Killers." As they drive along, the narrator is again able to take pleasure in the natural world. He also takes pleasure in the discomfort of the young man, whose "nose looked cold." The narrator displays a talent for simile, likening the young man to "the figurehead of a ship." Ever the keen observer, he notes the discomfort as well as the purpose of the Italian. Like Al and Max in "The Killers," he and Guy work to keep themselves entertained during this wait, but they do so without antagonizing or blaming each other.

224:22–225:10 **The woods were gone . . . "twenty kilometres with us."** With the woods and river behind them, the focus is on the road, the automobile, and the handicap that the passenger clearly has become. The radiator is boiling, and Guy's driving skills are severely tested as he works the speed pedals to the top of the range above Spezia and the sea. The ascension into Spezia tests Guy's skills as much as had the ascent—short, rounded turns dominating. The Fascist nearly turns the car over. Noting Guy's annoyance, the narrator puts the best possible light on the risk the Fascist is posing. Guy, of course, has been concerned with his own preservation on this ride. Guy's response (like the metaphor of the figurehead) points to the symbolic aspect of the narrative—a journey across Italy. Decisions about "self-preservation" can be far reaching, disastrous for self and for others. They mock Italy's part in World War I. The narrator and Guy see that this episode has meaning beyond itself. As the car rounds the curves, the drama is intensified by "deep dust," which also mars the beauty of the olive trees. But at last the perils of the ride end as the "guest" puts his head inside the window and declares that he wants to stop.

Confident, nonchalant about any peril on the ride, after reclaiming his suitcase, the Fascist explains that his departure just outside Spezia will keep Guy and the narrator from trouble with the authorities for carrying him. The reader will doubt the magnanimity behind the statement. Indicating other motivation, the Fascist quickly demands his package from within. Without speaking, the narrator obliges. His silence is appropriate to the terse request—kind for kind. The Fascist then reaches into his pocket, putting the trip on a monetary rather than a fraternal basis. The narrator's "Nothing" is puzzling to the Fascist, who asks for a reason. The narrator might explain that not all exchanges can be handled with cash, that some actions are not confined to "self-preservation." Ever reluctant to use language to express human warmth, the Fascist manages a "thanks." The narrator, who has traveled in Italy at an earlier time, knows that something is happening to language in Italy. The warmth of an earlier era has been replaced. The Italian looks "suspiciously" at those in the car. His glance judges them people not worthy of trust. The narrator's wave suggests a democratic spirit foreign to the Fascist. So he does not respond, and the car proceeds into the town. The narrator's prediction that the young man "will go a long way in Italy" highlights his conviction that the episode's meaning is far-reaching. Mussolini's party is the right arena for the young man who has been their passenger. Guy's understated factual line reminds the reader of the unpleasantness of the methods for future journeys in Italy—literal and figurative.

225 A MEAL IN SPEZIA

A subtitle marks a pause for the travelers. The word *meal* emphasizes the practicality of the goal. *Dinner* would be too elegant. The town takes on more meaning because it is the destination of the young Fascist—an environment that he seeks, that his party has transformed. "Che Ti Dice" coming immediately after "The Killers," the event takes on added force. The meal in Spezia now plays against Al and Max's meal in Summit, against "the big dinner." "A Meal in Spezia" could stand alone as a story.

225:11–23 **looking for a place to eat . . . went in.** Guy and the narrator are not seeking "dinner," but only a satisfactory meal, something to eat midday: it is bright and the people are out and about. The narrator provides an overview of Spezia, the outer scene against which the inner scene at the restaurant will be played, similar to the pattern of "Hills Like White Elephants," which may be still fresh in the mind of the reader of *Men Without Women*. Instead of the white of "Hills," the color highlighted here is yellow. The houses are yellow, and stretches of dust abound. Black is the color that contrasts with it—and the dripping from the hand-painted *vivas* suggests haste and little concern for aesthetics. The stenciled portraits of "eye-bugging" Mussolini detract from the charm of an earlier Spezia. The prominence of icons of political figures plays against the Sunday motif of the journey. The state has become the prominent force in Catholic Italy. Though the people are "all out for Sunday," there is no mention of the church. The narrator's omission is a telling silence. He puts emphasis on streets and motion. He and Guy must move close to the curb to avoid being hit by the tram. The first words of the episode ("Let's eat") are appropriate to the dark comedy of the meal in Spezia. They also tell us that Spezia has nothing that would entice the travelers to linger. Guy's wish for a "simple" meal is similar to a contemporary traveler's decision to opt for fast food and getting on with the journey. The choice of restaurants is another comic moment, familiar to any weary traveler. Standing opposite two restaurants, Guy and the narrator must make a choice. Like Robert Frost's diverging two roads, there seems to be little difference between them. But a smile from a woman standing in the doorway of one of the restaurants makes all the difference (from across the street the travelers cannot get too careful a view). The narrator carries with him the newspapers he has just bought. That the purchase is for multiple papers reveals his keen interest in knowing "how it is" in Spezia, in Italy, and elsewhere.

225:24–42 **It was dark . . . "This is complicated."** From the bright square, the travelers enter the "dark" room, requiring an adjustment of perception, a kind of reading different from newspaper reading. But the narrator and Guy are accustomed to careful noting of surroundings. At the back of the room, deeper in the shadows, one presumes, sit three "girls" and an old woman. How young the girls might be or their relationship with the woman is not evident. But there is no indication that they are dining or enjoying each other's company—they only "sit." A sailor seated at a table opposite them also "sits"—neither eating nor drinking. "Further back" is another young man—"smartly dressed" in a blue suit, "clean-cut looking" with "pomaded and shining" hair. He writes at a table. The description of the "clean-cut" young man alerts the reader that he is likely a pimp—overdressed, flamboyant. The paragraph highlights isolation, mystery—not the ambience of a bustling restaurant. The mystery clears for the reader as it did for the narrator, who maintains the pose of the detached observer, one not easily surprised. "Light" enters the room. Food is present in a "show-case"—a front for prostitution. The "girls" with the old woman now have functions. They take turns standing in the doorway. No longer "across the street," the two men notice that the girl at the door wears nothing under her housedress. The one who takes the order brazenly puts her arms around Guy, but the men show little reaction. When the old woman calls the girls back to the table, it is clear that she is the madam. Responding to Hemingway's piece, Guy Hickok reminded Hemingway that the girl had not put her arms around him (Reynolds, *American Homecoming* 130); Hemingway's license here punctuates the reality of Italy in 1927 that he found.

With no doorway except the one into the kitchen, the space conveys confinement. The curtain over the doorway contrasts with the door of beads so important in "Hills." It bespeaks the seedy. The waitress brings spaghetti from the kitchen and a bottle of red wine—a simple meal, surely. When she sits down at their table, she intrudes on their space as determinedly as had the young Fascist. The two travelers play with the irony of their wish for a simple meal. It, and by extension Spezia, is complicated.

225:43–227:12 **"What do you say?" . . . the lady said.** Because the men have been speaking English, the waitress understands little, if anything. She speaks in Italian, which the narrator, but not Guy, can understand. (The narrator's Italian may demonstrate more fluency than Hemingway achieved in his months in Italy, and that would be part of the joke in "Italy 1927.") The language differences set the tone for the ensuing comedy, one that gives the controlling hand to the narrator. He picks up on the waitress's guess that they are German—"South Germans," he declares, "gentle, lovable people." The Germans had been a formidable foe of Italy in the Great War; in the new Italy the waitress intuits a German presence. On this day, certainly, the Italians have displayed nothing of the gentle or lovable. Guy, dependent on the narrator's translation, looks to his friend for an explanation of the girl's forward behavior. Although Mussolini has abolished the brothels, the oldest profession does not go away; it merely plays according to new rules—like a restaurant meeting a fundamental need. The waitress emphasizes what she has to offer—leaning forward on the table, she suggests that sex may be better fare than spaghetti. But this waitress is no great beauty, and her uneven looks get close scrutiny. She is drawn to Guy, not the narrator, and the narrator amuses himself by teasing the waitress that Guy "adores" her. That the waitress here claims to speak German—though she earlier mistook English for German—adds to the ridiculousness of the situation, as does the narrator's use of *lady* as a label, suggesting "lady of the night." She does not pick up on his joke of citing Potsdam as his native city. That would have the home base of these "South Germans" close to Berlin, far from southern Germany. Nor does she catch his irony when he praises "this so dear Spezia." Guy would like an end to the game; any excuse would do. The narrator prolongs it, telling the girl that Guy is a "German misogynist." Probably she does not understand the meaning of *misogynist*, and her "ardor" continues as Guy's anger mounts. The lady may be amusing herself when she calls attention to the travelers' quarrel.

The lady hopes to win her client, affectionately describing him as a *bambino*, translated for us as "beautiful boy." Thirty-eight-year-old men may be handsome but seldom look like boys. Reporting that Guy enjoys being taken for a traveling salesman in France, the narrator clarifies for the reader that Guy has an appreciation for the ladies and appreciates his reputation as a lothario. The narrator has fun telling Guy that he is a "beautiful boy"; Guy alters the edge of the comedy, asking who says so: the narrator or the girl. And he can pretend to be asking for information. Two men traveling together for ten days can be open to interpretation, especially in this episode that brings sexuality to the fore. The narrator's presence on this trip is a puzzle—and the title *Men Without Women* suggests complexity. In point of fact, Hemingway made the trip that led to the story at Guy Hickok's invitation to be his interpreter, but also because he needed time away from the women in his life. He went to take a look at Italy and to interpret for Guy, but also for male camaraderie.

Guy knows, of course, that the narrator has no romantic interest in him. The narrator builds on the jest that Guy might have to leave him behind, emphasizing thereby the political theme of the story: he ironically labels Spezia "a lovely place." Pleased to have Spezia so described, the girl can flaunt her patriotism. Her words emphasize how successful Mussolini's propaganda has been. Nationalism and superpatriotism are hallmarks of Fascism. Guy's remark that Italy "looks like her country" is a scathing judgment of such nationalism.

Duration is important to the effect of the "simple" meal in Spezia. The narrator is probably more curious than hungry when he asks for dessert. The question marks a movement toward conclusion. Italian chefs take pride in a meal's final course, but because the restaurant is a front for other activity, the option is simple—then quickly complex. Bananas will do for Guy because they have skins, protection from the germs of Spezia. The "lady" is delighted that the "beautiful boy" accepts the phallic fruit as she again embraces Guy. Readers of the time might hear echoes of the popular song "Yes, We Have No Bananas." Banter about whether Guy does or does not "take bananas" plays on the earlier banter about sexual orientation. When Hemingway wrote "Che Ti Dice la Patria?" the song "Yes, We Have No Bananas" by Frank Silver and Irving Cohn was widely popular. Guy ends the banana banter by telling his friend to say that he takes a cold bath every morning. The cold bath is an established formula for young men who need to control their sexual urges. The lady does not know the joke.

227:13–40 the property sailor . . . looking after us. Marking the end of the banter with the girl and the end of the meal, the narrator casts his eye on the rest of the room. The sailor remains a mere fixture of the property, unheeded, joyless. The reckoning, the bill, is typically a significant moment in Hemingway's work. The narrator's request signals finality; he uses no grace note. The girl had been working for other expenses. Even now, she keeps trying, even holding that narrator's hand as she suggests a quickie: "To stay a little while is nice." The "clean-cut young man" is part of a dirty business, and he has good judgment that the girl lacks. The two men are not amusing to him and will not be of value to the establishment—nor to the values of the new Italy that the establishment embodies. Because the girl is not easily dissuaded, he will repeat his words that the two men are "worth nothing." The narrator, however, tries to leave her more gently. Affirming the need to travel by day and play by night, he cites Pisa or Firenze (Florence) as the desired destination. In a sense he covers their tracks, for the travelers have already been to those cities, as the third part of the story reveals. He pretends to want to go deeper into Italy, when their direction will be out of Italy. He and Guy do not seek the "amusement" that the women of this restaurant represent.

As the narrator and Guy pay the bill and stand up, the girls and the old woman sit down—save for one girl now on duty at the door. The property sailor remains isolated. His head in his hands, his posture suggests his spiritual emptiness. Gestures, not speech, tell the story in the final paragraph. Now silent, the girl brings the change. The travelers leave their tip (they will follow protocol) and depart, the simple meal ended.

Back in the car, the engine going, the men share a moment of relief—the moment of departure at last. But life at the restaurant goes on—the girl at the door looking for the next prospect. Next to her is the "lady" who waited on the men. By waving to her as the car pulls away, the narrator recalls the humor of the scene. Although the girl does not wave, she looks after them—a humanizing moment. The final tone is melancholy, even ominous. The narrator and Guy may be on their way, but the girl is going nowhere. Nor under Mussolini, we sense, is Italy.

227 AFTER THE RAIN
From the "dirty" inner-weather of "A Meal in Spezia" to the concluding section of Hemingway's triptych plunges the reader into the stormy outer-weather.

227:41–228:8 raining hard . . . blew across the road. The passing through the suburbs of Genoa immediately confirms that the destinations the narrator recited in Spezia were not truthful. The dust of the first section of the story gives way to heavy rain and mud in the third segment. The Ford proceeds slowly behind tramcars and trucks that splash mud onto the sidewalks. The splash is considerable, as is indicated by the necessity of the townspeople to step inside doorways. Under other circumstances the view of the Mediterranean would be appealing. But we read this scene as ominous—most of all for the men coming home from work and the people they represent. The "big" sea is "running"; waves break, and the wind blows spray against the car. In a short time, something radical has happened, not to just this particular spot but to Italy. The "discolored" sea blows across the road. With Robert Frost's sonnet "Once by the Pacific" in mind, we might think of the scene as "Once by the Mediterranean." In Frost's words, "Someone had better be prepared for rage" (l. 12).

228:9–23 A big car . . . a travelling-bag with them. Someone with power and authority drives the "big" car that rushes by the Ford. The travelers are caught in circumstances they cannot very much control. A disturbing "film" spreads over the windshield. The stop at Sestri for lunch is partly to escape the weather, but the weather inside the restaurant is equally unpleasant. The symbolism of that outside scene pervades the inside of the restaurant, as the travelers look at their muddy car parked near the sea. The distance between sea and land is minimal. Inside the restaurant, one can see one's breath. This meal focuses on the basics—and the experience lacks the duration of the previous restaurant scene. Dialogue—brief and business-like—is implied. A waiter rather than a "waitress" serves them. The narrator pronounces the *pasta asciutta* "good," but the wine bitter, like alum. The beefsteak and fried potatoes are ordinary fare. *Asciutta* means "dry"; nothing here marks flavor or supports the traditional Italian reputation for exceptionally flavorful food. Like the restaurant in Spezia, this one is not bustling with activity. But the only other diners touch us on a compassionate level. A middle-aged man and young woman are eating at the "far end" of the restaurant. They want to be alone, and we—like the narrator—wonder about their story and are tempted to create one. The age difference strikes us. They eat without talking. Though we see the man shaking his head (a negation that goes with her black dress), they hold hands under the table, but they seem sad. The traveling bag between them suggests departure. Are they running away? Where will they go? The reader of *Men Without Women* will likely recall the American man and the "girl" from "Hills Like White Elephants." Nor can we forget the meal we just left in Spezia, nor the agonizing dinners in "The Killers." All those meals are in sharp contrast with the special grace of Manuel's supper at Zurito's in "The Undefeated."

228:24–32 **I read the account of the Shanghai . . . "to steal anything," Guy said.** With no counterpart to the "lady" in Spezia, the narrator translates for Guy from the newspapers about fighting in Shanghai. In the context of Mussolini's nationalism, the reminder of violence in the world accords with the spray from the turbulent sea and prepares the reader for the confrontation with the Fascist that will end "After the Rain" and "Che Ti Dice la Patria?" Inadequacy has characterized the entire journey, so when Guy needs a restroom, he must leave the restaurant—led there by the waiter. Meanwhile, the narrator, attuned to the rules of Mussolini's Italy, cleans off the windshield, headlights, and license plate. As the two men drive away, with sardonic humor Guy reports that the waiter not only took him to the restroom but remained with him. Suspicion of the foreigner, not courtesy, was at work.

228:33–229:11 **As we came . . . "got way out."** The weather again serves to emphasize that the car and the two travelers are at risk—as is a society. Alone, the two men can talk about their situation, an exchange that displays the good spirit of their relationship. The narrator is a literary person, and the dialogue has a flavor similar to that between Bill and Nick in "The Three-Day Blow" in *In Our Time.* Were they to drown here, they would end in a grand romantic mode—and the joke is effective because both men write, though they certainly lack the fame of the English poet Percy Bysshe Shelley. Guy can be as literary as the narrator. He points out that Shelley drowned in Viareggio, which is south of Spezia. Shelley's idealism and philosophy of individual expression and freedom have no place in Fascist Italy, hence the force of Guy's question: "Do you remember what we came to this country for?" The mention of Shelley is not incidental to theme. If we consider the narrator Nick or Nick-like, the line resonates on a couple of levels. With Ag and Luz, Nick (or his avatar) had thought that Italy had brought him his love of loves, as "A Very Short Story" recounts in *In Our Time.* In "The Three-Day Blow" Nick remembers the wish to go to Italy with Marge—Italy was the cherished destination. Now the narrator and Guy, especially with the image of the unhappy couple in the cold restaurant before them, realize that the romantic glow is gone from Italy. Male camaraderie has not been sufficient to make their excursion to Italy more than a business trip; they have not found what Bill and Nick had in "The Three-Day Blow" or what Nick found in "Big Two-Hearted River." On the political and the personal levels, Italy has not this time given what they sought. But they have another story to tell, the one in the reader's hands. Guy is eager to see the end of the trip that continues to disappoint. The narrator's response is a caution: Ventimiglia is the coastal town right on the border with France. Given what the day has brought, they must expect other hazards, and Guy admits immediately that driving this coast at night can be difficult.

Because it is early afternoon, there are several hours of daylight ahead, especially with the sun out. The blue sea is also a good sign, though the union of the brown water and the blue water beyond the cape reminds us of the threatening waters that morning. If Guy must keep his eyes on the road, the narrator is free to give us the details (the water, the tramp steamer) that affirm the artist's eye. Guy looks to his friend for the larger expanse. Throughout the story the narrator sees and hears for Guy. Guy imagines the larger map as he posits that the next big cape will put Genoa out of sight. Like a child eager to reach a destination, he is eager to make progress. The narrator's lines create the sense of duration: Genoa will be in sight for a long while. When they can no longer see Genoa, there is a small moment of triumph, and a gentle exchange reminiscent of the ending of "The Three-Day Blow" and Nick's consolation that he could go into town on Saturday night. The narrator gets the last word in the little game that has meaning beyond the literal.

229:12–230:5 **an S-turn . . . "gets dirty again."** The S-turn sign and the words *Svolta Pericolosa* (a dangerous turn) follow the narrator's words pointedly—that way out is hazardous. Not only does the road curve but the wind picks up. Since the mud has dried, the wind picks up the dust, playing against the ominous dust that set the tone for the beginning of the story. The dust of part I prepared the reader for the young Fascist, and here the dust leads to another such man, one with more authority. This one rides a bicycle and has a heavy revolver clearly in sight. This S curve has a new danger. As the car passes the Fascist, he can see that the license plate is French. Italy appears to be conspiring against the foreigner. The arrival of the train has caused the gates across the road to be lowered and Guy to stop the car, giving the Fascist policeman time to catch up. The travelers' instinct all along has been to be responsible and courteous. Now they confront a policeman determined to exercise his power at their expense. The dust on the plate is minimal, but the Fascist's version of truth brooks no disagreement. Though the narrator wipes off the plate, the Fascist insists on the fine, which rises with every objection. Power is to be enjoyed, and the policeman enjoys it. The Fascist, with little sense of where Italian roads might lead, feels clever in using the narrator's words to set his trap. Any answer to the question will be the wrong one. The reader of the story sees these roads as highly metaphorical. Hemingway will soon be probing similar Italian roads in *A Farewell to Arms*. The narrator knows he is caught but feels compelled to assert that the Italian roads are dirty, which by now carries huge meaning for the reader. There is more than a touch in the narrator of Jack Brennan's tough rhetorical stances in the story that follows, "Fifty Grand." When the Fascist doubles the fine, he spits in the road—punctuating the fine with the insult, ironically making the road more "dirty." The narrator knows he has been beaten but wants to put a little fear into the Fascist, if he can. So he asks for the signed receipt. Always a keen viewer, the narrator notes the characteristics of the receipt book. That there is no carbon to record what is on the offender's ticket makes clear that the system invites corruption. There is no surprise in the narrator's declaration that the receipt says twenty-five lire, undoubtedly the standard fine for a dirty plate. Isolating the line, Hemingway gives fictional duration to a scene that was likely over quickly. The duration highlights the corruption on display. Italian roads having been made metaphorical, the narrator calls attention to the police-man's "beautiful" Italian smile. What is happening here has meaning beyond the petty injustice. "Che ti dice la patria?" the line asks. The amount on the receipt is kept from the narrator's view, and the price on the receipt is likely beyond the Fascist's view as well. The Fascist thinks, of course, that he has won in every way, and he gets the last words—which are in the imperative.

230:6–12 **We drove . . . the people.** Even though Guy does not like to drive at night, he wants more than ever to get out of Italy and so drives two hours after dark. The men are happy to sleep in Mentone, France. Though they arrive in the dark, Mentone seems "very cheerful and clean and sane and lovely." Those qualities did not mark their path in Italy, which the narrator then traces. Their entry point had been the same as their exit point, carrying them to Pisa and Florence and across the country to the Adriatic at Rimini and through several towns. The listing of the towns carries great beauty—a poetry of a heritage that gave much to Western civilization. In ten days, they would have spent a great deal of time in the automobile. The narrator implies that the last day is a fair sample of what they experienced on those other days. That the trip was short he admits, but for a keen observer (like himself) there was ample opportunity to gauge conditions of the people and the state. The irony is heavy.

FIFTY GRAND

If "The Killers" may be said to promise a story about a boxer, "Fifty Grand" may be said to fulfill the promise. Its length made placing it in a magazine difficult (though it was published in the *Atlantic Monthly* and *La Nouvelle Revue française* just months before publication in *Men Without Women*), but Hemingway declared that it was the kind of story that was easy for him to write. His task was made easier because when he wrote, boxing was a popular sport in all social classes and an important arena for intercollegiate competition—as the history of Robert Cohn of *The Sun Also Rises* reminds us. "The Undefeated" had posed a much more difficult task, for Hemingway was dealing with competition that readers knew primarily through his work. "Fifty Grand" allows opportunity for readers to find the differences and the similarities between the two arenas. Boxing pits man against man: it is the only sport in which an aim is to cause a concussion in the opponent.

The getting and spending of money is a major theme in Hemingway's writing. (In his 1977 topical biography *By Force of Will: The Life and Art of Ernest Hemingway,* Scott Donaldson titles two of his chapters "Money.") The title "Fifty Grand" boldly highlights the theme that is implied but not mentioned in "The Killers." We never hear the cash register ring in that story, and no one mentions money at the diner or at Hirsch's. But the story is a striking evocation of Herman Melville's truth: "There is nothing nameable but that some men will undertake to do it for pay" (*Billy Budd* 61). In "Fifty Grand" the money is up front, but the words *double cross* are not used. With "Che Ti Dice la Patria?" and its revelations about the realities of the "civilized" world that the young innocent of "The Killers" comes to intuit, Hemingway might have expected the reader of *Men Without Women* to make that Nick story a steady reference for "Fifty Grand."

Fifty thousand dollars was a great deal of money by the standards of 1925. Adjusted to October 2007 value, the figure represents roughly $600,000. That would be more than Jack Brennan could afford to lose. Given the odds of two to one for Walcott, Jack will collect $25,000. But the point, as the title emphasizes, is not what Jack wins, but what he does not lose.

231:1–16 **"How are you going?"** . . . **"That kike!"** No other story in *Men Without Women* (or any in *In Our Time*) opens with dialogue. ("Today Is Friday" gives the reader the stage setting before the first Roman soldier speaks.) The first-person story implies a listening audience more than a reading audience. The dialogue in a men's gym is clipped, unadorned. "The Undefeated," the other long story of *Men Without Women*, places emphasis on seeing; "Fifty Grand" emphasizes listening.

The conversation being reported is barely underway, the narrator's question making clear that this question follows a preceding question, Jack's inquiring how the narrator is "going." The word *going* may be roughly equivalent to *doing*, but it is appropriate to a story that deals with Jack's departure from the world of boxing. That the question is not shared with the reader implies Jack's interest in the narrator, his interest in a fellow boxer. But Jerry, the narrator, does not want to tell his story, but Jack's. The reader will judge Jerry's character and reliability as narrator by his reactions to Jack. By the end of the story, we will have a definitive answer to the question. Jack knows how to take care of himself. And he understands how to use language for dramatic effect. He answers Jerry's simple question with another question, putting the focus on his opponent. He gives Walcott his due but takes a longer view: he doesn't think that Walcott will last. He is not soothed by Soldier's fawning assessments nor by Soldier's advice that Jack handle Walcott the way he handled Kid Lewis. Mention of Lewis gets a quick response from Jack and shows his fire. When Jack mockingly picks up Soldier's bird-shot metaphor, we suspect that he won't be easily played—by Soldier or anyone.

The narrator's voice is one that builds trust; his judgment seems measured. His opinion that Walcott may be easy to hit proves to be quite accurate. Jack need not be disgraced in this fight. Using the narrator's first name for direct address, Jack indicates affinity with Jerry that he does not share with Soldier, whom he never addresses by name. Jack is another of Hemingway's aging protagonists, and the reader of *Men Without Women* will place him next to Manuel Garcia. For them, the important thing is to endure. Although Jack realistically reckons with his opponent's youth and ambition, he sees the possibility that he could beat Walcott (with luck, perhaps), but he won't accept Soldier's easy rhetoric. Although there is no tag for the line about Kid Lewis, we recognize Soldier's glib voice. Jerry does not give advice; he recognizes that advice is not what Jack needs. The nickname *Kid* links Lewis with Walcott, now at his youthful prime. Triumph is not what the name evokes for Jack. Lewis was not an opponent who won his respect, as he shows in his choice of epithet. *Kike* is a noun referring derogatorily to a Jewish person. Jack shares in the prejudices of his time. Given Jack's concern with money, and the stereotypes surrounding Jews and money, this label has ironic force.

231:17–19 **The three of us . . . had been drinking.** The paragraph identifying characters and place divides the opening scene. Had it come first, the paragraph would signal a reading audience; placed here, it indicates a more local audience, one familiar with Hanley's. Jerry's audience comes from the boxing world. Reporting on events that led up to the Brennan-Walcott fight and to the fight itself, Jerry gives an insider's view to friends, and he is a splendid raconteur. Hanley's attracts not only boxers and their managers but "broads" as well. In the 1920s, women seldom went into taverns and saloons—certainly not unescorted. We would not expect to find Jack Brennan's wife in such a place—and he would not want his daughters to be there. Because the "broads" have been drinking, their tongues have been loosened. The "broads" help reveal the culture of the boxing world.

231:20–232:2 **"What do you mean, kike?"** . . . **when he wanted to say it.** The dialogue at Hanley's before the paragraph indicating a precise setting raises the issue of Jack's stature and prospects as a boxer; the subsequent conversation pairs this with Jack's attitudes toward money. "Fifty Grand" will revolve around two topics: his prospects as boxer and his concern with money.

A "lady" does not interject her views into conversation at an adjoining table. The broad is also a regular at Hanley's, and she knows who Jack is, and she knows about his reputation as a "spender." She does not mind hurling an insult at someone who is unlikely to buy her a drink or purchase her services. Jack is not like other boxers, she has reason to know. The reader would know from the name *Brennan* that Jack is probably Irish. That the broad uses it as an insult underscores how ethnically conscious the streets of New York were and still are. Jack is not eager to trade insults with the woman, but she senses the derision and presses for verbal battle. Jack gives his opponent another chance to avoid that battle and prepares to leave. But she fiercely attacks. She ridicules not only Jack but all Irishmen as anti-Semites. Mocking Jack as tight fisted, she overreaches by bringing Jack's wife into her attack, questioning Jack's authority in his own house. Bringing Ted Lewis back into the conversation, she insults Jack's ability as a fighter. But Jack delivers the last "blow," and he is easily the winner. (If Jack's retort silences the woman, her objection to Jack's slur of Lewis surely earns her some points.) Quickly, decisively, he brings the encounter to an end, silencing his opponent as he will later silence the verbose Walcott. The brief scene at Hanley's sparingly and effectively establishes strong character lines and prefigures the plot of the story. Jack's leadership is evident: he decides when it is time to leave, and Jerry is all admiration: "That was Jack." For Jerry, the episode captures Jack's essence. Jack, Jerry surmises, makes his words count. Jerry praises a honed intelligence ("he could say what he wanted to") and Jack's expert timing ("when he wanted to say it"). For a boxer, timing is crucial.

232:3–16 **Jack started training . . . like it any, though.** Jerry's story keeps strict chronological order. To prepare for the challenge of fighting young Walcott, Jack begins training at Danny Hogan's health farm. The choice for Danny Hogan's is his, a choice appropriate to Jack's Irish heritage. *Jersey,* rather than *New Jersey,* would be the designation of the blue-collar New Yorker and of the boxing world. Jerry approves of the choice of Hogan's. It is good for the trainee to be away from the crowd at Hanley's and the city. It is "nice" at the health farm, but Jerry has no problem reading Jack, who isn't happy away from home. Jack is "sore" (read "angry") and grouchy most of the time. The adjective *sore* is also appropriate to the physical demands of training for the aging boxer. Jerry identifies the basic cause of Jack's malaise: he misses his wife and kids, though it is unlikely that Jack actually talks about them much. It has not been necessary for Jack to say that he likes Jerry and Hogan, or that Soldier Bartlett is getting on his nerves. Jerry provides a useful maxim, one based on some years of experience. The challenge to the "kidder" is to know when his stuff goes sour. (Soldier is woefully inept at recognizing that moment.) Whereas Jack knows how to say a thing, when he wants to, Soldier does not know his moments. He is "always" kidding. Soldier's deficiency is not something that Jack alone finds awry; Jerry pronounces Soldier's wit not very funny, not very good. *Kidding* always implies a put-down of some sort. "Sort of stuff" is not high literary style, but Jerry is a good rhetorician who recognizes that a solid example is in order. Jerry's example is meant to be a summary of many instances. What is most striking about the example is that it is the opposite of what Soldier had spouted back at Hanley's: "He can't hit you, Jack." Now Soldier taunts that Walcott can hit, and often. Why the change? the reader wonders.

232:17–32 **One morning . . . "sick of you."** Following the representative example, Jerry recounts Soldier's dismissal on a particular morning, one that Jerry remembers vividly. The early morning trek has been planned to promote endurance and speed. Jerry picks up the narrative for the return trip, clarifying the regime that they were following. Jerry admits that Jack was not fast on the road. He gives a sense of the effect of the morning on Jack by keeping the emphasis on the pounding routine, a beat accented by the information that Soldier is "kidding" Jack the whole time. We get no example of the kidding, but Jerry makes clear that Soldier is kidding Jack about his "speed"—hence, his vulnerability. In the extended paragraph describing the road workout, Jerry provides no speech in the paragraph, giving the sense that Jack has been biding his time, waiting for the moment when he will again speak decisively and make his words count. Calm, deliberate, his mind is in good order, if his speed is suspect. In a quick sentence, Jack dismisses Soldier. Soldier is stunned. He has not been able to read Jack's silence or the effects of his "kidding." Jack displays no anger, just firm decision, as he advises Soldier to stay in town. Pressed, as he was in Hanley's, Jack states what should have been clear to Soldier, that he is "sick" of hearing Soldier talk. Soldier misses his opportunity to depart with some small dignity and picks up on Jack's "sickness" and taunts that Walcott will make Jack a lot sicker. But Jack maintains his calm and again has the last word: "But I know that I am sick of you." Jack's single use of *know* contrasts with the multiple uses of it by the American man in "Hills Like White Elephants." Jack has no doubt here; repetition is not part of his strategy. His disposing of Soldier parallels the ending of the scene at Hanley's.

232:33–43 So Soldier went off . . . "See you then." Jerry, the peacemaker, accompanies Soldier to the train station. "Good and sore," Soldier can only affirm that he was "just kidding," marking himself as a man who doesn't know much about how to use words. The point is that Jack *has* "pulled that stuff." Soldier has no means of retaliation any more than did the "broad" at Hanley's. His line is the equivalent of an inept "You ain't firing me; I'm quitting." Jerry maintains his good nature and honesty. He acknowledges that Jack is "nervous and crabby" but still a "good fellow." He won't betray his friend. What makes a "good fellow"? Certainly, Jack does not meet the standard concept of the jolly good fellow. That would be someone who is generous, laughing, perhaps a jokester. The evidence of the story is not yet sufficient for the reader to judge the merit of Jerry's judgment, but it invites reflection on the concept of the good fellow. In any case, Jerry's loyalty is not compromised. Jerry leaves Soldier to his bitterness; he understands Soldier's limitation (his insensitive "kidding") just as he understands Jack's nervousness and crabbiness. Soldier warms to Jerry's good nature, repeating the friendly "so long" and calling Jerry by name. He would like to see Jerry in town before the fight, but Jerry's loyalty is with Jack. Soldier is now calmer. Jerry's even manner has had its effect.

232:44–233:9 He went in . . . "a cold one, though." The paragraph recounting the train's departure and Jerry's return to Hogan's is a model of efficient prose. Everything is clear and direct—no decoration. The scene reflects the rightness of Jack's dismissal of Soldier. From that unpleasantness, Jack turns to the pleasure of writing to and thinking about his wife. Jerry does not disturb the peace, gets the papers, and on the other side of the porch sits down to read. He respects Jack's privacy. Hogan reads the scene and knows that he should speak to Jerry, not Jack. Hogan has noticed Soldier's departure, but he has waited for Jerry to return to get the story. Hogan, unlike Soldier, can read Jack's mood. Jerry's answer rejects "jam" as an explanation, for that would suggest confusion, mixing. What Jerry has seen—and reports to Hogan—is deliberation and decisive action and Jack's avoidance of verbal turmoil. Hogan's tact and his perception should not surprise us. Jack trains at Hogan's because Hogan has these virtues. Jack is not interested in gathering admiring entourages around him. He prefers a select company—his letter writing pointing to his focal "liking." When Hogan describes Jack as a "cold one," we read *cold* as a reflection of personality as he relates to others, but the adjective also comments on Jack's mental efficiency, to his calculations and decisiveness. Jerry affirms another side to Jack: loyalty. Hogan has known that side too and makes clear that he is not criticizing Jack, but describing him. Jack is not like most of the boxers he has known.

233:10–25 **Hogan went in . . . "see him doing it?"** Hogan has done nothing to disturb the calm on the porch. Jerry continues to read the newspapers. He has time to savor the fall weather and the "pretty nice-looking country." The hunter in Jerry is stirred, and when Hogan comes to the door, he asks what game might be out there. Jerry's connectedness to the natural world predisposes us to continue to find him a reliable narrator, to sense those qualities that have made Jack and Jerry get along so well. But Hogan quickly checks Jerry's dream. This is not "the last good country," as another Hemingway story might put it. The bucolic mood broken, Jerry quickly changes the subject to the horses. Speech continues to be in the stichomythic pattern—terse and direct. Jerry reports the newspaper item that the jockey Sande "booted three of them in"—or rode three horses to victories yesterday. Because Hogan says that he got that news last night on the telephone, it is clear to the reader and to Jerry that betting on the races is habit with Hogan. (The competitive instinct of hunting seeks other outlets.) There is understatement in Hogan's "Oh, I keep in touch with them." But Hogan's betting is not the chief interest of the story—Jack's is. The narrative quickly turns back to him. Jerry's question lets us know that, like Hogan, Jack has played the horses. Hogan knows a good deal about how important money is to Jack. Price is something he has had to negotiate with him. He cannot envision Jack betting at the races. Jack's history with horses prepares us for Jack's bet that is at the center of "Fifty Grand." When it comes to money, Jack is not a high-risk investor.

233:26–34 **Just then Jack . . . "Lost money."** As if in answer to Hogan's question about seeing Jack betting at the races, he appears, wearing old pants and boxing shoes. His asking Hogan if he has a stamp for his letter provides a highly comic moment. Good-naturedly, Hogan offers to mail the letter, saving Jack the pennies that a stamp would cost. Jerry wants Hogan to know that he had not been wrong about Jack's betting at the races. He asks the question directly, setting us up for another theatrical moment, and Jerry skillfully leads his audience there. Jack is characteristically minimalist with his words, offering nothing other than what is asked. The exchange climaxes when Hogan asks why Jack stopped betting. Two words suffice: "Lost money." Jack abandoned that habit as decisively as he dismissed Soldier.

233:35–42 **Jack sat down . . . "That's so."** Although resting, calm, Jack appears to have a lot on his mind. Hogan, sensing the burden, offers a chair. Jack's quick "No" is in character, but Jerry and Hogan sense that he is not "fine." Jerry tries another approach—accenting the natural world—to help make Jack feel better, if not "fine." Jack himself identifies what will make him feel better. He yearns to be with his woman. His career, he knows, is nearing an end. What he has built with his wife will be his support in the time that follows. The verbalization of the admission provides something of a shock, coming from this tough ("cold," Hogan has said) boxer who has not been one to offer information. Although Jerry reminds him that the separation will last only another week, it is clear that Jack has already been away from his wife for some days. Another week can seem an eternity, as Ernest Hemingway experienced in the hundred-day wait that his first wife, Hadley, imposed before he could resume being with Pauline Pfeiffer (who would eventually become his second wife) and during other separations from his women. Jack recognizes Jerry's attempt to be comforting, but his line is tinged with awareness of what this waiting will be.

233:43–234:10 **We sat there . . . "tired all the time."** Jack may get along with Hogan, but Jerry is the confidante. The scene on the porch provides a turn to the confessional mode that is rare in *Men Without Women*. (Manuel Garcia shares nothing of his inner life with Zurito, the character most like Jerry in "The Undefeated.") Jack now approaches the larger part of the burden of the coming week—the fight and how he will acquit himself. Jack does not use the word *fight* or *bout*. He is more concerned with who he is than with the outcome of the fight. When Jerry tries to be diplomatic, Jack cuts through the evasion and insists that Jerry state his professional judgment: Jack is not ready for this fight. When Jack confesses that he is not sleeping, he takes his place with numerous Hemingway protagonists. In the Hemingway canon, the phenomenon marks the character as central, worthy of the reader's compassion. Jack may be a man without a woman during the course of the story, but he is a man who very much needs a woman—and his declaration would come only under very private circumstances with a trusted confidante. Jerry is awkward in his attempts to be constructive; his advice plays to the comedy of the story. He advises Jack to bring the wife out: sexual intercourse is usually prelude to contentment and sleep. Jack is surely not too old for sexual activity, but the missing of his wife goes beyond the sexual. So Jerry tries again, giving the advice more typically given to the adolescent with raging testosterone: take long walks and get "good and tired." The point is not so much that Jerry isn't able to solve the problem, but, comedy aside, he is the vehicle that permits Jack to voice what he normally would not.

234:11–35 **He was that way . . . "He'll pick him."** Having shared this rare moment with the private Jack, Jerry represents it as typical of Jack's dark mood. His colloquial "you know" reminds us that Jerry is speaking his narrative. Since Jack can't sleep, Jerry notes, he wakes up tired. A boxer who can't shut his hands can't make a fist, nor can he take hold of something. During this week Jerry and Hogan often discuss Jack's unpromising condition ("stale as a poorhouse cake") and anticipate the coming fight, and Jerry shares the exchange between the two as the training week nears its end. A poorhouse cake is one that has been given to an institution for the indigent precisely because it is a "day old" or more. "Poorhouse cake" also keeps the monetary theme before us. Walcott is the new kid on the block. Jack has seen him only in the gym. That Jerry has not seen him is, then, no surprise. Hogan, however, has had a good look at Walcott. From his perspective, the difference between the two combatants is vast.

Philosophically, Jerry accepts that "everybody's got to get it sometime." Diminishment and defeat are the norm of experience. But Hogan thinks not of the magnitude likely to ensue. Ever practical, he too has his eye on the financial line. Jack is in such sorry shape that the farm will be criticized for failure to do its job—and Hogan's business might suffer. It is also clear that Hogan takes pride in his product. He is a professional. Dwelling on the negatives of their professional verdict, Jerry is building a good story. The odds against Jack seem overwhelming. In the tradition of much sports literature, the reader likely expects, therefore, that Jack will prevail. Hogan makes precise what the judgment of the experts (usually suspect in Hemingway's world) is and why the farm may get a black eye. But the reader knows that fights and games sometimes disprove the prescience of the experts. (End of season polls often have little resemblance to preseason polls.) But sometimes the experts are right. Hogan insists that Jack is woefully out of shape and not ready for the fight with Walcott. For the tale's sake, Jerry plays devil's advocate. His protest does set him up to look good at story's end, the single person to give Jack a chance. Because the issue between Hogan and Jerry is extended, Jerry's loyalty will be remembered.

The errors of the critics—a pronounced motif in "The Undefeated"—is a comfort to Jerry as he recalls the Willard-Dempsey fight. Jess Willard had won his heavyweight title by knocking out Jack Johnson in the twenty-sixth round of the fight held in Havana, Cuba, in April 1915 under a broiling sun. Debate followed as to whether Johnson threw the fight. Willard defended his title only once, losing to Jack Dempsey in Toledo, Ohio, on 4 July 1919. Willard collected his largest purse from that contest, $100,000. He took a severe beating in the fight and surrendered after the third round. Tall and slow moving, Willard disliked training and training camp, disliked boxing. He was in the sport for financial gain. In Toledo, his failure to prepare led to the severe beating. Dempsey fractured Willard's jaw and knocked him down seven times in the three rounds. Aspects of Willard's career are reflected in Jack Brennan, though by story's end Hemingway will have highlighted telling differences. Ring Lardner (1885–1933) first earned fame as a sports columnist for the *Chicago Tribune.* As a young man, Hemingway was very familiar with Lardner's columns and stories about sports figures. Lardner's stance was cynical. Because Lardner enjoyed satirizing sports figures, he is ripe for Jerry's aspersion. Hogan reflects accurately that Dempsey did not knock Willard out and then switches his pronoun reference back to Lardner. All in all, it's a muddy, unclear response to Jerry's indictment of the columnist.

Jerry gives himself the last word on the sports writers. The breed is dependably deficient in Hemingway's work, reflecting his steady distrust of reviewers and critics. (The writer of "Fifty Grand" counted himself an authority on boxing and continued to think of himself as that. Shortly after the publication of *The Harder They Fall,* Budd Schulberg's 1947 novel about boxing, Schulberg was in Key West and eager to meet Hemingway. At the meeting, Hemingway insulted Schulberg by immediately questioning his boxing knowledge. Schulberg recounts the episode and its lingering effects in the lead essay of his 1995 *Sparring with Hemingway and Other Legends of the Fight Game*.)

Hogan takes the conversation back to Jack and the present moment, asking for Jerry's professional judgment on "Jack's shape." Many readers of the 1920s would see the parallels to Jess Willard before Toledo. His professional judgment invoked, Jerry has to acknowledge Jack's sorry state. And this is not just a fight to be lost; it's a career that's over: "He's through." But the public pontificators annoy Jerry. He anticipates that "Gentleman Jim Corbett," now retired from boxing, will predict that Jack will win. Corbett died in 1933. We never discover whom Corbett picks. What is important is Hogan and Jerry's shared sense of where the coming fight is going.

234:36–46 **That night Jack . . . "I suppose. Sure."** Jack's insomnia a day before the fight can only confirm Jerry's sense that it's "all over." We are one week beyond the first porch scene, when Jack confessed his insomnia to Jerry and the cause of it. Back on the porch with Jerry, he can again verbalize what it is that he "thinks about." His thoughts revolve around two poles: his dedication to his craft (boxing) and to his wife and children. Manuel Garcia of "The Undefeated" was concerned with the professional arena exclusively. Jerry's question—"What do you think about, Jack, when you can't sleep?"—reverberates throughout *Men Without Women*. It is implied for Ole Andreson in "The Killers" and hauntingly central in "Now I Lay Me," the last story of the book. Only someone who has Jack's confidence would dare ask this personal question. Jack's specificities are revealing. Anyone listening to Jerry's tale would be struck by the revelation of Jack's properties in Florida and the Bronx as well as stocks. In today's parlance, Jack has a diverse portfolio. His financial worries and stinginess seem excessive, considering his resources. His enmity toward Lewis, rekindled by the scene at Hanley's, resurfaces. The context makes clear that this admission is more than a reminder of Jack's anti-Semitic streak: Kid Lewis embodies qualities that Jack envies. The British fighter was a great favorite in America (as the women at Hanley's illustrate) for his fighting style and his enthusiasm. His many boxing wins place him among the most financially successful boxers of his era. His era was long. When Lewis retired in 1929 at age thirty-five, he had won three British titles, two Empire titles, three European titles, and a world championship. Lewis, like Jack, is near the end of his tenure at the moment of "Fifty Grand," and Jack realizes that his legacy will not be as lasting. But more than a career drives Jack, and his worry for his wife and "kids" puts into perspective his worry about his properties and his stocks. Jack's response to Jerry's attempt to give solace is predictably sardonic. Jack knows that there may be more sleepless nights after the fight.

235:1–17 **He was sore . . . slapping the rope hard.** Jerry uses brief staccato sentences—subject (Jack's name once, but otherwise a pronoun) and verb, one adverb (*just*)—to create a sense of Jack's soreness—his mind-set, his speech. Jerry's sentences portray negation and minimal movement. Jack didn't work out; he moves around "a little"; he shadowboxes "a few" rounds but doesn't look good doing it; he skips rope "a little while" and "couldn't sweat." All the signs agree: Jack will lose the fight. More briefly, Hogan and Jerry again assess Jack's state. Accustomed to seeing boxers work up a sweat, Hogan thinks total rest would be better than the half-hearted attempts at discipline he witnesses as Jack skips rope. That Jack doesn't sweat puts him outside the pale of training. (A week earlier Jack could not close his hands after the run.) Hogan leans toward physical explanations and worries that Jack might have "the con," consumption (tuberculosis). Hogan's hypothesis is reasonable. Pulmonary tuberculosis remains a common and deadly infectious disease; loss of appetite is one of its symptoms. There is, it is clear, every reason to be concerned about Jack's health—as there was for Manuel Garcia's in "The Undefeated."

Jerry and the reader know that Jack has worries other than making weight. Jerry recognizes the inner void that Jack deals with, a resignation akin to that of Ole Andreson: "He just hasn't got anything inside any more." Vigilant ever, Jack skips over to interrupt the dialogue between Jerry and Hogan. His "buzzards" is in part playful direct address, but he recognizes that they are pondering his collapse the way buzzards keep a watchful eye on wounded prey. Hogan does not equivocate from his initial judgment: Jack should cease working out, though he softens it with "You'll be slow." Jack's terse and ironic response is authentic Jack Brennan, and he punctuates his irony by continuing his routine. Advice is not something Jack seeks or, as it turns out, needs—as he asserts by "slapping the rope hard," disregarding, for the moment at least, Hogan's counsel.

235:18–40 **That afternoon John Collins . . . "a look at him," Steinfelt said.** The arrival of John Collins, Jack's fight manager, and two as yet unidentified "friends" marks a major turning point in the story—an arrival that despite its factual tone seems ominous. Collins "showed up," suggesting that Jack has not been expecting him. Collins makes no preliminaries to Jerry, seeing him exclusively as functionary. Jerry's report that Jack is up in his room, lying down, evokes the image of Ole Andreson, in a similar setting, expecting visitors from the city who mean him no good. Collins expected his man to be training. Jerry might have told Collins that Hogan advised that workouts should cease, but he offers nothing more than has been asked.

Jerry is willing to share information with Collins, but he does not wish to be frank about Jack before strangers with no right to an answer. His hesitation adds to the sense that this is not a friendly gathering. But he does the reasonable thing and trusts Jack's manager with the verdict that Jack is not in good shape. Collins wants specifics and is not surprised when Jerry says that Jack is not sleeping. Jerry's concern is obvious, though Collins is unimpressed with his judgment. And he seems not to be worried, because Jack has "never been right" in the ten years he has been his manager.

The ensuing laughter from the mysterious companions is their first vocal expression since they arrived. Somewhat belatedly, Collins introduces Jerry to the "fellows." That one is named Morgan and the other Steinfelt, an obviously Jewish name (aspersions at Hanley's about Jewish acquisitiveness introduced the story), suggests the nature of their visit: money. Collins keeps the introductions formal: Jerry is "Mr." Doyle, paralleling Mr. Morgan and Mr. Steinfelt. Since the report on Jack that John has just received is grim, Collins's identification of Jerry as Jack's trainer has an ironic side. But the introductions are pro forma; Morgan and Steinfelt are not interested in Jerry—and their manners contrast with his. Like Collins, they want to "take a look" at Jack.

235:41–236:5 **We all went upstairs . . . "in the daytime for?"** The transition to the upper room is stark, simple. The forthcoming scene in the upper room being crucial to the story, the transition helps mark that drama. In a story accented by Jewish presence, the scene plays against the Passion story that is central in "Today Is Friday," wherein Jesus is likened to a boxer.

Collins's question about Hogan's whereabouts, although casual, hints at the purpose of the visit. The trio will want a very private setting. Similarly, Hogan's question about the number of Hogan's clients at the moment may be mild curiosity, but who might or might not know about the visit may be more than that. That Hogan's business has not been booming has also suited Jack's purposes. He would not want to have trained with a crowd. The transition ends with a question: "Pretty quiet, ain't it?" These are the first words we hear from Morgan, the only words he or Steinfelt says directly to Jerry. Jerry's quiet affirmation prepares us for the greater quietness of the next minute—a dramatic pause that anticipates a narrative silence about what transpires in the upper room.

236:6–16 **John turned . . . "Of course not."** The paragraph format for the three-sentence stage direction emphasizes the importance of the visit about to transpire and invites the reader to intuit the mind-set of the man on the other side of the door. Ever tactful, Jerry gives the obvious explanation for the silence following the knock on the door, but he does not mention who asks the colossally stupid or insensitive question about why Jack might be asleep. Morgan or Steinfelt might easily ask the question. Collins would know that a boxer is not in training every minute, that rest is also part of training. If Collins asks the question, it would be clear that he knows little or nothing about his boxer. Hemingway's reader recognizes the irony of the line—a line that evokes the spiritual angst of Nick Adams, Jake Barnes, Ole Andreson. The answer to the question would hardly be one the questioner would grasp.

The visitors' entry is an intrusion, an invasion of privacy typically not lightly made. The reader may recall Hogan's advice that Jack should rest at this point; the visitors are disrupting needed therapy. Since Jack has told Jerry that he misses the wife, the arms around the pillow reflect that emptiness. Collins is the only one present who would deliver the rude awakening. Jerry's narrative emphasizes how deep a sleep Jack has been experiencing and makes clear how valuable this sleep is. It releases Jack from worry about the fight, his family, all the other things he worries about. But Collins is insistent that this meeting take place. When Jack sits up and looks at the company, we may well wonder what he sees, what he makes of this moment—the three unexpected visitors, looking like the three ravens of the old ballad. We may also ponder what the three unexpected visitors make of the unkempt boxer wearing his cheap sweater.

Jack's response to being awakened is at once a curse of protest and a line that can be read as prayer. Collins's attempt to calm Jack's anger may be a warning that he will lie when convenient, but it counts among the story's jokes, one that Jack does not find funny.

236:17–34 **"You know Morgan and Steinfelt"** . . . **"out here all right."** Ever the ironist, Jack quickly passes over the insincere greetings and vents his frustration to Collins. Small talk is not Jack's forte. He resents the neglect from his manager, who has left Jerry and himself to deal with reporters—something he knows he is not good at, ironist that he is. Characteristically, he chides Collins as more than adequately paid. Collins has his excuse for his absence, and it may have validity. The important point is that Jack sees that his welfare is not Collins's major concern at the moment. Collins's answer has inflamed Jack, as his "What the hell" and "Why the hell" underline. Twice Jack underscores financial concern by noting the cut Collins gets. Jack wants his money's worth: Collins should be here at Hogan's. When Collins attempts to calm Jack by noting Hogan's steady presence, Jack irritably declares Hogan as dumb as he is. Jack may not be gifted in the realm of public relations, but the story repeatedly—finally climactically—illustrates how smart Jack is. Mimicking Steinfelt's accent in his narration to us, Jerry recognizes that Steinfelt wants to defuse Jack's anger with a new subject, and he knows that Steinfelt's new topic of conversation, Soldier "Bahtlett," is not a happy choice. Jack's sardonic response gives raconteur Jerry another good moment.

236:35–44 **"Say, Jerry," John said** . . . **"find Hogan," I said.** Collins begins to "manage" more successfully, rearranging the scene. The agenda for the meeting is about to get more serious. More than wishing to see Hogan, Collins wishes to get rid of Jerry, who knows that he is not a major player in the scene. A storyteller with a good sense of detail and a good sense of timing, he is the major player in the outer frame of the story. He pauses as Morgan and Steinfelt look at each other, as the single-sentence paragraph about them reveals. Jack senses the shifting balance, and he anticipates a confrontation he won't like. Collins's admonition for Jack to quiet down is a stage direction necessary for a reader to imagine the tone, the vehemence, of Jack's previous line. Jack dreads the private conversation Morgan and Steinfelt plan.

Jerry's readiness to find Hogan permits Jack to save his dignity. Jerry's departure, so simply announced, creates for the story an important absence for the narrative. The crucial scene of Jack's meeting with the visitors cannot be reported. There is no indication either that Jack ever tells Jerry who said what at this meeting. The reader has just witnessed how reluctant Jack is for this meeting to happen; his temper and short fuse have been evident. The reader is invited to imagine the missing scene. The best help for that imagining comes at the end of the story. But the reader can never know very precisely what happened at the meeting.

Because the smart money is on Walcott to beat Jack (as the crowd's roar of approval when the men enter the ring attests), Steinfelt and Morgan see a way of making lots of money by putting their money on Jack. This is not what they tell Jack. They let him think that their money is on Walcott. They now scheme in an attempt to ensure the result they wish. Perhaps they offer Jack money for betting purposes to go with any he has of his own. In return, they may want a guarantee that Jack will lose the fight. Jack agrees, but perhaps not immediately; he is concerned with his inner integrity. But he knows that he cannot beat Walcott, and so he rationalizes what he sees as a good business deal. He does not think that he is really betraying himself. He will fight a good fight, believing that Walcott's youth and preparedness will wear him down. He will go down in dignity and pick up extra money.

If Jack's mind is working well in this exchange, Steinfelt and Morgan have miscalculated. If they want Walcott to lose, they need to get him to foul Jack—which apparently they do, worried that Jack is putting too much into the fight. If Jack has $50,000 bet on Walcott and Walcott loses, they will realize more than they would have otherwise.

The reader has no certain way of knowing why they did what they did, though it will seem apparent later that greed and poor judgment about boxing cause the manipulators to lose. It also becomes clear that the visit to the upper room is prelude to colossal betrayal.

Long after the publication of the story and years after Hemingway's death, Kenneth Lynn (1987) and soon thereafter Michael Reynolds (1989) posited a new biographical reading. Behind the "contract" with Steinfelt and Morgan, Hemingway was replaying the contract that he had had with Horace Liveright, his publisher for *In Our Time,* a contract that Hemingway judged Liveright had not honorably met. Thus, Liveright's "betrayal" justified his own machinations to move to the house of Scribners, hence the pronounced racist edge to the story. Liveright, like Steinfelt and possibly Morgan, was Jewish, and the Judas of this reading.

236:45–237:5 **Hogan was out . . . came over to me.** Jerry meanwhile finds Hogan, just as he was ordered. There is ample time for him to watch with amusement the "health-farm patients" take their lesson in the manly art. Sending his "gentlemen" to the shower, Hogan adds a comic pause before Jerry reports.

237:6–21 **"John Collins is out" . . . "those sharpshooters."** If Jerry is curious about what is going on in the upper room, Hogan has also been thinking about the three visitors. He had recognized Happy Steinfelt and Lew Morgan (he gives Jerry the first names that Collins had not when he made his introductions) and twice labels them "sharpshooters." His scorn is evident. Is the name Steinfelt meant to suggest Gertrude Stein? (Hemingway would play an elaborate game with her name in *For Whom the Bell Tolls*.) Does the name Lew Morgan carry an implied rhyme of "Jew" Morgan?

237:22–238:7 **After about thirty minutes . . . "So long," Jack said.** Hogan's distaste for the scene in Jack's room is strong. Wishing to end the charade he and Jerry have had imposed on them, he is prompt in reporting in the prescribed time frame but in no mood to play further games with the "sharpshooters." His anger reflects his sense that the events in the upper room besmear the sport of boxing. That Steinfelt is the one who unlocks the door clarifies whose agenda has controlled the now concluded meeting. Hogan cannot be surprised that the visitors have no real purpose in summoning him. Jerry freezes the moment of the entrance: Jack sitting on the bed, Collins and Morgan in chairs, and Steinfelt standing. Collins and Morgan lighten the mood by addressing Hogan as "Danny." Morgan furthers that goal by shaking hands with Hogan. Steinfelt declares that the purpose of the summons is celebration. Silent on the bed, Jack is noticeably alone. "He ain't with the others," Jerry remembers. Jerry's dramatic sense causes him to make this the moment to contrast the sharply dressed visitors with Jack's garb and his unshaven face. Jack and the loyal Jerry do not further the spirit of the fete; each takes only a single drink. Now standing, Jack refuses another and again delivers one of his memorable one-liners: "I never liked to go to these wakes." The visitors laugh, but not Jerry, and it is likely not Hogan. The "they" who are "feeling pretty good" are the three who drive away. Jack refrains from waving back. His "So long" to Morgan and Steinfelt is indeed final. He will not have to deal with them again.

238:8–13 **We had supper . . . "Sure," I said.** Jerry reads Jack's moods ably. He does not attempt to cheer Jack, as Soldier might have done. Jerry likely had some conversation with the health-farm patients, whom he pronounces "nice fellows." On the porch after dinner, he waits for Jack to suggest a walk, the possibility of conversation.

238:14–23 **We put on our coats . . . in the doorway was Hogan.** The evenings are already cool and call for a coat. A good walk is supposed to be conducive to sleep, an obvious objective for Jack. But the walk is not pleasant, as the two men encounter steady traffic that causes them to have to interrupt the walk to step to the side of the road. The big car forces them into the bushes—and Jack is not much given to being pushed aside by big cars. The incident carries echoes of the car that brought Collins, Steinfelt, and Morgan. The walk has not produced conversation, either—as we might expect from a walk in the dark that covers over a mile and a half. Patiently, Jerry continues to take his signals from Jack. A side road and a shortcut across a field take them back to Hogan's, lighted now "up on a hill." Standing in the front doorway, Hogan is a comforting figure.

238:24–240:44 **"Have a good walk?"** . . . **"Good night," said Hogan.** The evening walk having failed to tire Jack enough for sleep or provide opportunity for him to unburden himself to Jerry, Jack will turn to alcohol to numb himself enough for the sleep that regularly eludes him—and certainly would this night of nights: "I'm going to sleep tonight." Jack knows how to reach the goals he sets for himself. The extended drinking scene that follows consists primarily of dialogue. It evokes a similar scene in "The Three-Day Blow" in *In Our Time.* In it two close adolescent friends, Bill and Nick, explore the art of drinking and conversing. Admitting to liking liquor "pretty well," Jack eventually calls Jerry "the only friend I got." When Jerry rejoins Hogan at the end of the scene, Hogan asks if Jerry got his "boy friend" to sleep. On one level, Jerry is Jack's caretaker, as Bill is Nick's, but Jack is the one who shapes the scene, much as Bill does in the earlier story. Humor is less prominent in "Fifty Grand," but it helps set the scene. When Hogan asks if Jack wants some ginger ale with the liquor, Jack asks, "What do you think I want to do, get sick?" Hogan has already called Jack "the doctor." Liquor is the prescription. It should not be taken carelessly. Jack declares that he wishes "to take it slow and easy." Jerry drinks considerably less than Jack in the scene, drinking with him for companionship's sake. "I don't need it," he tells Jack, who pressures him to keep pace. Liquor loosens the tongue, and Jack confronts the theme of corruption in the world of professional sports, confirming Nick's view when in "The Three-Day Blow" he declares to Bill: "There's always more to it than we know about" (86). When Jack declares that he likes liquor "pretty well" and that if he hadn't been a boxer he would have drunk "quite a lot," we hear echoes of Nick's report that his father claims never to have taken a drink at all, a choice Bill justifies by noting the doctor's profession. Jack declares, probably for the first time, that he has paid a high price as a boxer. "You know I missed a lot, Jerry." In "The Three-Day Blow" Nick in his cups can sadly acknowledge that his father "missed a lot" (89). Had the doctor been able to relax with drink, he might have been able to share his sense of what he has missed (realities strongly suggested in "Ten Indians"), as the equally private Jack Brennan is here able to utter, and likely they are very similar items. Jack worries about his daughters and their feelings for him; he greatly misses his wife, her companionship, her place in his bed. Hemingway here writes out of his own intimacy with profound feelings of loneliness and self-doubt, vividly his during the famed separation from both Pauline (soon to become his second wife) and his first wife, Hadley, and their son, Bumby. Five times he tells Jerry that he can't have any idea what it's like to know such separation. Near the end of the lengthy scene, he connects this absence with the inability to sleep, twice more telling Jerry that he "ain't got an idea" what that's like. The repetitions accent the effects of liquor, but they have a purpose exceeding that. Before falling asleep, Jack thrice declares to Jerry that he's "the only friend I got." Practical Jerry has thrice advised Jack to add some water. Having no need himself to drink to drunkenness, he is there to help Jack undress and get into bed for the blessing of sleep. In "Ten Indians," Hemingway chose to leave us imagining the doctor's loneliness as he went to his solitary bed at story's end. A rejected ending portrayed the sleeplessness of the doctor—denied in all the published stories of a friend like Jerry who could listen without judging (Smith 197–98).

240:45–241:5 **In the morning . . . "still sleeping."** Jerry's appearance at eight indicates a night of rest for him. Reasonable as always, he has his breakfast and then sees the equally dependable Hogan already has his two customers at their routines. Confirming to Hogan that Jack is still sleeping, both men take satisfaction that Jack's goal of the past evening has been realized.

241:6–18 **I went back . . . Hogan went out.** Both Jerry and Hogan are pleased that Jack sleeps until 9:30, and both check on his condition. Hogan credits the success to the "good liquor"; characteristically, Jack delays payment—drawing, perhaps, a smile from Jerry's implied listeners. Good businessman that he is, Hogan proceeds to inquire about the time of the planned departure. The night after the binge, Jack has need to talk more. His request that Jerry sit down is Hogan's signal to depart.

241:19–242:2 **I sat down . . . "a good show," Jack said.** Wise in the ways of drunks, Jack wishes to know how he behaved last evening and what he told Jerry. Never evasive, Jerry goes quickly to the main point: the wager of fifty grand on Walcott. Jack has mixed feelings about his wager, and in trying to convince Jerry, he is trying to convince himself that he acted honorably, telling Jerry in full sobriety that he couldn't win the fight. Though he acknowledges that fifty grand is a lot of money, Jerry can't let Jack off the hook: "As long as you're in there you got a chance." Jack is destined to struggle with moral ambiguity. (In "The Doctor and the Doctor's Wife" in *In Our Time,* Dick Bolton forces Dr. Adams to face a similar ambiguity about the company logs on his beach.) Jack is determined, however, to "give them a good show." Walcott will know that he has been in a fight.

242:3–7 **After breakfast Jack called . . . "only costs two cents."** Jerry's audience doubtless smiles at Jack's penury over his reluctance to make long-distance telephone calls. The scene also accents that the day at hand carries special meaning. Whatever happens this day will be for the wife he so misses. Daily letters accent devotion as much as stinginess. Letters are more planned than telephone calls and can be reread. Surely the wife has also been writing letters to Jack. That Jack is careful with money is scarcely news, and but the tip of this iceberg. Hemingway, it should be noted, was an inveterate letter writer. Hadley and Pauline—and his other two wives—would so attest.

242:8–15 **Hogan said good-by . . . "for the rubbing."** Jerry is nothing if not thorough in his narrative—as this account of the departure illustrates. With these lines cut, the main line of the narrative would not be affected, but the episode does deepen our understanding of Jack and our sense of Jerry as a reliable narrator. Jerry senses that Bruce is disappointed in the tip Jack gives. Jack notices Jerry's disapproval and Bruce's disappointment. Jack's defense is that the rubbings are covered in the bill from Hogan's; the tip is for the trip to the train. The point is that Jack sees the disappointment, and on some level he has doubt about his "generosity" to this black man. Because Jerry provides us with his name, Bruce is more than "the nigger rubber"; likely he has financial concerns more basic than Jack's.

242:16–39 **On the train . . . "Number 238, Mr. Brennan."** Likely, however, Jack does not reflect on injustice to Bruce on the train ride to town. (Hemingway is surely accurate in portraying the ability of the more affluent to ponder only briefly the plight of the poor.) But Jerry senses that he is deeply disturbed—and though the registering at the Shelby Hotel provides another instance (with comic tenor) of Jack dickering over prices, it is not money that occupies his mind. He wants to believe that his wager of fifty grand does not compromise the integrity of the coming fight. His silence on the train reflects his inward struggle over his meeting with Collins, Steinfelt, and Morgan. Staying at the Shelby is an unnecessary expense since he lives in town. But he does not wish to share his grouchy self with his wife as the fight approaches; he is willing to spend money to keep her and his daughters at a distance from the brutality of the boxing world. The invitation for Jerry to stay with him so that he can "get my money's worth" provides another comic moment for the story, but the reader senses that Jack continues to need Jerry's comforting presence.

242:40–45 **We went up . . . something to eat.** Jack's judgment that the room is "pretty good" reflects his satisfaction in getting his money's worth. Jerry gets to have a part in the bargain, for Jack lets Jerry provide the tip to the expectant bellhop.

242:46–243:9 **We ate a lunch . . . "one thing," Jack says.** Jack is not given to departing from the familiar. Both he and Jerry have frequented Jimmy Hanley's, a favorite with boxers and trainers, so it is not unexpected that Collins would also be there. But Jack is more interested in eating than in talking with his manager—for whom Jack now has little respect or confidence. And Collins has little confidence in Jack as a boxer. Knowing that Jack is a natural welterweight (between 136 and 147 pounds) who has not gained weight at Hogan's, his inquiry is pro forma. But it leads to the line that emphasizes Jack's current state as an aging boxer: "Well, that's one thing you never had to worry about." Now, of course, Jack has much to worry about, some of which he has confided to Jerry.

243:10–33 **We went around . . . "go and eat now."** The scene at Hanley's leads easily into the official weighing in at Madison Square Garden. Had Jack been concerned with weight, he would not have had lunch before getting on the scale. The drama at the scale is part of the psychological warfare that is part of boxing. Walcott has already been weighed when Jack arrives. When Jack steps on the scale and the bar does not move from the 147 mark, Walcott's manager, Solly Freedman, presses to know Jack's weight exactly. Jack's aggression is visible in his compliance and then in his insistence that Walcott get back on the scale. His grinning opponent is only four ounces from the top welterweight limit, and he takes pleasure in telling Jack that he is going for lunch now. In the ring, Jack can expect more than the four pounds he has spotted Walcott. The "match" here gives Jack his first look at his opponent and allows Jerry to describe Walcott to his listeners. Jack has the edge in height (half a head), but blond Walcott has "the widest shoulders and back you ever saw." With a "plenty marked-up" face and the wide shoulders, he appears a formidable opponent.

243:34–44 **Jack got dressed . . . "All right."** In the dressing room, Jack gives Jerry his assessment. Walcott is "tough-looking," but he sees that Walcott "ain't hard to hit." When Collins appears to check on plans and arrange for evening dinner together, the scene takes on an ominous note. Asking Collins if he "looked after everything," Jack receives an answer that he might later remember, as Jerry has: "It's all looked after."

243:45–244:34 **Jack took off his shoes . . . taxi was waiting.** Jack is portrayed as calm and controlled as he spends the afternoon waiting. The weighing-in experience does not have him worried. Having announced that he was going to lie down in his room, he does that, and neither he nor Jerry nor Jerry's audience is surprised. Then everything goes Jack's way. Playing cribbage, he wins three dollars from Jerry, a dollar and a half from Collins, the expenses of dinner from Collins, and two-and-a-half dollars from Collins. And everything has been according to Jack's time schedule. Collins, having arrived in heavy rain, is the uncomfortable loser of the afternoon. "Jack was feeling pretty good." The autumnal rain has not harmed Jack's spirit or afternoon. Ever protective of himself, he changes to a jersey and a sweater so that he will not catch cold. In this scene, Jack is the man who cannot lose.

244:35–45 **We rode down . . . "You can't tell about the weather," Jack says.** As usual, Jerry's matter-of-fact reporting conveys more than he realizes. The heavy rain (often ominous in Hemingway's work) does not affect Jack negatively. Rather, the rain accents his status as a boxer, and he takes pleasure in the "good crowd." The rain has not kept the crowd away: Jack will fight to a full house. Inside the Garden, with Jerry, we look from the heights through the dark to the lighted ring—where ability and character will be tested. If an outside fight in good weather would have drawn an even larger crowd, as Collins suggests, Jack's almost trite observation about the uncertainty of weather not only suggests his prudent side; it also comments on the fight that will take place in the ring.

244:46–245:5 John came to the door . . . "He's just gone down," John said. Collins is now busy with the practical details in the last moments of waiting—the activity that dominates so much of this long Hemingway story. With his handlers, he comes to the door to get Jack. The boxer, dressed for the fight, sits in his bathrobe, waiting for the moment to head for the ring. Watching Jack as he sits looking at the floor, Jerry senses the emotion of the waiting boxer. Some of the hidden feeling is conveyed in Jack's first words to his manager: "Is he in?" He does not use Walcott's name. Walcott the man does not matter to Jack; for him, boxing has not been so much a beating of someone as a testing of self.

245:6–21 We started down . . . each other luck. The arrival of the boxers in the ring has its own drama, one that Jerry has observed often. So has Jack. His first words to Walcott are to mock him for aiming to be a "popular champion." Walcott has received a "big" hand, Jack a "good" hand. The crowd's money, it is clear, is on Walcott. Jerry observes that an Irishman always gets "a pretty good hand." The Irish in the crowd acknowledge their own, even as Jerry reminds us that socially, the Irish are below the Jews and the Italians. Considering money or ethnicity, it is clear that appreciation of the art of boxing is a compromised affair for the crowd. Fallible as the crowds watching Manuel in "The Undefeated," this one, Jerry reports, takes the preliminary encounter between Jack and Walcott as "gentlemanly" conduct—certainly what Walcott has aimed for by holding the rope down for Jack to get into the ring.

245:22–33 Solly Freedman came over . . . lad who brought the gloves said. The "gentlemanly" exchange as Jack's hands are bandaged allows for more "trash talk." When Freedman, Walcott's manager, comes over to question the amount of tape being used on Jack, after inviting him to feel the tape, Jack tells Freedman not to be a "hick." (Collins has not inspected the taping of Walcott.) Asking Freedman about Walcott's nationality, Jack insinuates that his behavior so far has been a bit strange. Freedman doesn't know his nationality and comically suggests "some sort of Dane." The boy who brings the gloves identifies Walcott as Bohemian. *Walcott* is not, of course, a Bohemian (Czech) name. It originated in England. That boxers often adopt ring names contributes to the theme of authentic identity at the heart of the story.

245:34–45 **The referee called them . . . "moving pictures of this."** Summoned by the referee to the center of the ring, the boxers continue the comedy of showmanship (Walcott) and insult (Jack). For the second time, Walcott tells Jack to be himself, which is exactly what Jack is doing when he calls him "popularity." Jack seizes on the issue of Walcott's identity, implying the "Bohemian" chose that name, the name of a "nigger" boxer—the social group that would be placed beneath the Irish. Jack, like Hemingway, knows boxing. Joe Walcott, the "Black Demon" of Barbados, was welterweight champion of the world from 1901 to 1904. Walcott resists the racist goad but soon goads Jack by grabbing Jack's arm and asking if he can hit if Jack so holds him—which Jack recognizes as grandstanding.

245:46:13 **They went back . . . left hand in his face.** After a preparation that insists on duration, the story suddenly erupts into the action of the boxing. The only language that matters now is Jerry's, and we have been with him long enough to recognize him as someone who knows boxing and boxers. Jerry's praise is high: "There wasn't anybody ever boxed better than Jack." The styles of the two fighters are as different as their social graces. Walcott is a "hooker": "All he knows is to get in there and sock." Jack is more studied. Early in the rounds he presses Walcott's weakness: a left into his face.

246:14–19 **After about four rounds . . . He's a socker.** There is no hiding that boxing is a blood sport. Although by the end of four rounds Walcott's face is "all cut up" and he is bleeding badly, he is able to counter with hard body socks, which Jerry makes vivid by reporting that the blows can be heard in the streets outside. Walcott is the bull here, and Jack the matador who draws blood. Jack had promised to give the crowd a good show, and the crowd is getting it.

246:20–32 **It goes along . . . the same thing again.** Jerry appreciates the fine detail of Jack's art. Jack wastes no energy; doesn't move around much; and, matador-like, remains calm in close. His left continues to be his prime weapon, but he is alert to the damaging variation of an uppercut with the right to the nose. When the profusely bleeding Walcott wants to smear some blood on Jack's shoulder, Jack is able to lift the shoulder to get the nose again and then use his right once again to the nose.

246:33–42 **Walcott was sore . . . "My left's getting heavy."** Like a bull who has been thoroughly worked over, after five rounds Walcott is fiercely angry. Jerry continues to admire Jack's control: he fights with his mind rather than his emotion. The contrast with Walcott provides the opportunity for Jerry to explain the virulent scorn of Kid Lewis back at Hanley's. Jack had never been able to force Lewis into the angry reaction Walcott now displays. If Jerry is able to cut the anti-Semitic sting a bit, he makes clear that the epithet was a cover for his frustration at encountering competition with a boxer whose temperament matched his own. Jerry's praise for Jack's performance through seven rounds is high: Jack is an "open classic boxer." Fighting ever with his intelligence, Jack knows in the seventh that his left is weakening and so prepares Jerry for the remaining rounds.

246:43–247:5 **From then he started . . . "My legs are going bad."** The transition soon becomes marked as the younger fighter asserts his force. Blows that previously "just missed" are now hitting, and Jack takes "an awful beating in the body." Body blows are bloodless but still very telling. After the eleventh round, Jack alerts Jerry that his legs are also weakening. He knows that he cannot last.

247:6–19 **Walcott had been . . . want to be knocked out.** No longer setting the tone of the round with his left, Jack concentrates on blocking blows from the "socking machine." By comparing Jack to a baseball catcher who pulls the ball back to take some of the shock, Jerry highlights a certain grace in Jack's taking the blows. But as he rubs the fluttering muscles in Jack's legs between rounds, Jerry is keenly aware that Jack is suffering. When Jack asks Collins how the fight is going, Collins's answer is not what an encouraging manager in a legitimate fight would say. Collins does not appear distressed when he says Walcott will win, and Jerry seems to sense that his reading of what happened at Hogan's is on target. Realistically, Jack knows that the fight will now be judged in Walcott's favor, as he has bet his money. He can live with this because he knows that the turn for Walcott is not because he is throwing the fight. Meanwhile, for Jack the important thing is to endure. He does not want to go out on a knockout: "'I think I can last,' Jack says. 'I don't want this bohunk to stop me.'" When used by other nationalities, *bohunk* is a mocking term for a Bohemian. That Walcott may have no Czech blood is irrelevant. The term is useful to Jack as he reduces his opponent to the "other." But Jerry's narrative amazingly transcends Jack's words, catching an inner calm and dignity in Jack that evoke the strength of Manuel in "The Undefeated" and the determination of Nick Adams in "Big Two-Hearted River" in *In Our Time*: "He wasn't strong any more. He was all right though. His money was all right and now he wanted to finish it off right to please himself." Jerry Doyle's reporting surprisingly creates the poetry we often encounter in Hemingway's prose.

247:20–29 **The gong rang . . . while he counted.** The eleventh round is crucial for Jack's goal and for Walcott's. Jack's left is not what it was, and after Jack comes with his left, Walcott is able to pound Jack's body and, after Jack misses with a right, bring Jack down. Had Jack stayed down, Walcott would have been declared winner. His emotion runs the risk of betraying the scheme of which he is a part. Taking the opportunity to shorten the round, Jack remains down through the count of eight. Walcott appears caught between wanting to finish Jack off and wanting to complete his contract with Morgan and Steinfelt. But he might just be giving the fans a good show. Here Nick's words in "The Three-Day Blow" about the darker side of baseball find correspondence.

247:30–38 When Jack was on his feet . . . mouth come open. Solly Freedman's warning to Walcott indeed seems admonition not to let emotion rule his head, advice that leads Walcott to foul Jack flagrantly, five inches below the belt, into the soft underbelly. This should bring the ruling of a foul and declaration of Jack as winner.

247:39–46 The referee . . . Jack says to Walcott. In a brief second, amidst the intense noise of the crowd, Jack must counter with intelligence, and he wills himself not to fall down, wills the blow "a accident." But he now realizes that he has been double-crossed. In the "undefeated" mode, he declares himself "all right" and once again proves able to "say what he wanted to say" at this moment (232): "Come on, you polak son-of-a-bitch." Jack's earlier epithet for Walcott, *bohunk,* becomes *polak,* now a more virulent term of derision because it is direct address. Reading the glance at Collins, Jerry may wonder if the referee is innocent of the planned outcome for this fight, but Jack's quick response has decreed that the fight continue. Collins's emotions also become problematic. Unless he was party to the double cross, he also has put money on Walcott. If his money is on Jack or his loyalty with him, he would have wanted Jack to be declared winner on a foul. But here the listener (or reader) cannot be sure.

248:1–7 John was hanging . . . "you slob," he says. Although Collins was primed to have the fight end with the flagrant foul, Jack's not having fallen compels the referee to wave Walcott to further fight. When he sends Walcott back in with the insult, we realize that the eye contact with Collins does not involve complicity in the double cross. The referee desires a fair fight.

248:8–24 Walcott went in . . . "Walcott on a foul." In contrast to Jack's mental agility, Walcott is uncertain about which moves would now be "smart." Significantly, he attacks Jack's head. (Earlier he had concentrated on Jack's body.) Jerry mentions no blood—for Jerry, Jack's face becomes a mirror not just of Jack's physical pain but of his courage and determination. Visibly suffering, Jack shapes his own plan. When he starts socking low, he causes Walcott to cover low and then goes quickly to Walcott's head and then comes the left to the groin "right back where he'd hit Jack"—a payback that causes Walcott to go down and the crowd to go wild. Jerry's description of the last moments of the fight highlights Jack in full control. The referee and the judges must give the verdict that has become the intention of the quick-thinking Jack: "Walcott on a foul."

248:25–27 The referee is talking . . . "He'd lost it anyway," John says. Collins is dealing with the realization that Steinfelt and Morgan have not played fair. Walcott's "victory" is what he had been led to expect, but he had not expected the means that would bring it about. The referee's words further support his noncomplicity in the double cross.

248:28–249:3 **Jack's sitting . . . bet in the Garden.** For Jerry, it is not Collins's reaction that matters, but Jack. Jerry notices what few others do, the attention at that moment being on Walcott. No one speaks to Jack until Collins tells him to apologize to Walcott because it will "look good." Jack is not much interested in looking good, but the ironist in him is caught in his apology. The occasion provides another instance of his ability to sting with words. He tells Walcott that he hopes he "get[s] a hell of a lot of fun" out of his championship. Solly Freedman catches the irony and sting of Jack's message, is aware of the victory that is Jack's in defeat.

Walcott is certainly not having fun as he sits in similar physical pain. Jerry's eye has been on Jack's face, a barometer of his pain. Sitting in the chair, Jack is "holding himself in down there with both hands." When he goes over to Walcott, he holds with one hand under the robe. When he exits the ring, he walks in "that funny jerky way." As Jack makes his way to the dressing room, he may take some satisfaction in the considerable number of people who want to slap him on the back. He knows that he gave the crowd its money's worth. Having bet two to one on Walcott, the crowd has ample reason for satisfaction.

249:4–17 **Once we got inside . . . "It was nothing."** With Jack inside the dressing room, Jerry accents the price that Jack has paid, keeping us focused on Jack's face. Jack's pain is intense, and John sees the need for a doctor. Jack admits that he is "all busted inside." Whether his eyes are open or closed, his face, with "that awful drawn look," may seem a death mask. The moment is searing for John Collins, too. He apologizes to Jack for the double cross, but in minimal language, giving Jack another opportunity to display his irony: "You got nice friends."

The reader of *Men Without Women* might be tempted to view Jack as likely to find himself in circumstances similar to those of Ole Andreson in "The Killers." But Jack has provided Morgan and Steinfelt with the outcome that they said they desired. The story does not end with intimations of a revenge plot, but with tribute to Jack. His famous line "It's funny how fast you can think when it means that much money" has its own dark humor. Touching on the amusement that Jack's miserliness has maintained from the beginning of the story, the line also comments on the power of money in the sporting world and in the culture at large. Jack plays the games of his time exceedingly well, earning John Collins's tribute: "You're some boy, Jack." Jack's triumph is a fitting ending to the comedy of sport and self-definition, the counterpart to the tragedy of Manuel Garcia's return to the bullring.

A SIMPLE ENQUIRY

As Hemingway's "The Light of the World" in *Winner Take Nothing* is rooted in Maupassant's "La Maison Tellier," "A Simple Enquiry" took its inspiration from "The Prussian Officer," the lead story in D. H. Lawrence's 1914 collection, *The Prussian Officer and Other Stories*. Both stories have at their center a military officer who is drawn to a young soldier under his command. Lawrence's officer seems outraged at some "undiscovered feeling" linking him to his young orderly. Hemingway's Italian officer faces more honestly his sexual nature and can make the inquiry, whereas the Prussian codes desire in violence. At the end of "The Prussian Officer," officer and orderly lie "side by side in the mortuary" (33). Tonally, the stories are vastly different. Hemingway's story is understated. Overt action is minimal, but the reader may decide that a good deal has happened. Little is "simple" in "A Simple Enquiry."

Sherwood Anderson's story "Hands" also echoes in Hemingway's story. "Hands" is the opening story of *Winesburg, Ohio*, a work that Hemingway had read carefully. Anderson portrays Wing Biddlebaum, a high school teacher who barely escapes with his life when the community reads threat in his nervous hands. Anderson's understanding of Biddlebaum's repressed sexuality was not lost on Hemingway, as his artful attention to the Italian officer who makes the "simple enquiry" demonstrates.

Although the word *war* does not enter into Hemingway's story, World War I is important to its effect. Like "Soldier's Home" and virtually all of *In Our Time*, Hemingway's first short-story collection, "A Simple Enquiry" insists that war and the military are vastly different from what Harold Krebs's parents—or the citizens of Hemingway's Oak Park—have imagined. The men involved in those wars take their own complex natures with them. Their sexual longings will be pushed aside during battle, but in the sometimes lengthy periods of waiting, desire may become more manifest and a large part of a man's thinking. Desire blatantly obvious in the Left Bank cafés and dance halls of Paris sometimes exerts itself in all-male military settings. The theme would mark it as one of those stories that would not be published until it appeared in a book. That the book is called *Men Without Women* suited beautifully.

250:1–7 **Outside, the snow . . . another table.** The story will, the first sentence suggests, take place inside. But the world outside—the powerful forces of nature—shape what takes place inside. The snow is a powerful force. Here "higher than the window," it restricts those inside to seeing mainly the inside. The view at the window would be like a painting of white, ominous in its whiteness. Hemingway's readers know that the snow can also dictate the progress of war. When the snow is no longer a force, those inside will be engaged with the outside, with battle—perhaps injury or death. The sunshine pulls the eye to the map on the wall. The map is important to strategies of defense and attack in battle, at once relevant to forthcoming maneuvers inside the hut and to the outside, once weather permits. *Hut* emphasizes impermanence, the compromises of comfort inherent in war. The power of the sun is intense, accenting the whiteness of the view from inside and the impending melting that will eventually involve those inside more intimately with life-and-death struggle, significantly widening the trench. *Trench* is a loaded word here, reminding readers of the trench warfare that made the Great War, World War I, so horrendous. Resumption of hostilities is imminent. The specificity of a late March date affirms the coming release of nature—in fields of war and of love. The final two sentences of the paragraph stress separation—by rank and by location. A table is what we expect in a hut, especially in wartime and its need for quick improvisation. The major has, it is likely, made the military his career. The adjutant has no authority. He sits at another table—befitting the professional nature of the relationship. The sentences carry us clearly "inside."

250:8–20 **eyes were two white circles . . . "You will finish up."** It is now time to look at the chief character. The sentence emphasizes his eyes—seeing, his seeing and ours. His snow glasses in the long winter have given him a somewhat strange appearance. The white circles recall the threatening whiteness of the previous paragraph. Even more than the skiers of "Cross-Country Snow" in *In Our Time,* the major has been in the mountains too long. The image recounts personal ravage, but also the larger ravage of the continuing war. The considerable attention to the nose makes unmistakable its sexual connotations. The image recalls the missing nose of the wounded Italian soldier who walks the streets of Milan with Nick in "In Another Country." The swollen and blistered nose recalls a tradition going back to the Middle Ages that sees the state of the nose as the penis and the indicator of sexually transmitted disease. The major scarcely seems military as he tenderly oils his nose, perhaps even effeminately. *Stroking* as sexual activity is highlighted by the repetition of the verb, and the oil is conduit to sexual gratification. The action is careful. The major knows what is required, "only a film of oil" on the fingers. Although the action suggests that the major is experiencing pain and seeks relief, his careful oiling of his nose is in some measure performance for the adjutant. The oiling of the face becomes preparatory to other activity, perhaps to sleep, but not necessarily for sleep. The sleeping room, however small, moves the scene to a more private setting. The major states a goal, a wish to sleep, but it is one that is unrealized in the course of the story. The sentence in which the narrator reports that an adjutant is "not a commissioned officer" jars slightly, foregrounding the narrator's presence at a private moment. The narrator is not part of "that" army. (Lawrence's officer gives a strikingly different image. Tall, he has "a handsome, finely knit figure." His orderly admires the "amazing riding-muscles of his loins" [2].)

250:21–30 "Yes, *signor maggiore*" . . . "The major is sleeping." In military style, the adjutant, known to us by his duty as the major's assistant rather than by name, briskly assents to giving the major his rank, which is "major," or large. In a modest act of rebellion, the adjutant does not put action to words; instead he leans back and yawns. He is not overly intimidated by the major and sets out to read a "paper-covered book." His action suggests a rather assured position. His reading material suggests recreation, perhaps a novel. That he is a reader anticipates the worldly distance he maintains in the rest of the story. But the pleasure of reading will be postponed, denied for the course of the story. The action anticipates other postponement and denial. The lines echo Nick's setting up camp in "Big Two-Hearted River" in *In Our Time*. To create "the good place," Nick must first complete his work: "Now it was done. . . . That was done. . . . Nothing could touch him" (167). Then pleasure of a high order follows. The change in lighting as the sun sets affects the mood inside the hut and reminds us of the larger realities that surround the scene. The setting of the sun accompanies the entrance of a soldier, a reminder of work, duty. The entrance carries in some cold air, and the placing of the branches in the stove emphasizes a contrasting sense of temperature. The soldier's task of gathering wood and then stoking the fire makes creating comfort one of his responsibilities. The tension between comfort and discomfort is central to the story. The soldier becomes a named character, and the name is likely his last name. *Pinin* is not a common Italian name; the consonant ending might suggest northern Italy. Pinin's rank is not specified. But we know that he answers to the major and to the adjutant. The adjutant offers a gentle warning. Perhaps he thinks that the major is sleeping, but he may be suggesting that the major is trying to sleep.

251:1–11 Pinin was the major's orderly . . . "and shut the door." The information that Pinin is an orderly again makes us aware of a distant narrator. Though he is often outdoors, dark-faced Pinin has been spared the harsher effects of the sun. As with many soldiers, *boy* is sometimes an apt signifier for those who bear arms. Pinin is intent on doing his tasks well and then retreats. The major has heard the soft tones; he is not asleep. We learn the adjutant's name when the major asks him to tell Pinin to see him; only the major remains unnamed. Like Pinin, the adjutant's name, Tonani, is not a common one in Italy and, given the military setting, is likely a family name. If a first name, Hemingway might have heard somewhere the informal name for *Anthony,* which is *Tonano.* The adjutant answers the major's call using his rank to address him, and rank here seems threatening in its privilege. Officers lying on their beds do not typically call others to their bed chamber. What emotion does Pinin feel as he receives this summons? Curiosity? Might he expect commendation? Rebuke? The narrator does not say, though a soldier receiving this news would ordinarily be somewhat apprehensive. He takes a walk toward the more private and the unknown. The half-open door suggests that the major has been interested in what transpires in the outer room. The knock and the question emphasize the decorum of correct procedure. For a moment longer, Hemingway keeps the emphasis on the outer room and rekindles interest in the adjutant's perspective. If Pinin is uncertain about the reason for the order to see the major, the adjutant may or may not be, but he knows that he is not supposed to know what is transpiring.

251:12–37 **Inside the room . . . "You needn't be superior."** Behind closed doors, the authority figure commences an interrogation of a subordinate, an interrogation that quickly becomes an attempt at seduction. The word *bunk* connotes isolation and reminds us of the primitive nature of the hut: the officer is not very privileged, a fact reinforced by the makeshift pillow. Intended for holding supplies, a rucksack is made of canvas. Pinin will stand by the bunk until the conversation ends; the major can use a quiet voice for their conversation. A strange sentence sets the tone: "His long, burned, oiled face looked at Pinin." The reader is well aware of the major's face; the lines indicate what Pinin sees—the major looking at him. The power of the gaze will be a dominant motif for the rest of the story. Pinin likely finds the face as unattractive as the reader did upon confronting the narrator's opening description of the major. The narrator also notes the hands lying on the blanket. Hands can be used for grasping and are typically very important in lovemaking, already intimated in the major's oiling of his nose. The narrator makes a point of having the major's eyes pause at Pinin's hands.

Like Max of "The Killers" in a somewhat different play for power, the major will mainly use the interrogative mode. Pinin has been introduced to us as a "boy." Confirmation of his age, nineteen, highlights the significant difference in age between the two. When the major asks if Pinin has ever been in love, he uses syntax strange to the native English speaker: "You have ever been in love?" not "Have you ever been in love?" It reminds us that the characters are not speaking English, but Italian; the oddness of the syntax also highlights what a strange moment this is for Pinin. The question is hardly "military." Pinin scarcely knows how to respond to the strange question from his officer, but the major may take some encouragement from the statement. There may be many kinds of love—including, of course, boy-man love. But the major knows not to approach the boy-man possibility yet.

Pinin is not quite comfortable with the word *love*. From the major's perspective, Pinin's response is something of a tease. When the major moves toward greater precision—"with a girl"—he uses a pause that more pointedly implies alternative loves. Curiously, his question is in the past tense (had been in love). Asking if Pinin is in love might have provided opportunity for quick closure. (Lawrence unequivocally states that his young soldier and his girl are in love [9].)

Informed that Pinin has been in love with a girl, the major moves into present tense—opening the way for bisexual experiences. Since he reads Pinin's letters, he knows that Pinin does not write the girl. In wartime, especially, censorship prevails; private lives are monitored. The major's lines make clear that he has not been reading Pinin's mail primarily with military interest. The verbal is not Pinin's gift; hence he does not write his girl. The major can speak with nuance; Pinin cannot. He is likely a conscript and not highly educated, but he knows he is being toyed with.

When the major gently gives Pinin opportunity to reveal any ambiguity about his feelings for the girl, Pinin does not hesitate. When the major, still in a calm voice, calls to ask if Tonani in the next room can hear, his question seems geared at assuring Pinin that he has privacy. The major does not wish to end the interrogation. He is not satisfied with Pinin's answer. It seems clear that Pinin's voice never conveys shock or disgust. The silence from Tonani adds to Pinin's discomfort—and the silence opens up various possibilities. In part, it is a come-on. Tonani may not hear the words, or he may and yet know that he is not expected to respond. He would not likely reveal that he has been privy to the conversation. Seeming to ensure privacy, secrecy, the major says, in essence, "Nobody knows or will know." Then he makes the "simple" inquiry at the heart of the story. By now surety has become a key issue of the story. Certainly, the major is trying to cast doubt on the surety of Pinin's love for the girl. When Pinin gives the direct, simple answer, he repeats the key word *sure*. The direct eye contact is powerful when the major asks if Pinin is "corrupt." His choice of the word *corrupt* carries a sexual connotation, revealing the cultural construct that makes the major view his own disposition as "corrupt." The forbidden sometimes carries allurement, and the major's voice here intends to entice. Probably Pinin intuits the major's meaning, but the word *corrupt* is not one someone from his social class would likely use. Soldiers and schoolboys have more direct and cruder language to use when discussing homosexuality. But for Hemingway's audience in 1927, the concept was in the main one that "dare not speak its name," words spoken by Lord Alfred Douglas and made famous in Oscar Wilde's trial for homosexuality. The major is not fully convinced of Pinin's innocence. The temptation of the straight person is often the morally superior stance. It is not a stance that the story seeks to allow the reader.

251:38–252:6 **Pinin looked at the floor . . . "when you go out."** That Pinin does not look at the major distances him from the major's appeal. Pinin senses the major's embarrassment. The direct look at the major might suggest a different message; the eyes—certainly in this story—are the eyes of the soul. The major's "looking" is intensely physical, intensely thorough, visually caressing. Ending the sentence describing that gaze with *hands,* Hemingway accents the tactical implications.

With some experience in seduction, the major again uses the pause to make the unstated the climax of his discourse of desire. The first is the pause while the major's gaze lingers over Pinin's body, and then the second is the pause at the end of the sentence. The major lives in a world in which homosexual people have to lie or hide their true emotions and wishes. The second pause allows for admission of what he hopes Pinin "really" wants. Pinin's answer is silence. He may not know what he "really" wants, but he does not want the major. For the third time, Pinin makes his statement without saying a word: "Pinin looked at the floor."

When the major leans back on the rucksack and smiles, the action reveals another pause even as it makes clear that the major's longing gaze at Pinin has involved motion, the lifting of his head from the rucksack. Pinin would have heard the motion of both the rising and the falling back. The simple smile (the first of the story) carries increased weight. The narrator identifies the meaning of the smile as relief, and the sentence slips into the major's point of view. He concludes that life in the army is too complicated (requiring games, indirection—especially in sexual matters); the narrator seems to share in the judgment about the complexity of life in the army and educates readers about realities very different from stereotypical images of the military.

Pinin has made his denials thrice through silence, looking "at the floor." It seems clear that no one has ever spoken to him in this way before. When the major calls Pinin "a good boy," we may hear some ambiguity. The phrase at once acknowledges Pinin's innocence, but the expression is also demeaning. *A good boy* would be more appropriate to a child. The major uses the appellation twice. For him, repetition is an important rhetorical device. The first repetition indicates that the major really does think of Pinin as a good boy, and it softens the tension of the preceding moments. The repetition of the caution about not feeling superior is a plea for understanding that carries with it a warning about the complexities of life in the military: another man may also make a play for Pinin, who is, we infer, handsome.

The single-sentence paragraph reminding us that Pinin stands beside the bunk accents Pinin discomfort. Silence remains his chosen stance in the discourse. But one might also read hesitancy in the posture, uncertainty—especially given his silences. Has Pinin continued to look at the floor—or does he see with the reader the major's hands, folded on the blanket? The major's speech is ingenious in a couple of ways. He promises to keep the "threatening" (or appealing) hands where they are and gives permission for Pinin to return to his platoon. But he also gives permission for Pinin "to stay." Pinin's self-interest (but perhaps not his self-respect) would be served by a decision to remain the major's servant. His self-interest also would be served by his discretion about the afternoon's exchange. Being the major's servant invites him to another kind of front, as Pinin seems to realize. Less is more with Pinin. He does not say thank you. Responding with a loaded question, "Do you want anything of me, *signor maggiore?*" he replays the title of the story. He is not ready to speak about the option of servanthood that the major presents. The major is ready for this session to end. It is the end of an episode, though not necessarily the end of the relationship. The major returns characteristically to the imperative mood. His order that the door be left open makes it clear that he does not wish Tonani to confer with Pinin.

252:7–14 **Pinin went out . . . he lied to me.** A good soldier, Pinin does as he has been told, and he does not stop to talk with the adjutant. When the conversation with the major ended, Pinin, standing by the bunk, sensed that he has been metaphorically undressed (he has felt the major's eyes on him even if he has been looking at the floor). He now walks "awkwardly" and "moves differently" because there has been arousal. This does not mean that Pinin is gay, but his walk shows the effects of the special ravishment he has experienced. The adjutant can see something of the emotional impact of the visit. The meeting with Pinin is probably not the only one of this sort that the adjutant has been privy to. Significantly, his position as adjutant makes him "less likely to be killed." He is one of the protected ones. Pinin returns to his chores. Whether he intended to or not, his return with the wood feeds the embers of desire, as the ending of the story reveals. That the major looks at his helmet and snow glasses brings images of war and the military into juxtaposition with the image of desire and rest, the bunk. In the army, life is indeed too complicated for him. So the story ends in uncertainty as he ponders the possibility that Pinin has lied to him. The fire will receive more fuel.

In *Death in the Afternoon* Hemingway would embed an account in peacetime of the seduction of a younger man by an older man. The older American man derives his power from money rather than military position. At first the younger man resists but later seems fully acceptant of a homosexual life. Probably Pinin will not accept the major's offer to become his servant: there seems to be too much of "the unhampered young animal" (to use Lawrence's description of the orderly, Schöner, in "The Prussian Officer" [39]) for him to choose the bondage that the major invites. But Hemingway has brought Pinin to a moment of awareness and of choice. As he did in "Hills Like White Elephants," Hemingway ends his story leaving his reader to contemplate a defining and uncertain juncture in the life of his character.

The Puerta del Sol. The opening story of *Men Without Women* takes the protagonist and the reader to Madrid's central square, to the very heart of Spain. We view the Puerta del Sol in the 1920s as Manuel Garcia would have seen it, as Ernest Hemingway first saw it. Photo courtesy of the Museo Municipal de Madrid.

The picador: "Zurito sat his horse, measuring the distance between the bull and the end of the pic. As he looked, the bull gathered himself together and charged, his eyes on the horse's chest." In the photo, the picador Anderson Murillo takes similar aim at a charging Marqués de Domecq bull. Madrid, May 27, 1994. Caption by Allen Josephs, photo from his book *Ritual and Sacrifice in the Corrida*.

The matador: "He felt the sword go in all the way. Right up to the guard. Four fingers and his thumb into the bull." In the photo, matador César Rincón sinks the sword in a spectacular kill with a Marqués de Domecq bull. Madrid, May 27, 1994. Caption by Allen Josephs, photo from his book *Ritual and Sacrifice in the Corrida*.

The railway junction at Casetas: We know from an unpublished fragment that Hemingway changed trains here in July 1925 and that his wife Hadley made a remark about the hills looking like white elephants, thus providing the setting and the title, but probably nothing else, for "Hills Like White Elephants." The station faces northeast across the Ebro River to the chalky-gray eroded hills running parallel on the other side. The table where the couple sat would have been on the platform along the far end of the building (visible in the photo), and the man had to carry the bags around the building to get to the other track for the "express from Barcelona," which went on to Madrid. Caption by Allen Josephs; photo courtesy of Allen Josephs.

Early twentieth-century interior of Windemere, the Hemingway cottage on Walloon Lake, Emmet County, Michigan. Here we have a rare view inside the cottage (a national historic landmark). Its rustic quality emphasizes the marked contrast to the genteel norm of Oak Park, where the famed architect Frank Lloyd Wright designed numerous Oak Park houses. Summer months summoned the Hemingways to the woods, to the lake, and to nearby rivers and streams. Like Hemingway, young Nick Adams spent his summers in the woods of northern Michigan. And if we may judge from the Nick Adams canon, Nick was outdoors as much as possible; "Ten Indians" is the single finished Hemingway story that takes him inside the Adams cottage. Photo from the Marceline Hemingway Sanford Collection, courtesy Ernest Hemingway Foundation of Oak Park.

Parlor fireplace inside Windemere, the Hemingway family cottage. Although this fireplace had decidedly practical function in the early years of the twentieth century, the hearth serves widely as universal symbol of home and fulfillment. The image never attracted Hemingway (as it did Hawthorne); "Ten Indians" suggests the reasons that Nick Adams was in this trait like his creator. Photo from the Marceline Hemingway Sanford Collection, courtesy Ernest Hemingway Foundation of Oak Park.

600 N. Kenilworth Avenue, Oak Park, Illinois. Ernest Hemingway moved into this house when he was eight years old. Following her father's death, Grace Hall Hemingway used her legacy for the construction of a house she herself designed. It included a large music room off the left side of the house. Many years later, subsequent owners removed the music room. Photo from the Marceline Hemingway Sanford Collection, courtesy Ernest Hemingway Foundation of Oak Park.

Ernest Hemingway, 1918, back in Oak Park following his brush with death on the Italian front. Looking very military, he returns to his high school—an easy walk from the family home. Domestic structures visible in the photo accent the solid values of the community. Photo from the Marceline Hemingway Sanford Collection, courtesy Ernest Hemingway Foundation of Oak Park.

TEN INDIANS

As Paul Smith has made clear, Hemingway struggled to write "Ten Indians." Three manuscript versions all end very differently. He was uncertain about where he wanted to take the biographical material that lay at its heart. Smith argues that he settled the uncertainty by using James Joyce's "Araby" from *Dubliners* as his prototype. In both stories a young boy loses his romantic innocence. Like Joyce, we might add, Hemingway provides a strong national dimension to his portrayal of lost innocence. Andre Dubus, who prized Hemingway's short stories and ranked them above those in *Dubliners,* would have us find a more human, more compassionate protagonist in "Ten Indians" than in "Araby."

The title "Ten Indians" is at once stark, suggesting a tale that will portray ten Indians. But the story that unfolds has more to do with how a white American youth responds to one of the ten Indians. The title alludes to the song familiar to generations of American children. The song counts down from ten little Indians to one to none. This title, like the title of the last story in *Men Without Women,* "Now I Lay Me," evokes the world of childhood. Though the characters in the story are all based on actual people known to Hemingway in Michigan, the events of the story may be entirely fictional. Joe Garner is based on Joseph Bacon, who farmed near the Hemingway cottage on Lake Walloon. As Constance Cappel Montgomery has reported, he had four sons (Carl and Earl among them) and four daughters. Carl was a close friend of young Ernest. (Carlos Baker's biography calls the father Henry Bacon, as do critics who rely on Baker's account rather than Montgomery's study of the locale and its records.) Prudence Mitchell is based on Prudence Boulton, who was two years younger than Ernest; there was no Prudence, Montgomery found, living in the Indian camp near the Hemingway cottage.

Of the fourteen stories in *Men Without Women,* "Ten Indians," set in the middle of the collection, takes us closest to the natural world. Unlike *In Our Time, Men Without Women* is overwhelmingly cast in urban settings.

253:1–7 **After one Fourth of July . . . on the wagon box.** The opening sentence introduces several important motifs. The Fourth of July is both the major national holiday and a major family day, especially in the early years of the twentieth century, as Eugene O'Neill dramatized in *Ah, Wilderness!* That Nick Adams is the focal point of the story is immediately made clear, but he doesn't need a last name here; he is with Joe Garner and his family—in a sense one of the Garner family, though the sentence emphasizes his separateness. The reader may well wonder why on this day Nick is not with his family. It has been a full day: the Garner wagon comes home "late" from town. Indians also make it into the opening sentence: the Garners have passed nine of them, drunk, along the side of the road. The holiday celebrates the nation's independence from Great Britain. The birth of the nation, joyously being celebrated by the Garners and other Americans, is no cause of joy to the Indians. Rather, it calls for alcohol to blunt their sense of loss. On some level, young Nick recognizes their loss. He has silently been keeping count when Garner removes the ninth inebriated Indian from the rut in the road. Roads came from the white man, and the ruts in this rural Michigan road suggest the ruts created by other large wagons as they made their way west on their way to fulfilling what came to be known as Manifest Destiny. More often then not, the Indians blocking the path could be tossed aside—preferably out of sight, exemplified in Joe's dragging the ninth Indian "into the bushes."

253:8–21 **"That makes nine"** . . . **"Them Indians," said Mrs. Garner.** If the opening paragraph of the story evokes national memory, the first segment of dialogue conveys Nick's immediate memory of the recent experience with the ninth Indian. Joe Garner's announcement that the recently removed Indian is the ninth drunk Indian they have passed prepares us for the story's tenth Indian. Mrs. Garner's "Them Indians" suggests the educational level of the Garners and the prevailing attitude of whites toward the native peoples—an attitude that fails to comprehend the tragedy these people have experienced, an attitude that implies that the Indians are deficient and were somehow not worthy of the land. Nick, by contrast, is thinking of the Indians as individuals. When he looks back, he does so to ascertain who the Indian is: he can affirm that it is not Billy Tabeshaw, the Indian boy who is about Nick's age, to judge from "The Doctor and the Doctor's Wife" in *In Our Time*, where Hemingway first presented Billy. Frank Garner did not see the ninth Indian and assumed that his father was killing a snake, an instinctual solution for dealing with perceived threats to a family or a nation's progress. Joe Garner uses Frank's words to highlight the scourge of alcoholism for native peoples; killing snakes describes the alcoholic's delirium tremens, famously used by Mark Twain in chapter 6 of *Huckleberry Finn*. Pap Finn is convinced that snakes are crawling over him and will give him no respite. Attempting to rid himself of the snakes, he nearly kills his son.

253:22–27 **They drove along . . . in the wagon again.** The paragraph evokes travel of an earlier era and helps define the Michigan of Nick's youth. The world here suggests the reality of the early years of the republic. We are far from the suburb of Summit of "The Killers" or the Chicago that Nick will identify as his home in "The Light of the

World" in *Winner Take Nothing*. On a sandy road, the horses must pull hard, and so the boys walk for a while, as early settlers of the nation often did. At the top of a hill is a schoolhouse, emblematizing the theme of Nick's education and the perceived value of formal education. In the Michigan woods, Nick learns lessons very different from those encountered in a classroom. By having Nick look back to view the lights of Petoskey and Harbor Springs, Hemingway provides a precise location for his story, the terrain the Hemingway family knew well. That the lights of the towns are visible emphasizes that the Garners have made a full day of this Fourth.

A traveler wishing to retrace the Garners' journey would drive along U.S. 31 from Petoskey and exit at Resort Pike Road and proceed to the road's ending at Walloon Lake. (The white wooden schoolhouse on the hill that Hemingway mentions and used to thematic purpose in the story survived the twentieth century, though it eventually ceased to operate as a school, but was razed in the twenty-first century. Constance Cappel Montgomery includes a picture of it in her *Hemingway in Michigan*.) A right turn places the traveler on Lake Grove Road, which quickly takes one to the rear of the Hemingway cottage. For the modern traveler, the six to seven miles from Petoskey to the cottage, named Windemere by Grace Hall Hemingway, are easy ones. The emotional miles for Hemingway in 1947 when he and Otto Bruce made a nostalgic trip to Windemere were more complex.

253:28–254:2 **"They ought to put some"** . . . **into a clearing.** The seating arrangement is revealing. The Garner parents sit "close together." Joe Garner is not one of the men without a woman. (In "The Short Happy Life of Francis Macomber" Hemingway uses the seating arrangements of the Macombers to create images of a very different kind of marriage on a very different kind of excursion.) Nick's position between the two boys suggests that he has been warmly accepted into the family. Mrs. Garner's comment on the gravel not only underscores the condition of the road; it also reminds us of the effort required for this outing.

254:3–14 **"Right here was where"** . . . **"smell about the same."** Skunks more than Indians are likely to be run over in northern Michigan, and their scent will mark that spot long after the incident. With an ironic rejoinder, Joe can squelch the minor argument of his sons over the location where he ran over the skunk: there is, in fact, no "good place" to run over a skunk. Such incidents usually happen at night, the time when skunks prefer to hunt. When Nick innocently reports that he saw two skunks just last evening, he opens himself up for probing and for teasing. What was Nick doing out at night? That he reports seeing a pair of skunks anticipates the report of a sighting of another couple. In both sightings there is some uncertainty about just what the viewer saw. When Carl says that Nick probably saw raccoons looking for dead fish, Nick speaks forcefully: "I guess I know skunks." (Challenged, Nick's father will likewise strongly affirm the identity of the couple he has seen.)

Carl is delighted to turn Nick's affirmation into adolescent teasing, linking the odor of Indians and the odor of skunks. Mrs. Garner accepts the mother's role of curbing teasing. Her son has overstepped the bounds of acceptable banter.

254:15–25 Joe Garner laughed . . . "ain't my girl," he said. When Joe laughs, Mrs. Garner protests her husband's response—her authority is being undermined; the laugh is a minor betrayal. Joe placates her by changing the slur on Indian smells to something more serious, the possibility that Nick has a romantic attachment. By using the softer version of Nick's name (Nickie), he accents Nick's youth and the warmth of their relationship. Nick's "No" is a less-than-honest answer to Joe's question, but it is not unusual for denial to be part of the games boys play when other boys or adults tease or seem to tease them about their romantic interest in some girl. In *The Descent of Man and Selection in Relation to Sex*, Charles Darwin instructed numerous writers of fiction in the complex patterns of sexual selection. Bert Bender in *The Descent of Love* makes a strong case that Hemingway was among the distinguished company of late nineteenth- and early twentieth-century writers who played on the Darwinian theme in sophisticated ways. Without a doubt, sexual selection (through the ages smell has long been an important factor in such selection) is key in "Ten Indians." When Frank speaks up, supporting his brother Carl's claim that Nick has an Indian girl, Nick is quick to deny it. Carl's claim that Nick sees Prudence Mitchell every day also brings a denial, and Hemingway's paragraph recounting the denial is instructive. It begins with "I don't." It ends with "She ain't my girl." (Nick's *ain't* would not be the verb he would use in the doctor's house, but it shows how easily he can slide into the Garner world.) This is denial writ large, but between the disavowals is a sentence describing how happy Nick feels during the banter. Hemingway observes that Nick is sitting between Carl and Frank, suggesting that he is a favorite of both brothers, but also that he is at this moment special, a victor of sorts: the victorious male, dominant in his sexuality.

254:26–32 "Listen to him" . . . "Look at your pa." Carl is not ready to surrender, but he might better have remained silent. Siding with Nick, his mother pronounces her son a loser in the sexual competition: Carl can't "even" get a squaw. Her words sting (much is captured in a sentence—and paragraph—of just three words: "Carl was quiet"). The sexual loser is prone to ridicule, as Robert Cohn discovers in *The Sun Also Rises*. When Frank adds his taunt—"Carl ain't no good with girls"—Joe Garner realizes that the game has gone too far. But his words of comfort are ambiguous. "You're all right, Carl" might convey that Carl's moment will come, but the sentence also suggests that not being good with girls may not be a handicap. "Girls never got a man anywhere" places the men without women in a category with some merit. The sentence meant to be playful forecasts later developments in the story.

254:33–42 **"Yes, that's what" . . . "the way to talk," Mrs. Garner said.** The Garner parents can banter playfully about sexuality; the affirmation of their relationship is mirrored in Mrs. Garner's moving closer to Joe. The exchange is pleasing to Joe, much as Nick took pleasure in being teased about Prudence. In contrast to Carl, the father is affirmed as sexual conqueror, someone who has had "plenty of girls" in his time. He pretends to be ripe for future conquests and jokingly warns Nick to keep careful watch over Prudie. His comment affirms that an Indian girl would be okay. The Garner parents have made a concerted effort to put Nick at ease, to keep his Fourth "happy." When Mrs. Garner whispers to her husband, it is about their own sexuality, which remains vibrant. Joe wants to keep it that way, leaving Prudence to Nick as he anticipates a sexual ending to this Fourth of July. The Garners' discourse contrasts markedly with Nick's later conversation with his own father and that father's lonely finale to the Fourth.

254:43–255:6 **The horses were pulling . . . pouring kerosene on the wood.** On the last leg of the journey, we are reminded of the effort required for the Garners' outing—a transition from the world of celebration to the world of work and responsibility. Joe's words to the horses announce that the morrow is a workday—for the horses and for the family. When the wagon arrives at the farmhouse, duties commence. Mrs. Garner quickly readies a kerosene lamp to provide the necessary light. (Electricity will mark an ending to the nineteenth-century world.) Carl, Frank, and Nick all assume tasks. After helping unload the wagon, Nick opens the door to the kitchen to find Mrs. Garner building a fire in the stove.

255:7–22 **"Good-by, Mrs. Garner" . . . "Good-night, Nickie."** Well-mannered Nick has stopped to thank Mrs. Garner for the hospitality. Her fondness comes through as she twice addresses him as "Nickie." Nick is more than perfunctory: "I had a wonderful time." Nor is Mrs. Garner perfunctory. Nick is a family favorite. He would like to accept her invitation to stay for supper, but he also feels a pull to other obligations. His father, Nick feels confident, will have waited for him. Mrs. Garner understands that pull and sends him off with a request that on his way he send Carl up to the house. The request may stem from her sense that she needs to reestablish communication with the son whom she has wounded. The request also reminds us of the ending of "The Doctor and the Doctor's Wife," when Mrs. Adams requests that her husband send Nick to her. In the barn, Nick keeps the bridge to the Garners in good repair by telling Mr. Garner and Frank, who are busy milking the cows, that he had had a "swell time." Carl, perhaps nursing his hurt feelings, is nowhere to be found. When Nick asks that they "tell Carl his mother wants him," he echoes Mrs. Adams's words to the doctor: "tell him his mother wants to see him." Nick's "his mother" is natural under the circumstances—as Mrs. Adams's words are not. She lays claim to a possessive power, setting up an authority not found in Mrs. Garner's "send Carl up to the house." As Nick leaves the Garners, Mr. Garner affirms the family affection with a "Good-night, Nickie"—a wish that will not be fulfilled.

255:23–30 **Nick walked barefoot . . . went in.** Hemingway provides a striking paragraph of transition as the story moves from the Garners to the Adamses. It recounts a different kind of journey, a journey more primitive than the pioneer-like journey from Petoskey. Nick walks barefoot along a path through the meadow, the elemental feel linking him to the earlier world of the Indians—a world with which he has much affinity: "The path was smooth and the dew was cool on his bare feet." Describing the ravine, the swamp mud, the climb up through the beech woods, Hemingway emphasizes not only Nick's comfort in the natural world (he moves at ease, though it is now night) but also the great psychological distance between the Garners' life and the life found in the cottage at the end of the story's second journey.

When Nick arrives at the cottage, the story pauses briefly to frame the scene through the front window: his father sits by the table, reading by the light from the big lamp. In a story set in evening and ever-increasing darkness, Hemingway continues to play with images of light. A lamp summons light and dispels darkness—metaphorical as well as real. The image anticipates the task that Nick's father has set for himself; he will need all the wisdom that he can find. The paragraph ends with a return to movement, the real end of the second journey as Nick enters the cottage. (The noun *cottage* contrasts with the Garners' *farmhouse*. The Adamses, the reader is reminded, are summer people.)

The entrance marks a dramatic moment in the Nick Adams stories. This is the only time in any Nick story that we see Nick inside the family cottage. In "The Doctor and the Doctor's Wife" he has declined his mother's invitation to enter this cottage. The posthumously published "The Last Good Country" begins with Nick hiding in the woods because the game warden has gone to the cottage to arrest him for shooting a heron; Nick tells his sister Littless, his informant of events in the cottage, that he has decided to run away. (Littless would be happy to go with her brother.) We never see Nick inside his parents' town house in any story, nor do we see him in one of his own after he marries and becomes a parent. (In "A Day's Wait" in *Winner Take Nothing*, the father, often considered to be Nick, and son seem to be guests: "At the house they said the boy had refused to let anyone into the room" [333].)

The prototype of the Adams cottage is the Hemingway cottage, which Dr. Hemingway constructed in 1899, the year of Ernest's birth. It was modified through the years as the family grew. The Hemingway cottage was placed on the National Register of Historic Places on 24 November 1968. In a letter dated 15 August 1949, Hemingway told his sister Sunny she need not fear that he would sell Windemere, the place where the Hemingway children were happiest.

255:31–37 **"Well, Nickie," his father said . . . "out to the kitchen."** The narrative echoes the "Nickie" of the Garner parents, as Nick's father aims for a similar kind of warmth. Nick's father asks a question that Nick will long remember: "was it a good day?" Nick's affirmation catches the fervor of his declarations to the Garners. Twice he uses the adjective *swell*, a word that corresponds nicely with youthful enthusiasm. The father's parental concern (more motherly at first than fatherly, perhaps) comes out in two additional questions, both having to do with creature comforts. That Nick has left his shoes at the Garners recalls his comfort there; it is a place to which he will certainly return. But the father wants this abode also to be a place where Nick wishes to be and so invites him into the kitchen.

255:38–43 **Nick's father went ahead . . . "It's grand."** When Nick said good-bye to Mrs. Garner, she was in the kitchen, setting the fire in the stove so that she could prepare supper. In a striking contrast to that image, Nick's father (though like Mrs. Garner also the bearer of a lamp) enters the kitchen to lift the lid from the icebox. The fare here will not be hot. The scene unfolding carries tension. Cold chicken, a cold glass of milk, and cold pie can be delicious fare, and Nick's response shows his appreciation. Literally, the food that Nick gets is not cold; iceboxes do not have the efficiency of the modern refrigerator. What Nick gets is standard picnic fare; the contrast with Mrs. Garner's kitchen alerts the reader that the scene is ambiguous. There is a caring father here, but the care also carries disturbing elements. (Ernest's father was adept in the kitchen, unlike his mother. Carlos Baker recounts how the still single Clarence astonished his hunting companions in the Great Smoky Mountains with a fresh blackberry pie baked on the campfire, fare to accompany stewed squirrel [Baker 2].)

255:44–256:1 **His father sat down . . . "Five to three."** The two-sentence paragraph emblematizes the powerful role that the doctor has played in Nick's life thus far. ("Indian Camp," the first Nick story, ended with Nick in the stern of the boat; "with his father rowing, he felt quite sure that he would never die" [70].) The transition here is immense. In "Indian Camp" Nick had been on an outing with his father; a few years later the outing has been with others. We now get a sense of what Nick's day with the Garners was like. They watched a baseball game, known then as the great American pastime. (The designation persists, but some now would claim football or basketball first.) The mention of baseball reinforces the national implications of the story. Probably the ballpark was also the scene of evening fireworks. Petoskey lies at the mouth of the Bear River at the southeast shore of Michigan's Little Traverse Bay; it is the county seat of Emmet County. In *In Our Time*, "The Doctor and the Doctor's Wife" ends with Nick choosing to go into the woods with his father. "Ten Indians," the Nick Adams story next in a chronological study, finds Nick's father (whom we soon learn has been wandering the woods alone) requesting information about Nick's day spent some distance from home territory. After this night, Nick's view of his father will never be the same. So far the father has been asking all the questions, Nick providing answers. His question about the game ends this series, a series in which the questions veil what is on the father's mind.

256:2–4 **His father sat watching . . . huckleberry pie.** The moments of silence here prepare us for the reversal of the questioning pattern in which questions originate with the father. The now silent father watching the hungry son eat has doubtless made the son a bit uneasy; he senses something in this body language. This is not, after all, a shared meal, what Mrs. Garner had offered. Nick's father breaks his staring when he pours Nick some milk and serves him pie. Because he does not talk or return to his reading while Nick eats, we sense that he has an ulterior motive— especially when he offers Nick a "big piece" of huckleberry pie. At the same time, we do sense great caring. The watchfulness and generosity seem maternal. The last sentence of the paragraph catches that love. The fact that the pie is huckleberry is separated from the act of cutting. Huckleberries grow wild in Michigan forests; into the twentieth century, huckleberry picking was often the occasion for a family outing. Huckleberry pie counted as a treat of summer bounty. (Few twenty-first-century readers of "Ten Indians" have savored huckleberry pie.) Possibly Nick's father gathered the berries for this pie. In the absence of a mother, the father likely baked the pie. Here the pie is both a gesture of love and propitiation.

256:5–9 **"What did you" . . . Nick eat the pie.** Nick breaks the uncomfortable sense of excessive parental hovering by asking a question. The question conveys the close bond that Nick has had with his father. The young teen inquires about the parent's day, a question made more genuine by the noun of address. More typically, a young teen son does not think to inquire about what his parents have done while he has been away. Nick's question is one, however, that he might wish that he had never asked. His father's answers are at first factual, brief. He is reluctant to report on how he has spent his Fourth of July. Nick must keep asking questions. The minimalist answers do alert Nick to the undercurrents of the scene, especially when his father continues watching him eat his pie.

256:10–19 **"What did you do" . . . not looking at him.** Sensing that there is more to his father's day, Nick initiates an insistent line of questioning about the afternoon— putting his father in the role of reluctant teenager, reluctant to talk not only about what he has been doing but especially about sexual matters. Nick's father exemplifies Victorian reticence on the parental side of sexual matters. By not looking at Nick after making this revelation, he underscores his embarrassment. The father's revelation that he had taken an afternoon walk near the Indian camp alerts the reader and Nick to sexual dynamics. Although the opening movements of the story provided images about Indian heritage and identity, discussion of them led to the talk about Nick's relationship with Prudence and interracial sexuality. His father's answer quite naturally turns Nick's mind to the tenth Indian of the story, Prudence. He may wonder, as might the reader, why his father chose that direction for his walk. Nick must work hard to get the information he seeks. He deals with parental evasion. When asked if he had seen anyone, his father falls back on the impersonal racial generalization: the Indians were all in town getting drunk. When pressed, he admits that he saw Prudence; pressed again, he not only answers Nick's question about where she was but adds that she was with Frank Washburn and that "They were having quite a time." This, we sense, is the information that Dr. Adams has been waiting to give his son ever since he came upon Prudence and Frank.

256:20–33 **"What were they doing?" . . . "I guess so."** The questioning here continues to accent the reversal of child-parent discourse. Nick must be insistent to get the confirmation he seeks. His father's discomfort is palpable, and he is forced into evasion and lies, and the lie is not natural to him. He does it unconvincingly. He declares that he doesn't know what Prudence and Frank were doing, that he only heard them, that he didn't see them, and then that he did. He cannot use medical or everyday English words to describe what they were doing, nor can Nick. Struggling to specify the sexual act of betrayal (from Nick's perspective, of course, not necessarily from Prudence's), Nick can only ask if they were *happy*. His adjective is appropriate to the Fourth of July, which celebrates the right to life, liberty, and the pursuit of happiness. Happiness has become a more difficult pursuit for Nick on this hitherto "swell" Fourth of July. We sense that exchanges with his father will never be the same after this night.

256:34–40 **His father got up . . . cleared off the table.** Leaving Nick to ponder Prudence's betrayal, his father chooses to leave the cottage, seeking his own comfort in the out-of-doors, giving Nick leave to shed his tears alone. He is gone for some minutes; when he returns, he finds Nick staring at his plate—the plate of a deception. Hemingway echoes a scene from "Soldier's Home" in *In Our Time* when Harold Krebs stares at the "bacon fat hardening on his plate" (115); in that scene, Krebs's mother prepares a bountiful breakfast for her son then launches into her agenda without giving her son the leisure to eat it. The "food" that the doctor had prepared having been ingested, Nick is eager for no more. The doctor, of course, offers Nick literal food again—a second piece of pie. But when he picks up the knife, his gesture appears threatening. And the doctor is again the one asking questions. His "Have some more?" is another way of asking if Nick will continue to see Prudence. Twice Nick says, "No"—he does not want another "piece." The pun is not one that the doctor would use or likely be aware of, but the narrator is. The *no* is the word that the doctor wants to hear from his son. Women can hurt you; certainly he does not want Nick to continue his relationship with Prudence. His immediate objective achieved, his father can clear off the table, leaving Nick's plate where it is.

256:41–257:4 **"Where were they"** . . . **"heart must be broken."** Nick is one of those destined to think about things. As if to check on the veracity of his father's story, he asks where Prudence and Frank were cavorting. Imagining the scene (perhaps the spot where he and Prudence have been together), Nick continues to look at his empty plate. His father gently suggests that his son go to bed, ending the sentence with a gentle, loving "Nick." The doctor has proceeded this evening out of concern for Nick, although not with unquestionable wisdom. Nick meekly agrees, but he does not soon fall asleep. He hears his father moving around in the living room. The father cannot settle into quiet reading, though Nick seems not to be thinking of his father's frame of mind even if Hemingway signals that the reader should do so. Instead, Nick is thinking of his own loss. The theme of the broken heart aligns Nick with the protagonist of Joyce's "Araby" in *Dubliners,* who at a very young age loses the innocence of early romance. Hemingway's narrator views the youthful heartbreak with amused sympathy. Especially with a protagonist easily identified with the author, it is important that the author not surrender to self-pity.

257:5–13 **After a while . . . was broken.** The concluding paragraph carries great lyrical beauty as it echoes many of the images of the story, ending with the third ring of the broken heart image. Its lead sentence echoes the drama of his father's part in Nick's education on this day commemorating independence. We are keenly alert to sound as Nick hears his father from the living room blow out the lamp and go into his room. Something has been extinguished in their relationship, and we are keenly aware that the father goes into his room alone—one of the men without women in this collection of Hemingway stories. And though Nick ceases to think of his father, the reader senses that aloneness. As Paul Smith has discovered, deletions from earlier versions made specific the father's loneliness and burden of betrayals; Hemingway wisely elected to make that suffering a hidden part of the iceberg in this story. It is enough that the reader sense that on this night the doctor will find sleep no easy ally. The sounds of the natural world replace the pain of human voices and their revelations and evasions. The wind in the trees brings comfort and welcome coolness. We are again told that Nick's face is in the pillow, as if he wishes to hide. Prudence and her meaning do not go away, but "finally" nature's balm of sleep comes. When Nick awakes later in the night, he hears the wind in the hemlock trees, hemlock useful for the image of deep sleep, ultimate forgetfulness. That sound against the lapping of the waves on the shore again carries Nick back to sleep. The final sentence of the story gives the images greater force; there is a "big wind blowing" and the waves are running high on the beach. Nick will certainly recover from the disillusionment that he has experienced, but he will also remember it, remember how "his heart was broken." The images of lake and shore remind us of the ending of "Indian Camp"—both of the terrifying images of love and sexuality there, suggestions of betrayal and abandonment, and of parental miscalculation. Now, however, Nick no longer relies on the assurance of the rower of the boat. He will be able to take the oars himself.

A CANARY FOR ONE

Immediately following his story of adolescent heartbreak Hemingway placed another story about heartbreak and betrayal. The characters in "A Canary for One" are adult. The plot is again double focused. In the foreground is the story of the young woman who is to receive the canary of the story's title, a substitute for the Italian man whom the American mother deems unworthy of her daughter. In another key, the story replays Dr. Adams's steps to separate Nick from Prudence Mitchell (also from another culture). The implied story of "Ten Indians" is the doctor's own lonely marriage. In "Ten Indians" Nick's mother is alarmingly absent; in "A Canary for One," the father of the heartbroken daughter is also absent and never mentioned, and his wife plays a role much like the doctor's. By the end of "A Canary for One" it is clear that the narrator's separation from his wife is the real story. Satire controls the foregrounded plot; Hemingway aims for something deeper in the larger structure and accents that in the emotional jolt of the final sentence.

The title of the story plays against the popular song "Tea for Two." The 1924 song (words by Irving Caesar, music by Vincent Youmans) has remained a romantic favorite. It contrasts with the song of childhood that Hemingway evoked in "Ten Indians," and ironically the pain of romantic love and marital love in "A Canary for One." The song's refrain runs: "Picture you upon my knee / just tea for two and two for tea, / Just me for you and you for me alone."

258:1–5 **The train passed . . . below against rocks.** In "Hills Like White Elephants" a man and a woman wait for a train; at the end of the story, the train arrives. The reader is left pondering where besides Madrid that train will take the couple. Although the American couple central to "A Canary for One" is not mentioned in the opening paragraph, the image of the train on its demanding schedule may well evoke the earlier story. The train passes house, garden, trees—traditional emblems of the American dream. The images anticipate the Americanness that Hemingway stresses in the story. The paragraph ends with images that suggest violence: "cutting" through red stone and clay. And "far below" are the sea and rocks. Across that sea lies America.

258:6–8 **"I bought him"** . . . **"sings very beautifully."** The first words of the story take the reader to the story's title, though the word *canary* is not used. The speech helps identify the origin of the journey in Italy. Palermo is in Sicily, so the canary is undergoing an arduous journey. That the narrator identifies the speaker as "the American lady," rather than "woman," makes her somewhat suspect. Her first words evoke the decisive nature of the woman: she is able to take an action and to move quickly. Her "we" might suggest that she was traveling with others, but she is in fact traveling alone. She sees herself as a shrewd dealer, proud to let her listeners know that she can strike a bargain. The reader may also ponder the reasons that the lady travels alone; she would have been absent from mate or other family for some time. The reader will also come to assess the song this caged bird sings. (Canaries who sing most are single, not caged in pairs.)

Did Hemingway know Paul Laurence Dunbar's poem "Sympathy"? The poem appeared in 1899, the year that Hemingway was born, and African American Dunbar was widely read by both whites and blacks in the early years of the century. Although "Sympathy" was not in his high school curriculum, Hemingway may have come across it. (Michael S. Reynolds lists the texts for Hemingway's high school English courses in *Hemingway's Reading, 1910–1940: An Inventory* 40–41.) The poem is appropriate to Hemingway's story all the way to its last line. The poem opens: "I know what the caged bird feels, alas! / When the sun is bright on the upland slopes" (ll. 1–2). Whether Hemingway knew Dunbar's lines or not, he seized on the metaphoric implications of the image.

258:9–14 **It was very hot . . . gray-stone hills behind them.** Here it's an adverb Hemingway repeats, *very*, in the opening sentence of the paragraph to emphasize the confined hothouse atmosphere of the sleeping compartment. The American lady finds the atmosphere congenial. She makes it more tomb-like by pulling the window blind down, blocking out even the occasional view of the sea (from whence all life originated). The lady never mentions the heat, and only the narrator calls attention to it. It is the narrator who notes the open window opposite the glass on the other side of the *lit salon* (sleeping compartment). He surveys a scene that sends mixed messages: dusty trees and an oiled road, but also fields of grapes. The "gray-stone" hills behind confirm the invitation to find parallels with "Hills Like White Elephants."

258:15–24 **There was smoke . . . did not hear them.** The paragraph shows a narrator intent not on interpreting but on coolly reporting what he sees. What he withholds, we later discern, bears significantly on what he reports. The arrival in Marseille takes the narrator and the other characters across a border, into "another country." A journey from which there seems no turning back is underway. (The train makes its way through a maze of tracks, arriving where it should, and for only a specified time.)

The smoke from the chimneys indicates a burning. The narrator keeps his eye on the American lady, reporting her nervous activities with precision. He knows already that she is "a little deaf," information he received from the talkative lady. The narrator does not report what his wife does at the stop; he prefers to keep his eyes elsewhere. The inability of the lady to hear may not be her problem alone. It may be a problem for the wife he doesn't mention, as well as himself. Their relationship (unmentioned to this point of the story) has reached the point where they are not even talking to each other.

258:25–28 **The train left . . . sun on the water.** This is the first sentence to call attention to the narrator as a character in the story. "Looking back," he sees not just the town but the harbor, the stone hills, and—hauntingly—"the last of the sun on the water." On a train going relentlessly forward, the narrator is "looking backward" at his own history, one he does not care to mention. In contrast, the American lady is quite vocal in her "looking backward."

258:29–259:2 **As it was getting dark . . . the house burn.** His eyes again forward, the man recounts the journey to Avignon. The image of the smoke from the tall chimneys in Marseille has prepared the reader for stronger images of burning and destruction, their center a burning farmhouse. Of the many domestic items that have been spread along the roadside, the narrator calls attention only to the bedding (primary symbol of a married relationship). The curious observers are not only those the narrator notes, but other observers of his own failing marriage.

259:2–8 **After it was dark . . . was with them.** The stop in Avignon is of short duration; in the dark the narrator observes the bustling platform activity. He observes people exiting and entering the train. Since he notes that "Frenchmen" are returning to Paris, he marks himself as an outsider. The French newspapers accent the difference. The narrator is reading the platform scene as text. Five sentences deal with the presence of several "negro soldiers" and the "short white sergeant" with them—a contrast within a culture. Rapid change and new contrasts characterize the post–World War I era. Old verities are called into question. Oddly, the narrator asserts that the "negro soldiers" were "too tall to stare." That is a relief to him—staring implies inspection, judgment; he keeps our focus elsewhere. In the preceding story, Nick felt discomfited while his father sat quietly watching him.

259:9–17 **Inside the *lit salon* . . . waited for a wreck.** The new age is one of speed and rapid change. Speed, like change, is alarming for the American lady, who cannot sleep as the train rushes through the night, and she fears a "wreck." Her sleeplessness echoes the doctor's in the previous story. The lady has been protective of the canary, putting him in the corridor that leads to the washroom. The narrator does not yet know how the canary figures in the woman's plans. Strikingly, the paragraph reports on two occupants of the *lit salon* but says nothing about the other two beds that the porter has prepared, those for the narrator and his wife.

259:18–25 **In the morning . . . nearer Paris.** The paragraph announcing the arrival of the morning is something of an aubade, one that is intensified (again) by what is not said. There is still no mention of the other two occupants, though their beds have again been made into seats. The focus is on the American lady—largely because the narrator prefers to keep attention on her. The real direction of the paragraph (and the story) is framed by its opening and closing phrases: in the first sentence the train is "near Paris"; at the end of the paragraph, "the train was much nearer Paris." That reality carries intense emotion for the as yet unnamed occupants of the *lit salon*. The narrator reminds the reader that the lady has not slept, but he is essentially reporting that neither he nor his wife has slept. Having completed her morning toilette, the lady looks "very wholesome and middle-aged and American"—as apparently the unnamed duo does not. The image of the canary "shaking his feathers in the sunlight" also plays against the emotions of the other travelers.

259:26–30 **"He loves the sun" . . . "singing now."** The American lady, not her companions, is inclined to speak—to exercise that American power of positive thinking. Citing her love of birds, the American lady states the purpose of her journey and the bird, a gift for "her little girl." Her appellation for her daughter accents another American trait: prolonging childhood and adolescence. Her daughter, the reader will discover, is not a "little girl." And the "one" for whom this canary belongs already has him.

259:31–38 **The canary chirped . . . talking to my wife.** This midstory paragraph provides positive identification of the other passengers. It is now clear that the narrator is a participant in the story he tells, and he increasingly becomes the major participant. He reports a "chirp," not singing. (The American lady, we know, does not hear well and misinterprets in a metaphorical, if not literal, sense the song of the caged bird.) The chirping canary does not cheer the narrating husband, nor does the chatter of the "wholesome" American lady. As he had in Avignon, he prefers to look outside. The inside of the train from the start has been confining, even claustrophobic. The narrator hates being a captive audience for the American lady; his wife bears the conversation with more grace. The Paris destination is again emphasized; the train continues relentlessly to that destination, passing through the Parisian suburbs ("outside of Paris towns," the narrator calls them). Identification of the river and the "carefully tended forest" suggests restful escape from the confining *lit salon*. In the towns the narrator also observes advertisements on the tram cars for alcoholic beverages; the last he mentions, Pernod, is the most potent of them. The drink calls attention to another kind of escape from the *lit salon* and all it represents. The availability of alcoholic beverages and the prominent advertisement of them are a marked contrast to the "wholesome" American scene. The narrator's observations peak with his report that the sights all look "as though it were before breakfast"; clearly, the day will soon provide other sights and rhythms.

259:39–45 **"Is your husband" . . . my English character.** When the American lady asks the wife if her husband is American, he can no longer treat her conversation as white noise. The use of the word *husband* to describe him strikes him as somewhat strange, and this may well be one of the last times that the wife will be able to find this word the right appellation. Like the lady, the couple are Americans, pushing to the fore the question of identity and values. The husband's reluctance to enter into conversation and his propensity to look out the window have made him seem reserved, English. The question of identity—husband or otherwise—he makes part of a game. His use of the English *braces* mocks the lady, who has been more than willing to fill the void of conversation between the couple that the story has implied. Amusing himself, he aims to keep the conversation away from the topic that has kept him awake that night.

259:45–260:2 **The American lady . . . talking to my wife.** The narrator emphasizes the severity of the lady's deafness (figurative as well as literal) and his scorn for her, since he keeps looking out the window. The lady prefers to talk rather than to listen.

260:3–7 **"I'm so glad" . . . "her away, of course."** This story accents American identity, which involves (especially following World War I) a sense of superiority to European values. The wife listens to the lady's maxim that "American men make the best husbands" with more than the lady's account about her daughter as reference. Someone reading the stories of *Men Without Women* consecutively may impose another historical dimension—the superiority that white Americans have felt to "them Indians." From the lady's perspective, her daughter crossed a cultural taboo by falling "madly in love" with a man from Vevey, and so she takes her decisive action, one that leaves her daughter with a broken heart, much as the doctor's action leaves Nick in "Ten Indians."

260:8–14 **"Did she get" . . . "suppose not."** The wife's question may be the most poignant of the story. Survival of the broken heart is central, as in "Ten Indians." The American lady's report alerts the wife and her husband to what is likely ahead for both of them. The American lady has a problem, and she would like to make amends. Her action has had a profound effect on her daughter. (Those reading "A Canary for One" autobiographically must consider not only the end of Hemingway's marriage to Hadley but the decision of Grace Hall Hemingway—on whom the American lady may be partly based—to evict Ernest from the family cottage when he was twenty-one. Some damages are impossible to repair.) The lady, by talking, seeks to convince herself of the rightness of her interference in her daughter's romance, not wishing to go beyond her friend's statement. Although the "deaf" American lady has received mainly ridicule and scorn from readers, the story does invite a measure of sympathy for her, certainly pity. She has lost more than she can now confront. The end of her journey may have a large measure of regret. There are prices to be paid.

260:15–29 The American lady . . . their changing now. Direct discourse now would trivialize the central issues; so the narrator summarizes the lady's chatter. The paragraph suggests how quickly the lady can move from her daughter's suffering to the more mundane, her wardrobe. The wife can scarcely be much interested in the details the lady reports, but under these circumstances the narrator proves himself a good listener. The report is rich in satire. The *vendeuse* (store clerk) knows both the lady (not a particularly difficult read—unlike our narrator) and her tastes (bland in the extreme). In case her listener had any doubt, the lady makes clear that she lives in "up-town" New York and also (as in the purchase of the canary) that she is careful about money. Nor does she like change of any kind. Her daughter's love for a Swiss man signifies a huge change. What she reports about management of her daughter's wardrobe as well as her own marks her as domineering in the way that Dr. Sloper dominates his daughter in Henry James's *Washington Square*. The lady's "little girl" is now grown up, and, her mother declares, there is not much chance that her measurements will change now. The chilling line must be viewed in the context of the *lit salon,* where monk-like beds have been before our eyes. The change pregnancy would entail is the hidden reality behind this line. No more than Catherine Sloper might become pregnant will the lady's daughter. The American man of "Hills Like White Elephants" also resists such change. It is unlikely that the wife of the narrator misses the unstated or that she fails to think of her own measurements.

260:30–38 The train was now . . . eaten any breakfast. The first sentence of the paragraph carries an ominous weight—the long awaited, yet somehow dreaded, destination. The word *Paris* tolls like a bell. Following it, the narrator reminds the reader of the Great War and the changed world that follows it. He notes the many train cars in the station—cars (restaurant cars and sleeping cars) that will soon vibrate with the bustle of travel, taking some passengers to Italy. Other cars serve the suburbs; here the narrator again accents change. He is uncertain if people still ride on seats on the car roofs. The strange clause "if that were the way it were still done" suggests that psychologically he has been away for a long time. The narrator is well aware that the postwar world is vastly different from the one that preceded the war.

The final sentence of the paragraph has an even stranger syntax, echoing the emptiness he noted in the outlying towns in a "before breakfast loneliness." *Nothing* makes a lonely subject for the sentence that hungers for a living person or animal. Through three manuscript versions Hemingway had let this strange syntax stand. Scott Donaldson wonders if the reader might feel an existential *néant* or *nada*, which Hemingway would make memorable in the parody of prayer in "A Clean, Well-Lighted Place" in *Winner Take Nothing*. As Donaldson notes in his study of the manuscript versions of the story, from the start of the story, the narrator has used a prose marked by passivity and unusual constructions (205–6).

260:39–261:3 **"the best husbands"** . . . **"long walks together."** The lady attempts to assure herself that she acted wisely in Vevey, hence her refrain about American husbands. The use of maxim as hindrance to thought is similar to that of the neighbor in Robert Frost's "Mending Wall" and his iteration: "Good fences make good neighbors" (ll. 27, 45). The situation reverses that of Henry James's *Daisy Miller*, in which an American girl is deemed unsatisfactory wife material.

The wife's question reveals how much she is thinking of her own situation. She is interested in the daughter because she recognizes that the daughter's fate may suggest her own future. The lady's answer lets her know that broken hearts are not soon mended—and reveals a bit of the desperation in the lady's use of her maxim. The canary is planned as propitiation. The daughter's absence becomes a presence. She does not wish to travel with her mother, certainly not in Europe. The mother's solo traveling reveals something of her own desperation. Not only has she not gotten a son-in-law, she has also lost a daughter.

Were the lady swifter, she could see that the wife's question is designed to take her behind her maxim. Naively, the lady lists qualities that might please many a caring mother. Her daughter's suitor is Swiss (emblematic of solid values), on his way to being an engineer. His long walks with the daughter (Daisy Miller was also given to long walks) suggest their compatibility. The activity is vastly different from the travels of the American man and Jig in "Hills Like White Elephants."

The biographical critic will recognize parallels to the courtship and marriage of Ernest's sister Marcelline, who was but one year old when Ernest was born. In their very early years, Grace liked to dress the two as twins. Marcelline married Sterling Sanford soon after Ernest and Hadley married. Sterling graduated in mechanical engineering from the University of Michigan. Grace once solicited his aid to encourage Ernest to enter college. Sterling would eventually become expert in heating, air conditioning, and ventilation. He retired at age sixty-five following a successful career at Detroit Edison. The Sanfords had three children, who grew up making frequent visits to their Grandmother Hemingway. Ernest did not see his mother after his father's funeral, and his children did not know their Hemingway grandmother. Marcelline remained closer to her mother than did any of her siblings. That she did rankled Ernest. Marcelline's marriage fit the expectations of a good marriage that the traveling mother of "A Canary for One" would have wished for her daughter.

Marcelline told her story in *At the Hemingways,* published in 1962, the year following Hemingway's death. For the centennial of Hemingway's birth, a new edition
with fifty years of correspondence between the brother and sister was published in
1998. Appendixes include brief statements from Marcelline's three children, none
of whom ever met their uncle. John Sanford became a devoted reader of his uncle's
work and a stalwart in the Hemingway Society, and an invaluable source on the
fascinating family dynamic.

261:4–15 **"I know Vevey"** . . . **said my wife.** The wife's declaration speaks powerfully to
the core drama of the story. She is reading the lady's narration on an autobiographical
level. The American lady quickly returns the focus to herself and her daughter. But
her admission about the surprising turns of love might also be heard by the wife on
an autobiographical level. The biographical critic may find other echoes of Hemingway's life in the lady's confession. In Switzerland, Hadley Hemingway experienced a
surprise similar to the lady's. The echoing of three "Yeses" in these lines invites emotional hearing. From the factual "Yes" of the lady, we move to the honest affirmation
of the wife. The wife recognizes what she had at the Trois Couronnes (Three Crowns)
hotel. Love had made her feel royal. Whatever the pain of the present moment, that
time was "lovely" and cannot be taken away. The third *Yes* is the wife's last word in the
exchange.

261:16–22 **We were passing** . . . **"don't go so fast."** The present moment bumps
heavily against the magic of a lost time—as do the narrator's words: "There's been
a wreck." Instead of three crowns, there are three railway cars—badly splintered,
clearly beyond repair. The narrator's masculine voice seems harsh against the wife's
delicate "Yes." The lady's reaction to the wreckage she views suggests her fears about
her daughter but also that she belongs to a different era. Speed and the dominance
of technology (the *rapide*) mark the direction of the new century. The lady will not
be a participant in its rhythms. The American husband and wife face the challenge
of living beyond the new wreckage. Their silence makes open ended their resolution, but the wife's "Yes" (in sharp contrast to the lady's firm "No" to her daughter's
chance for happiness) suggests that she will do well.

261:23–27 **Then the train** . . . **"for your name."** The train is indeed now in Paris, the
end of the line. The station (gare de Lyon) appears dark. The husband, mostly silent
on the trip, does not speak here either. Handing the suitcases through windows
gives him something to do; words fail him and his wife. The "dim longness of the
platform" bespeaks emptiness and loneliness. Taking attention from himself, he
mocks the American lady as she commandingly latches on to one of three agents
from Cook's travel agency. The agent has encountered such women before; politely
but firmly, he proceeds to check his records.

261:28–33 **The porter brought . . . took the tickets.** The lady's name having been located, her *baggage* (the narrator's word is apt—the lady carries a great deal of it, and symbolically the couple does also) is placed on the cart. The narrator spares the reader the good-byes that he and his wife make to the woman. In a story in which listening is primary, those are not the words that should linger in our memories. That the platform is long (an observation the narrator repeats) makes the walk of the husband and wife especially difficult. The walk contrasts with the many happy long walks that the American girl and her Swiss suitor had taken. The repetition carries the added information that the platform is made of cement, adding to the sense of its coldness. As the couple follows the porter, neither speaks. We hear no good-byes. On French trains, surrendering the ticket at the end of the ride is common practice, but the narrator means for us to sense more than that. The exit is also an entrance, and a price has been paid.

261:34 **We were returning to Paris to set up separate residences.** The reader might well wonder how on a first reading he or she missed this. More than revelation, the line may be seen as confession—an admission that the narrator has not wanted to make. Focusing on the American lady, he succeeds for a time in keeping at bay his own character—which becomes the most compelling aspect of the story. The lady's faults are there for all to see, but he only suggests his own. His images convey his admission of failure. The word *Paris* in the final sentence rings with doleful finality. That the narrator ends the story with this confession gives a sense of his own strength—an honesty about self that we never sensed in the American lady but found in the wife's realism.

AN ALPINE IDYLL

Following a story set mainly in the confining space of a train compartment Hemingway places a story that offers expansion and openness. Even when the narrator of "An Alpine Idyll" and his skiing companion sit inside, the window is open. Unlike the preceding story, this one exults in life and gives attention to virtually all the senses.

There are, however, significant structural likenesses. In each there is a foregrounded story that veils the deeper story being told—and that story belongs to the narrator. In both stories the narrator is a careful listener. In "A Canary for One" he keeps to the background as much as possible, and by story's end, we understand why. In "An Alpine Idyll," the narrator makes us aware of his role in a much more open way and invites us to share an experience with him.

He listens to an "idyll," which can be either a short poem describing a picturesque scene of rural life or simply a scene of rural simplicity. The story that the narrator hears may be rural, but its meaning is scarcely simple.

262:1–10 **It was hot coming down . . . "They never answer," John said.** The first words of the story are spoken by the narrator, establishing his pivotal role as character as well as teller. He and his companion have been skiing in the Alps, but the season nears an end. It is spring, and the travelers feel the vibrant rays of the sun as they enter the village of Galtür, Austria, feeling not only the sun but the weight of the skis they carry. Against the sensations of spring and morning and the energy of travel the opening juxtaposes the conclusion of a churchyard burial. In greeting the priest, the narrator uses the south German and Austrian form of greeting: *Grüss Gott.* Although "Hello" would be the intended meaning, the American reader will likely hear "Great God," an apt reflection on the story that the narrator will soon hear. The first words of dialogue clarify the gender of the narrator's companion, identification that had been delayed in the preceding travel story. John and the narrator have been together here for some time, long enough to begin to notice local customs. Priests may bow to *Grüss Gott,* but they seem not to respond in kind. Noticeably, the narrator and John talk to each other—as the husband and wife do not in "A Canary for One."

262:11–20 **We stopped . . . "We don't have to do it."** The two men share a sense of returning to the world as they watch the grave being filled with dirt. In the pleasure of their mountain skiing, death has not been on their minds. In the vibrancy of the May morning, the scene looks "unreal." It will seem more so when the narrator learns that the peasant who completes the task of filling the grave is the husband of the woman who has died. The narrator's comparison of the spreading of the dirt to the spreading of manure evokes the sense of smell and of an interconnectedness of decay and life. The dialogue reflects the vitality of skiers, their youthful vigor, and their ability to respond appropriately to humor. The repetition of the word *imagine* sets the tone for the story ahead.

262:21–263:7 **We went on up . . . May morning in the valley.** Repetition plays a key part in creating the special rhythm and tone of this paragraph. Describing a month of skiing, the paragraph emphasizes the insistent sun that promises even more sun, fertility, and eventually summer. It is noteworthy that the two men are tired of the sun, but that they themselves have remained collegial—men without women for this month, and happily so. The high Silvretta Mountains have, in fact, become dangerous: it is too late to be in them. The threat of the avalanche, though unmentioned, is implied. But threat is not the primary emphasis of the paragraph. The telling image of the paragraph is their drinking snow water melted from the tin roof, its taste making clear that the skiing has become less than perfect. It is possible to do a good thing too long. If the narrator had had Robert Frost's "After Apple-Picking" at hand, he would have found it reflecting his mood. The speaker in Frost's poem has been a perfectionist about his work but, tired at the end of the season, admits: "But I am done with apple-picking now" (l. 6). Something of the same effect would be obvious from Frost's "Birches." The speaker there recalls the joys of swinging birches in his boyhood and then admits, "I'd like to get away from earth for a while / And then come back to it and begin over" (ll. 48–49). Hemingway's paragraph is, in fact, a prose poem. (There are many in the Hemingway canon.)

263:8–15 **The innkeeper sat . . . "this time of year."** The atmosphere is relaxed; both the innkeeper and the cook are at ease, and the arrival of the skiers does not cause them to jump to attention. A friendly greeting suffices. *Ski-heil!* is a greeting to a skier. The skiers betray their Americanness in their response. *Heil!* is not usually used by itself. With the German *schön* (beautiful), the narrator admits that although the skiing has been a pleasure, there is now too much sun. The lack of activity at the inn confirms that the season is essentially ended. The sun literally checks the skiing, but it represents as well the increasing demands of the world from which skiing has been an escape.

263:16–18 **The cook sat . . . letters and some papers.** The narrator and John have obviously returned to the inn from which they originally departed. They are expected.

That the innkeeper brings out their mail and papers suggests that the demands of the world from which they have been in retreat will soon demand their energies.

263:19–22 **"Let's get some beer"** . . . **read the letters.** Drinking beer and reading their letters, the two men create an image of quiet pleasure. The scene reflects their continuing camaraderie. It should be noted that in "A Canary for One" references to eating or drinking are minimal. Rather the tone is one of denial: the morning scene emphasizing a denial of breakfast. The narrator views advertisements for drink in towns along the way. The American lady drinks Evian water.

263:23–33 **"We better have"** . . . **"doing a thing too long."** The situation will be quite different in this story, as John's suggestion and their agreement indicate. The desire for the beer plants a significant element in the story. To this point the story has been without mention of women, and the girl who brings in the beer is the only one we actually see. But her presence accents an absence that becomes more prominent as the story proceeds. Her cheerful service gives added pleasure to the scene. Her noting of "many letters" suggests complications, commitments, and responsibilities as well as pleasures. In the mountains, with skiing the heart of the agenda, the men had been without beer—one pleasure for a time displacing another. *Prosit* is the German drinking toast: "Your health." The presence of the girl likely recalls another kind of pleasure as well, one that has been on hold. John admits to fantasizing about the beer—but no one mentions the absence of the company of women. John and the narrator here may recall that in *In Our Time* Nick Adams talks in "Cross-Country Snow" with his friend George about pleasures and denials. There Nick concludes: "There isn't any good in promising" (147). Here John summarizes a lesson: "You oughtn't to ever do anything too long." The two men are agreed on this matter. A woman is the subject long held at bay in that story—as is the case in "An Alpine Idyll."

263:34–45 **The sun came through** . . . **head on his arms.** This stunning paragraph highlights the pleasure of vision—artistic vision. The reader considering *Men Without Women* as a unity, especially one familiar with *In Our Time,* is likely to conclude that allusions to "Cross-Country Snow" are on target and that the unnamed narrator is Nick Adams—a man with a need to write. His vision is painterly. The narrator frames his view with the open window, like any good painter recognizing the special effects of light on his canvas as they shine through the open window. Reflecting the good effect of his skiing excursion, he calls the beer bottles "half full." He highlights the pleasure of the beer, accounting for the "little froth" because it is very cold. The outside scene is as delightful as the foregrounded beer bottles. He is amused to see through this frame a long log rising and falling at the mill "as if" unattended. The paragraph moves to completion with the emphasis on the sunlight shining through the empty beer glasses. The spell of the picture is about to break since the cook has come into the room and gone to the kitchen. That John is leaning forward with his head on his arms separates his seeing from that of the narrator. John is ready for sleep, the narrator for creation.

263:46–264:13 **Through the window . . . He was asleep.** The human element, minimized in the narrator's picture view, now takes dominance. The two men who enter the drinking room are familiar from the burial scene John and the narrator viewed. The narrator's use of the term *sexton* with its original meaning (gravedigger) is appropriate to the genre of the idyll. The bearded peasant and the sexton make a despondent pair—in sharp contrast to the arrival of the two skiers. That the peasant is despondent is not surprising, though the reader does not yet know that it is his wife's grave he helped fill. He is likely poor, but his dress for the funeral (an old army uniform with patches at the elbows) seems strange—certainly to an American observer. The role of the girl in the scene is noteworthy. The peasant does not seem to see her, an oversight that prepares us for the later shock in the story. Neither does the girl (so friendly in serving the skiers) here speak a word. It is up to the sexton to order the drinks for the two men; the peasant is in a daze. Although John is asleep, the narrator is keenly interested in the scene before him. He is like the husband in "A Canary for One" in becoming a listener, but from the start it seems clear that a reading of the peasant will be much more difficult than a reading of the American lady.

264:14–31 **The innkeeper came in . . . "Ja."** Strangely, the innkeeper says nothing to the husband. The narrator knows that the innkeeper speaks to the sexton in dialect, and he is not able to hear or understand much of the conversation. The libation does not loosen the peasant's tongue, and he keeps his own counsel. Finally standing up to give the signal that he is ready to pay the bill, the peasant finally notices the girl. As is frequent in Hemingway, the moment of paying is highly charged. A simple "*Alles?*" has a haunting ring as the only word the girl says to the peasant, and indeed he would like to pay for everything, and so he refuses the sexton's offer to cover the wine that he drank. Whatever compassion there might be for the husband is muted. No one tells him good-bye as he leaves. The peasant's departure causes the innkeeper to join the sexton at the table. The peasant is the topic of conversation, the narrator surmises. He again notes that the Austrians are talking in dialect. So the narrator can only ponder their discussion. The differing reactions of the Austrians—one amused, the other disgusted—puzzle him. When the sexton gets up and goes to the window, it is clear that there is more to be learned. The narrator's curiosity is further piqued. That the peasant has entered the Löwen reveals he has not been oblivious to the cold treatment he has received in the inn's drinking room. The tavern's name (Lion's) accents masculine power.

264:32–42 They talked again . . . still sleepy. The narrator remains the detached but accurate observer, adding that the innkeeper is tall and old (the sexton is short and sports a mustache). That John is asleep creates a contrast between him and the alert and curious narrator. About his business, the innkeeper, after commenting on the sleeping John, asks when they might wish to eat. The girl returns to the story—again ready to serve. After she brings the menu, the narrator awakens John. The meal will be delayed, however. Story rather than food is on the narrator's mind, and John is not yet fully awake. Hunger becomes good discipline.

264:43–265:21 "Won't you have a drink" . . . "too fast for me." The intrigued narrator invites the innkeeper to join them for a drink, knowing that such invitations invite confidence. He is rewarded almost immediately. Seated, the innkeeper makes a strong pronouncement, labeling all peasants "beasts." The narrator wishes to go from general to specific, and he adroitly mentions the peasant who has just departed, connecting him to the funeral. Thus comes the crucial bit of information: the person being buried was the peasant's wife. The narrator's simple "Oh" catches the power of that interjection, one that many writers have been able to use at moments of stark revelation, as when, upon discovering what his wife is seeing, the husband in Robert Frost's "Home Burial" utters, "'Oh,' and again, 'Oh'" (l. 17). The word accents the narrator's realization of the peasant's emotion. It brings to the fore the female presence prefigured in the girl who has served the skiers. But more than that, it checks the absence of women for the skiers during the month of skiing. The narrator must think not only of the peasant's story but of his own as well.

The innkeeper rushes to judgment—"An Alpine Idyll" should lead us to caution when confronted with such judgments, especially as they pertain to love. The innkeeper enjoys his moment of power, sensing that delay is a part of storytelling. The narrator's simple "Tell me" is central to the action of the story: telling and judging. Delay is also part of the narrator's tactic. In no hurry, after repeating his teasing "You wouldn't believe it," the innkeeper calls the sexton over. The innkeeper introduces the skiers to Franz, informing him that they have just "come down" from the Wiesbadenerhütte, another delay. The *hütte* signals temporary quarters, literally a hut; because it is named for the German town near Frankfurt, we expect quarters of at least modest comfort. The point is that they have been removed from the dramas of ordinary life. The narrator's manners and curiosity also add to the delay. After he accepts the second offer of a drink, the innkeeper turns to the matter of dialect—a further delay. The issue of dialect is appropriate, of course, to the theme of listening well, to understanding the terms of the discussion—which can be more than linguistic matters. John is far behind on the story that will eventually be told. "I can't understand it, anyway," John says. And though he does not understand the German dialect being used, he also does not share the artistic sensibility that has made his comrade so keen on hearing the story. He becomes a nonparticipant in the conversation.

265:22–266:16 "That peasant" . . . "'I loved her fine.'" The scene is set for sharing a strange idyll; the sharing requires two tellers. The innkeeper and the sexton differ on the details of the story that caused the innkeeper to label the peasant "a beast." The irate one, the innkeeper, aims at as dramatic a scenario as possible. The sexton aims for precision, naming a specific 18 December as the date of the wife's death—a detail he likely learned from the documentation necessary for the burial. With slight annoyance at Franz, the innkeeper declares the long delay between death and burial to be the point. Franz clarifies the mitigating circumstance: the peasant lives on the other side of the Paznaun Valley, of which Galtür is one of the more important villages. (Even at the end of the twentieth century, agriculture remained more important to the region than tourism.) When the narrator seeks assurance that it would be necessary to wait so long for burial, the innkeeper asserts that the reason for his disgust is not the delay between death and burial. Although revealing that the priest was reluctant to bury her even then, he again postpones sharing the reason for his disgust. Having been checked by Franz for his earlier inaccuracy, he turns the narrative over to him, showing his pique by admonishing that the sexton not speak in dialect.

The sexton also knows the merit of sustained narrative, and he reports dialogue skillfully to build suspense around both the discovery of the wife's disfigured face and the reason for the disfigurement. When the priest tells Olz, "I must know," the innkeeper is as caught up in the drama Franz relates as anyone, breaking in to cause further delay and to punctuate the shocking revelation. Franz and the innkeeper do not go beyond the literal meaning of the facts, but the careful reader will. The dead wife's heart trouble, considered in the context of *Men Without Women*, carries immense meaning. "An Alpine Idyll" plays against the plight of the American lady's daughter and the wife who hears her story in "A Canary for One," as well as on the narrator of that story, and on Nick Adams and his broken heart at the end of "Ten Indians." "Did your wife suffer much?" asks the priest. Olz's simple denial of physical pain is not an accurate assessment for a woman who was given to fainting in church and became too ill even to attend. Who suffers and how much become increasingly complicated matters in this story—as they are throughout all the stories of *Men Without Women*.

Although Franz may be amused by the story he tells, and the innkeeper appalled (the expected response), the narrator invites us to see a suffering Olz. Certainly, Olz is now grieved by his habit of having hung his lantern from his wife's frozen open mouth when he went into the shed to cut wood. Throughout his marriage he has been accustomed to regarding his wife in a serving role (the only woman we see in the story is the serving girl); unthinkingly, he takes that function for granted. He confesses to the priest that he doesn't know why he did it. It was, in part, habit. And was it possibly resentment at her illness, anger at her death? He cannot say, nor with assurance can we. There seems little reason to doubt his authentic: "*Ja.* I loved her. . . . I loved her fine." The husband of the previous story, or the mother of the story as regards her daughter, might say the same.

266:17–29 **"Did you understand it all?" . . . I said.** Understanding is the ultimate challenge of any good story. The innkeeper stays on the literal level, hoping that the narrator's German is good enough to grasp the narrative. The narrator hears "understand" in a deeper sense. He does not claim to "understand," but he does have the facts. Probably for his own good reasons, he does not rush to judgment. During the story of Olz and his wife, John has been disengaged, uninterested. His is a different kind of hearing—and he calls for attention to the too long delayed matter of eating. The narrator, however, is not quite ready to let the narrative go, wondering himself what to believe. The innkeeper is like the American lady from "A Canary for One," who repeats her verdict that American men make the best husbands: for the third time he declares that peasants are beasts. Neither he nor Franz senses the pain that may be in Olz as he goes up the street to the Löwen, seeking, perhaps, some clean, well-lighted bar as he ponders loss and guilt. (Hemingway would later, in "A Clean, Well-Lighted Place" in *Winner Take Nothing,* create the atmosphere of a bar that was also a spiritual retreat.) There is nothing more for the narrator to learn about Olz from these informants. He returns to John and food, but the story we have just read reveals that he recognized a story worth telling, one quite different from that which will circulate in the valley.

A PURSUIT RACE

In arranging the stories of *Men Without Women,* Hemingway followed the tale of burial in the Austrian Alps with another story of the macabre. From the start Hemingway recognized that "A Pursuit Race" would be difficult to place in a magazine and so had saved it for book publication. "An Alpine Idyll" almost met the same fate; it had not won acceptance at *Scribner's Magazine,* but because the editor, Paul Rosenfeld, had requested a story from Hemingway, it appeared in *The American Caravan: A Yearbook of American Literature* a month before its appearance in *Men Without Women.* Essentially, most readers encountered the stories not in isolation but in the context of the book. But there are parallels besides the history of publication.

If the sexton was "amused" over the death and burial of Olz's wife, macabre humor is plentiful in "A Pursuit Race." Although "An Alpine Idyll" ends with Olz's emptiness and grief and the narrator's own questionings, the narrative carries affirmation in its depiction of a writer discovering a story. "A Pursuit Race" likewise gives prominence to a sympathetic observer of someone in despair, but there is little to brighten the scene. The natural world is excluded, felt all the more keenly because it is so prominent in "An Alpine Idyll." The setting is confined to a bedroom; the bed in it seems a deathbed. Even more fiercely than the story before it, "A Pursuit Race" showcases the world of a man without women and without hope. The title of the story is ironic. Promising physical action, the story is cerebral. As in "An Alpine Idyll," the major action is listening.

Thus, setting and situation of "A Pursuit Race" also play against "The Killers." Ole Andreson's resignation to his fate is replayed in William Campbell's in "A Pursuit Race." Mr. Turner's attempt to alter Campbell's fate parallels Nick's futile effort to rescue Andreson.

267:1–11 **William Campbell had been . . . at Kansas City.** Four sharp sentences define a pursuit race in bicycle racing, a sport Hemingway came to know during his Paris years. They are sandwiched by sentences about William Campbell. Unusual for the book, and for a Hemingway story, in this story the central character is immediately given first and last names. The shaping of the paragraph around those names gives a finality to the paragraph that suggests a completed action, one from which the narrator is distanced. The paragraph highlights metaphor, for the story is not about bicycle racing. The metaphor belongs to the third-person narrator rather than to any character in the story. The paragraph observes a journey from east to west—the controlling direction of American history as well as the journey of everyman and everywoman. That William Campbell is caught by a burlesque show alerts the reader that a sexual theme will be an important factor in the pursuit race under scrutiny.

267:12–15 William Campbell had hoped . . . he was in bed. In his race for survival (economic on the surface only), Campbell has had only a slight lead over the challenge of the pursuing burlesque show. If Shakespeare liked to compare life to a stage, Hemingway turns the metaphor macabre. Life, certainly for Campbell, is more like a burlesque show—garish, tawdry, and marked by incident and the joke rather than by meaningful plot. The metaphor is close to and may echo scenes from T. S. Eliot's *The Waste Land*, especially the lines "and still the world pursues, / 'Jug Jug' to dirty ears" (ll. 102–3). Campbell has been caught before he can reach the Pacific (peace), the end of the race.

267:15–20 He was in bed . . . refused a drink. The objective, or distanced, narrator gives a summary of the burlesque manager's discovery of Campbell in bed—a joke on the face of it, since he is alone. The narrator puts aside suspense for resolution: Campbell has elected to withdraw from the race, finding consolation in drink. That the drink was under the bed lets us know that Campbell has long turned to the bottle for solace and that he has done his drinking in isolation. He is relieved more than dismayed to be caught in bed and offers the manager a drink, which he professionally refuses. The manager is Mr. Turner, not an intimate of Campbell's. Hemingway's choice of Campbell for the last name is another joke recalling tippling Mike Campbell from *The Sun Also Rises*.

267:21–268:3 William Campbell's interview . . . the texture with his lips. The narrator may easily call the meeting between Campbell and Turner "a little strange." Campbell responded to the knock with a cheerful "Come in!" He welcomes the knock. The reader is left to imagine the look on Turner's face as he enters to find chaos, "some one" lying in bed, covered by clothes. The someone is, of course, Campbell. Turner's voice likely conveys his response. Campbell's response plays on a fairly old joke. Rather than adding "I'm quitting," as the reason he can't be fired, he uses the metaphor from bicycle racing, which the reader understands but the manager of a burlesque company very likely would not. Calling Campbell "drunk," Turner can only state the obvious. He shows no gift for language; Campbell enjoys playing with it, as his metaphor suggests.

268:4–28 **"You're a fool,"** . . . **"been perfectly happy."** Turner turns off the electric light that has burned through the night, an action that connects Campbell to other scenes of sleeplessness already in Hemingway's oeuvre and anticipates the powerful foregrounding of the theme in the final story of *Men Without Women,* "Now I Lay Me." It is Campbell who can turn the merely factual (his arrival in Kansas City) into the bizarre by asking Turner if he ever talked through a sheet. Turner is not in the mood for humor, black or otherwise, but he easily makes obvious Campbell's pun. Campbell is overwhelmed by shit, as it were. His employment terminated, Turner has no leverage over him. The dialogue about knowing (or not knowing) recalls the professed certainty about "knowing" found in the American man in "Hills Like White Elephants." Campbell acknowledges a great void, an emptiness, a "nothing." Pulling the sheet up over his face, professing his love for it, Campbell dramatizes the familiar gesture at a death. The sheet has become a shroud, as Turner seems to recognize. A younger manager with "many things to do" would likely have walked out of Campbell's room in anger or disgust. But the vitality of his younger body now compromised by balding and a large stomach, Turner acknowledges a kinship with the wasted man in the bed. He drops his first appellation ("Mr. Campbell") for the more personal address "Billy" as he offers to help Campbell find a cure. Drunkenness permits Campbell's declaration that he is "perfectly happy." The repetition of *perfectly happy* echoes the dialogue of "Hills Like White Elephants," where Jig's lines are heavily ironical. Campbell's perfect happiness is an illusion. The inebriation contains, however, a resolution that carries the conviction of Herman Melville's dropout Bartleby the scrivener ("I would prefer not to"). Having seen the void, Campbell does not wish to take a cure. That declaration he repeats, the repetition aligning with being "perfectly happy." Happiness is an elusive commodity in Hemingway's work. Famously, Nick Adams finds it at the end of part I of "Big Two-Hearted River" in *In Our Time*—outside, in a natural setting, far removed from the human society in which Campbell is trapped.

268:29–41 **"How long have you"** . . . **a deep breath.** In short space, for a third time repetition accents the metaphysical reach of the story even as it reveals the shock of an outsider who comes upon someone who strikes him as totally altered—from the previously efficient worker to a Bartleby-like dropout. Such transformations are not, of course, as radical as they appear to the outsider; they involve process. As he did in his first speech of the story, Campbell turns to metaphor in an attempt to answer Turner's question. Creating a macabre picture, he describes the return of his "wolf," a personal wolf or demon that Campbell can only remove through drinking. The metaphor reveals an attraction and repulsion syndrome. Ernest Fontana has argued that Hemingway likely knew one slang meaning of *wolf,* an aggressive pederast, and that Campbell's older lover has given him a venereal disease.

268:42–46 "You got to take a cure" . . . Mr. Turner. Turner does not read sexual meaning into Campbell's metaphor. For him, Campbell's problem is alcoholism, and he urges treatment at the Keeley. The Keeley Institute was the first medical institution to treat alcoholism as a disease. Dr. Leslie Keeley opened the first of more than 120 Keeley Institutes in 1879 in Dwight, Illinois, a town close to Chicago and its suburbs. Favored by the rich and famous, the institutes spread throughout North America and Europe. After Keeley's death in 1900, his partners continued the work. The institution survived until 1966 (Warsh 346–49). Campbell has, of course, heard about the Keeley. Likely, he has heard many jokes about it (as surely Hemingway did in his youth in Oak Park). The name of the institute makes Campbell think of another familiarity, the poem "The Barrel-Organ" by the British poet Alfred Noyes. Though twenty-first-century readers may miss the allusion, most readers of Hemingway's text in 1927 would have been able to recognize the lines behind Campbell's "The Keeley . . . . It isn't far from London": *Come down to Kew in lilac-time, in lilac-time, in lilac-time; / Come down to Kew in lilac-time (it isn't far from London). / And you shall wander hand in hand with love in summer's wonderland; / Come down to Kew in lilac-time (it isn't far from London)"* (ll. 49–52). The Keeley has as much promise for Campbell as does Noyes's lilting invitation.

269:1–16 "Listen, you think I'm drunk" . . . "wolf out of the room." When Campbell denies that he is drunk—denies that he has a disease, Turner points to d.t.'s as proof. The term *delirium tremens* describes a condition of alcohol poisoning characterized by hallucinations, delusions, and incoherence. Campbell's talk about the wolf and the sheet are—for Turner—incoherence. Although his apostrophe to the sheet would seem further evidence to Turner of d.t.'s, Campbell teases Turner to build up to his surprise: that he is on cocaine, "hopped to the eyes." Shocked, Turner quickly protests, "No." He is being taken further from his world of assurances.

Campbell's declaration of love to the sheet accents how muted the references to women have been in this story, how much Campbell is a man without a woman. His job as an "advance man" literally keeps him running from women. The "pretty sheet" mocks the idea of the bed partner. Campbell wallows in his isolation; even the sheet is purchased love, which he likens to establishments in Japan that include sexual services in the price of the room. Campbell's address to Turner as "Sliding Billy" offers the reader additional surprise. Campbell, quite unashamedly, offers Turner the proof of his addiction, baring his arm to reveal the punctures. The point he wants to make to Turner is that his diagnosis of the single explanation (drinking) is insufficient. And there may be more than drugs to the explanation. Mr. Turner may not know that *wolf* can also denote an active sodomite. The story has switched emphasis and has become a story of education for Turner.

269:17–28 **"They got a cure for that"** . . . **"take to that stuff, Billy."** Turner's world-view has become seriously challenged; he wants to believe that there is a cure for drug addiction. The relationship between the narrator and the characters shifts bizarrely. The narrator adopts Campbell's appellation *Sliding Billy;* Turner calls the advance man *Billy;* having consistently identified the advance man as "William Campbell," the narrator switches to "Billy Campbell" when he observes Campbell caressing the sheet with lips and tongue. Campbell scarcely sounds drunk when he declares: "They haven't got a cure for anything." Turner is sliding from his certainty. Sitting on the bed, Turner reflects his growing doubt of the verities he mouths. The narrator has also been sliding. Campbell's command to Turner to be careful of his sheet amuses because the sheet is not in any danger and because of the double entendre. Even Campbell's declaration that there are no cures for anything becomes suspect. Turner craves a halt to such strange language and to the threat it carries.

269:29–39 **William Campbell shut . . . He stood up.** Nausea is a condition Campbell knows well: he knows that without drink, the nausea will increase. The condition highlights Campbell's self-loathing. Although Turner is fond of Campbell, he can only "watch." And then he must return to the details of living, the urgency of his duty.

269:40–270:5 **"Listen, Billy,"** . . . **"No. It couldn't have been about sliding."** Campbell and Turner are both named William; both can answer to Billy. Whereas *William* evokes a formal dignity, *Billy* evokes the child, vulnerability, the feminine side of *William.* Campbell and Turner share a business, a somewhat unsavory one; they have lived among people associated with drugs; they travel, are essentially rootless. We know them as men without women. Campbell identifies Turner's edge in his ability to "slide," to stay in the race, as it were. He provides what may be the most painful line of the story: "It's awful when you can't slide." Turner's simple "Yes" contrasts with his earlier warnings and advice; he acknowledges his brotherhood with Campbell and his glimpse at the truth that "It's awful when you can't slide." Campbell intensifies the moment, pushing Turner to articulate what he has glimpsed. Turner, however, draws back from that abyss and invites Campbell to resume his speech.

270:5–9 **"I'll tell you a secret"** . . . **under the sheet.** Campbell retreats from the topic of sliding. He issues a three-part warning, his words carrying the flavor of delirium tremens: beware women, horses, and eagles. Horses and eagles are commonly associated with speed, power, and beauty. Women have likewise been sources of inspiration and challenge for men throughout history. Campbell's pause before mentioning eagles would seem to set it up as the climax of his series, but this expectation is thwarted when he links horses and eagles, identifying horseshit and eagle shit as the result of loving them. (It may or may not be significant that *horse* can be a slang term for heroin and a drug addict.) Hence his preference for the sheet. Reluctant to talk about women, Campbell hides his head under the sheet.

270:10–12 **"I got to go"** . . . **"If you love horses—"** Neither amused nor enlightened, Turner wishes to depart. The narrator accents Turner's ability to "slide" by again identifying him as "Sliding Billy" Turner. Before Turner can complete this slide, Campbell provides a significant variation with his repetition. Rather than *shit* (the expected word when the series was first established), Campbell declares that the lover of women can expect a dose. Explanations for Campbell's behavior have moved from alcoholism to drug addiction to venereal disease. In the climactic position, the sexual issues might be the most pivotal. Less of the iceberg shows with this revelation. Campbell quickly rushes to attempt a replay of the consequences of loving horses. But Hemingway's reader may detect the ruse. Does it conceal a deep hatred for women? Or, as Fontana argues, is Turner's venereal disease a gift from his wolf, his older male lover? (Paul Smith notes that in the first manuscript, Campbell named his wolf "Horace" [181].)

270:13–18 **"Yes, you said that"** . . . **"to love this sheet."** Speech repetition is a common symptom of delirium tremens. Campbell moves the conversation from horses and eagles back to his new love, the sheet. The physical act of breathing on the sheet and stroking it with his nose come close to conventional foreplay—as a man might nuzzle a lover's breast with his nose (or penis) or whisper in a lover's ear.

270:19–22 **"I have to go"** . . . **"All right, you go."** Distancing himself as he moves toward the more subdued final moments of the story, the narrator returns to a formal "Mr. Turner." By now, it is noticeable that despite his declaration of impending departure, Turner has been reluctant to leave. Amidst the various mentions of "shit," Campbell is amused to foreground the euphemism "have to go." Such is the comedy of Campbell's endgame. But in a story wherein the protagonist lies before us in what seems a shroud, the universal requirement of death is also part of the euphemism.

270:23–27 **"Are you all right"** . . . **"I'll get up."** Turner still hesitates; his growing compassion is evident in the final quiet moments of dialogue. His addressing Campbell as "Billy" affirms his compassion for Campbell. The ending echoes earlier moments in the story as well as other Hemingway stories. Campbell's assertion that he has never been so happy echoes "Hills Like White Elephants." His declaration that he will get up around noon will suggest Ole Andreson's resignation to his fate in "the Killers."

270:28–30 **But when Mr. Turner . . . did not wake him.** Turner returns at noon because he cares. He is not just the business man. He has looked into the existential void. His involvement with Campbell has made him a more compassionate human being. The final line not only harkens back to earlier Hemingway stories in which sleeplessness is accented but sets the reader up for the final story of *Men Without Women*, the title of which, "Now I Lay Me," is also descriptive of "A Pursuit Race." Mr. Turner's return provides a coda heavy with benediction and finality: "Everybody's got to go"; "I was never so happy in my life"; "I'll just lie here for a little while," as if to say "Let me lie." The final sentence of the story has a solemnity that transcends the dark comedy and evokes a desire for the ultimate blessed sleep, one the French composer Gabriel Fauré captured in the final line of his requiem mass *Pie Jesu: Dona eis requiem sempiternam.* In English, that final prayer to "Blessed Jesus" reads: "Grant them eternal rest."

TODAY IS FRIDAY

The emotional step from "A Pursuit Race" to "Today Is Friday" is not steep. With the image of the shrouded, sleeping William Campbell vividly in mind, the reader of *Men Without Women* next ponders the death of Jesus of Nazareth, the young Jew who had promised rest to the weary and heavy laden, all the William Campbells of the world.

No single death in history is more familiar to the world than that of Jesus. By the Middle Ages, artists and writers were drawn to that death. During the Renaissance, painters, musicians, and poets often made it central to their work. Like the majority of his readers, since early childhood Hemingway had been aware of Jesus' death and the orthodox version of its meaning. Visits to the Art Institute of Chicago and the music he encountered at church and at home would have made him aware that the events of Jesus' life that he read about in the Gospels could be viewed in different ways. Later, as a young writer in the 1920s close to the pulse of high modernism, Hemingway was aware that all orthodoxies had been brought into doubt. He was also aware that Jesus' story was receiving various treatments from many of the writers in the vanguard. Any careful reader of T. S. Eliot's *The Waste Land*, the essential modernist poem, encountered a lament for a culture in decay without a vital Christian force. In 1923 Wallace Stevens in his poem "Sunday Morning" offered a more upbeat portrayal of the world without the Christian God. But Stevens's protagonist remains haunted by the tomb of Jesus in Palestine as she longs for "some imperishable bliss" (l. 62). Somewhat earlier, in 1909, Ezra Pound had published the hugely popular "Ballad of the Goodly Fere" in which he portrays a workingman's Jesus who stands up to the establishment and goes bravely to his death on "a tree" and whom the cowards cannot conquer. That Hemingway would wish to answer the artistic challenge presented by these (among other) writers and offer his own take on the Nazarene is not surprising.

But much more than literary challenge was involved. Hemingway undertook his rendition of the Crucifixion at a time when suicide seemed a way out of a heavy burden of guilt. He may have recalled that Judas Iscariot, overcome by guilt (a betrayal preceded by a kiss), chose suicide (Matt. 27.3), the single suicide in the New Testament. (Luke, however, in Acts 1.18 says that Judas dies when he "fell headlong" and his bowels "burst asunder.") Hemingway was in Madrid, separated from his wife Hadley but still loving her, and he loved Pauline Pfeiffer, whom he intended to marry, though he knew that he and Pauline had betrayed Hadley's trust. Marrying Pauline also meant embracing Roman Catholicism, a faith that would bring the icons of the Passion before him. Mass entails confronting the drama of the Passion regularly.

Hemingway may have chosen the format of a play for his story partly to reflect that drama. He counted "Today Is Friday" a story in the count for *The First Forty-nine*. (Its first publication had been in *The As Stable Pamphlets*—a substitute in response to a request for an essay.) Had he wished, he might easily have converted the format to make it look more like a conventional story. Similarly, "Hills Like White Elephants" might easily be made to look like a play. The blurring of genre lines was natural to Hemingway's modernism. Present tense in the title accents the ever-playing drama of the Eucharist that is imaged in the story.

271:1–4 *Three Roman soldiers . . . a little cock-eyed.* As is his wont, Hemingway sets the scene after the inciting event. (In "An Alpine Idyll," Olz's wife is being buried when the story begins; in "A Pursuit Race" the "race" is already over when Turner enters Campbell's room.) The first Good Friday is near its end at 11 p.m. The week of Passover was especially demanding for the Roman soldiers, occupiers charged with preserving the Pax Romana. The population of Jerusalem swelled as worshippers made their way to the temple, and the possibility for disturbance increased dramatically. Roman justice was quick and punishment severe. Crucifixion was a favored method of crowd control. Passover nearing its end, the soldiers may have placed a good many disturbers on crosses. The soldiers know all the discomfort of being unwelcome guests in a society of *Hebrews,* to use the term Hemingway knew from the New Testament (as the Romans called the Ancient Israelites Jews). The drinking place is simple, as the barrels along the wall indicate. Whatever rewards the soldiers find, they are scarcely ever financial. Since they are "cock-eyed," we know that they have been in the drinking place for some time. That they are weary is soon evident. Their condition invites comparison with Campbell's. Like Olz of "An Alpine Idyll," they seek escape through drink. Of the four Gospels, Matthew gives the most sustained attention to the soldiers. The number of the soldiers is indeterminate in all four Gospels. The three synoptic Gospels (Matthew, Mark, and Luke) highlight a centurion. (In the Roman army, the centurion commanded a unit of one hundred men.) The centurion's verdict is most dramatic in Matthew and in Mark: "Truly this was the son of God" (Matt. 27.54) and "Truly this man was the Son of God" (Mark 15.39). Luke's centurion responds: "Certainly this was a righteous man" (Luke 23.47). The three Roman soldiers may be viewed as a kaleidoscope of the centurion. The wine seller eventually addresses all three as "Lootenant."

271:5–11 **"You tried the red?"** . . . **"That's a nice little wine."** Red, the color of blood, dominates the story. Although soldiers throughout the ages have been smeared with blood, these three have been participants in a day to be forever associated with blood, blood that they have helped shed. Their clothes surely carry some of that stain. The synoptic Gospels all portray the drinking of the cup of wine as Jesus' blood "offered" for his disciples.

The soldiers are unnamed, merely "government issue." The second soldier's "ain't" reveals his educational level and alerts the reader that something other than the recounting of an old story is at hand. The idiom is contemporary. The effect of combat on men remained an important theme for Hemingway, who regularly saw military combat as a setting where manhood could be defined, "In Another Country" striking the theme early in *Men Without Women*. While we may here consider the military a group, the story requires that the reader distinguish between the three soldiers in the story. On the biographical level, the three are one and represent different sides of Hemingway's personality. In the Gospels, the conflicts represented in the three soldiers are paralleled in the psyche of the centurion.

The Hebrew wine seller gets named, bringing another George (also with no last name given) to the reader's mind, the waiter in "The Killers." Both Georges are accommodating to difficult customers. The title of the earlier story is immediately appropriate to this one. Both Georges serve killers.

271:12–17 **"Have a drink"** . . . **"makes my gut sour."** There is no indication that George takes a drink; probably he doesn't. He has business to attend to, and he likely has little affinity with the soldiers. That the first soldier makes the offer and then takes notice of the third soldier leaning against the barrel suggests a certain sensitivity in him. The third soldier's complaint of "a gut-ache" evokes Campbell's steadily increasing nausea, for which a drink can be only a "temporary measure." The first soldier commends the red wine for a third time. (The number three repeatedly links the story to its biblical foundation.) The second soldier's explanation of drinking water for his comrade's stomachache is far too simplistic (though drinking water was doubtless unwise, as Europeans had discovered); the reader is alerted to beware of the judgments of the second solider. American readers of *Men Without Women*, when it first appeared, were under the strictures of Prohibition, though some of them might have recalled that St. Paul had advised Timothy to "drink no longer water, but use a little wine for thy stomach's sake" (1 Tim. 5.23). The third soldier has had more than a little wine and knows that he needs another remedy. Hemingway lards his Passion story with humor

271:18–21 **"You been out here"** . . . **"to fix up his stomach?"** Many a soldier has tired under the strain of occupation assignments; the first soldier correctly seeks an explanation other than drinking water. He also recognizes the severity of his comrade's suffering and so turns to the wine seller for other remedy. The concept of gentleman is a conscious anachronism and contributes to the humor in what is finally a highly serious matter.

The soldier's "gut-ache" is a response to not only what he has seen but what he has done. In each of the synoptic Gospels, the soldiers mock Jesus; Matthew and Mark stress the zeal with which the soldiers carried out the Crucifixion, though the issues did not concern them. Once they had their orders, the soldiers became sadistic. (John alone downplays this aspect, probably because he wished to emphasize the rejection by the Jews.) The soldiers were, of course, exhausted, having crucified two other men this day in addition to Jesus, and may have faced similarly unpleasant assignments earlier in the week. Their behavior at Calvary is antithetical to the concept of the gentleman and exemplifies nothing "gentle."

271:22–272:3 **"I got it right here."** . . . *drinks the cup down.* The immediate reaction to the wine seller's bromide gives the soldier the most raucous line of the story. "Camel chips" are of a piece with the scatological play of Campbell. The wine seller's calling the third soldier "Lootenant" has offended some readers, striking them as anti-Semitic. Hemingway does mean to suggest a New York accent and to heighten the contemporary overlay of his recounting. The choice is part of his preparation for seeing Jesus in the stance of a boxer. George's use of rank in addressing the third soldier may echo in "Now I Lay Me" when an orderly addresses a despondent lieutenant, Nick Adams. The first soldier's admission of his need to be "fixed up" (confirmed by George's declaration that he is "in bad shape") aligns him with the third soldier and William Campbell and explains his empathy. In draining the bitter cup, the third soldier plays against Jesus' prayer in the garden of Gethsemane that that cup pass from him. In Matthew's Gospel, when Jesus passes the cup at the Last Supper, he admonishes his disciples, "Drink ye all of it" (6.27).

272:4–21 **"Jesus Christ"** . . . **"He was all right."** Jesus' name is heard here for the first and only time in the story. It would mark the first use of a profanity that became one of the most frequent in the Western world. It might also be read as prayer or confession, *Christ* meaning "anointed" or "messiah." All four canonical Gospels report the inscription on the Cross above Jesus's head: INRI, Jesus of Nazareth, King of the Jews. The inscription pinpoints the threat to the social order that the Romans perceived. The third soldier would have been witness to Jesus' being offered vinegar and gall during his ordeal on the Cross and may have been the one who proffered it; that he now thinks of Jesus while drinking this potion is not a surprise. With the utterance comes the heart of the dialogue as the soldiers discuss what they have seen today, the topic that they have needed to discuss but have avoided until this moment. The second soldier is quick with judgment: "That false alarm!" Somehow

Jesus deserved what he got, though Pilate declares in Luke's Gospel that Jesus has done "nothing worthy of death" (23.15). The second soldier pursues his point by asking why Jesus did not want to come down off the Cross. The biblical analogue is pronounced. In Luke, the soldiers are the ones who taunted Jesus to come down off the Cross (23.36); the net of taunters is larger in Matthew (27.40) and Mark (15.30), and John omitted the words that the second soldier recalls completely. The empathetic first soldier challenges that easy label of "false alarm." His judgment evokes a metaphor from the world of sports as he declares that Jesus "was pretty good in there today"—like Jack Brennan, perhaps. The boxing metaphor also plays against the philosophy of a "muscular Christianity" and the sermons Hemingway heard from the Reverend William E. Barton in his Oak Park church. (Barton's son Bruce was author of the popular *The Man Nobody Knows: A Discovery of Jesus*.) The second soldier is eager for debate. His line is hardly original when he asks why Jesus didn't come down off the Cross. (In the synoptic Gospels, the crowd taunts Jesus to come down from the Cross.) The first soldier is able to see beneath and beyond surfaces of pain. Declaring that getting off the Cross wasn't Jesus's "play," the first soldier sustains his sports metaphor. When the second soldier calls Jesus "a guy," like any other, he misreads badly. Exasperated with the second soldier, the first soldier looks to George for support, but he offers a response that would hardly seem unique in coming centuries. The wine seller professes complete neutrality. In "The Killers" George remains in the diner when Nick goes to warn Andreson. The wine seller's disavowal is most like the attitude of Sam the cook in "The Killers." A disenfranchised minority, Sam wishes to distance himself completely from the empowered. The second soldier blusters, but the first soldier is firm. His judgment on Jesus' performance repeated, it gains in dignity. The third soldier has been quiet, but on reflection he also gives a positive judgment. Jesus was "all right." The line can be read with different emphasis to give different meaning—a ploy by Hemingway that seems completely appropriate to the essential question the story raises: What relevance can the Christ story have in the modern world?

Hemingway skillfully plays against his biblical sources. Who Jesus is, messiah or other, is exactly the question that Pilate in all four Gospels attempts to mediate. Jesus refuses to give a direct answer to Pilate's question and becomes silent at his own trial. Others must answer the question that Pilate asked, as the soldiers attempt to do in "Today Is Friday."

272:22–28 **"You guys don't know"** . . . **"how he acted."** Outvoted, the second soldier steps back a bit from earlier vehemence, insisting instead that all people in that predicament act in the same way. Moving to the general, the second soldier manages nevertheless to bring to the fore the moments that the third soldier especially has been trying to erase through drinking. The first soldier again turns to the wine seller, who repeats his assertion: He didn't "take any interest in it." The historical irony here is keen. After the triumph of Christianity in Europe, the Jews will bear the stigma of Christ killers—often with catastrophic results. Addressing the first soldier as "Lootenant," more than ever George gives the impression of bowing too low. The first soldier, however, is not thinking of George's fawning, but remembering Jesus: "I was surprised how he acted"—not, it seems, according to the everyman script of the second soldier.

272:29–36 **"The part I don't like"** . . . **"good in there today."** The first soldier's surprise about Jesus's behavior brings the men to remember together the most horrific moments at Calvary. The soldiers are the ones above all others who see "what it's like when they first lift 'em up" and "the weight starts to pull" at the nails. Artists were adept at creating images of Jesus on the Cross, some of them vividly showing the nails through the hands. In the seventeenth century, the Flemish painter Peter Paul Rubens in numerous drawings and paintings strove to depict every section of the Passion with historical accuracy. Relevant to this passage in "Today Is Friday" is Rubens's famous painting *The Elevation of the Cross*. For the second soldier it is not the nailing on the Cross that is so horrendous, but the lifting up of the Cross. None of the Gospels mentions the lifting, and before Rubens it had not been of much interest to painters (Judson 61). In these short lines, Hemingway invites reader participation in those moments of nailing and then lifting. The second soldier shows here his most humane side, and that is useful for making the scene at the Cross more vivid. It is certainly so for the first soldier, who repeats for the third time (three is the sacred number in Christian art and thought) his tribute to Jesus: "He was pretty good in there today."

In *The Old Man and the Sea* Hemingway would later use the nailing at Calvary to accent a climactic moment in Santiago's story. Having killed the great fish, Santiago exclaims, "*Ay,*" when he catches first sight of the sharks set on devouring his marlin (118). The narrator reports that there is no exact translation for the word, but that it is the noise a man might make "involuntarily, feeling the nail go through his hands and into the wood."

272:37–45 *The second Roman soldier* . . . **"Just for two, George."** Enjoying the role of bad boy, the second soldier smiles at the wine seller because his companions share a view. He tries to make light of their sympathy—and produces yet another label, "regular Christer." The second soldier stands with the third soldier, who again affirms his judgment. Athletic about his drinking, the second soldier wants to keep the evening going. The third soldier, feeling no good effects from George's medicine, declines more drink—and a role in further discussion.

272:46–273:10 *The wine-seller puts* . . . **"pretty good to me in there today."** George, ever the careful businessman, listens to the conversation, and he is aware of time and regulations about closing hour—hence the smaller bottle of wine. He listens but takes no part in the conversation. Paintings of the Crucifixion frequently portray the grieving who most loved Jesus, including his mother. The soldiers would not know Mary, but they could not fail to note the impact of the group. Mary Magdalene (the one of legend) they have noted. Like Pound's Jesus, Hemingway's Jesus is a sexual being. The second soldier amusingly plays the macho lady's man. He brags that he "knew" her (in the biblical sense) before Jesus did. To the second soldier's declaration that Jesus brought the beauty "no good luck," the second soldier places Jesus in company with many of Hemingway's most noble characters: "Oh, he ain't lucky." It is a chief trait of his undefeated ones. On a realistic level, the second soldier's fifth declaration of the story's key line might reflect a drunkard's repetition, but on the whole he ranks with Hemingway's good drinkers.

273:11–20 **"What become of his gang?"** . . . **"pretty good to me in there today."** In the second soldier's question about Jesus' followers, the disciples become "his gang"; the noun (like the conversation about Jesus and Mary Magdalene) would surely shock the devout reader in America, though Hemingway is realistic in conveying Roman disregard for later pieties. A Roman soldier would have no reason to see any merit in Jesus' followers: they had encouraged a disturber of the status quo. And so in the synoptic Gospels, the soldiers enjoyed tormenting and mocking Jesus; in keeping with those sources, the first soldier proves himself a good observer when he declares, twice, that only the women stuck by Jesus at the Cross. The second soldier characteristically has a stinging label for the disciples: "a pretty yellow crowd." The first soldier keeps thinking of Jesus. His judgment about the Nazarene's conduct that day is no late realization; he recalls with satisfaction having pierced Jesus' side, an act of mercy to hasten death. (Only John's Gospel mentions that a soldier pierces the side, and he does so after the soldiers have determined that Jesus is dead [19.33–34].) It is not an action that the second soldier would have taken; compassion is not his way, especially when it is against the rules. For the fifth time, the first soldier offers his judgment that Jesus was pretty good in there today. In the fifth chapter of *The Garden of Cyrus*, the physician Sir Thomas Browne eloquently described the mystical significance of the number five, a favored number in the natural world as well as in the Bible. Hemingway may never have read Browne, but he was certainly aware that he was planting this repetition above the several other repetitions in the story.

Keeping his focus on the muscular Jesus, the boxer-like figure, Hemingway eschews the late touch by John, who places Jesus' mother among those who "stood by." It is not the figure of Michelangelo's *Pietà* he wishes to evoke. Similarly, his lean story omits any mention of the thieves who were killed with Jesus.

273:21–30 **"Gentlemen, you know"** . . . **"Put it on the bill."** The wine seller's words about closing doubtless reflect how weary he is after this long day and night, but even more important, his words evoke the ending of "A Game of Chess," the second section of Eliot's *The Waste Land*. There another bartender is insistently calling an end to drinking even as the poem comments on the moral decline of the age. But the first soldier, the Crucifixion so vividly in his mind, is reluctant to leave this wineshop, anticipating the old man of "A Clean, Well-Lighted Place" in *Winner Take Nothing*. After his third attempt for "one more round" fails, he abides by the will of his companions. The third soldier's declaration that he "feels like hell" is another anachronism and usefully incorporates another aspect of the suffering of Jesus. The contemporary slang suggests the idea that after his death Jesus descended into hell; the belief is regularly recited in the ecumenical version of the Apostles' Creed but some denominations omit it, and it did not find a place in the Nicene Creed. The word *hell* knolls frequently in the last lines of the story. The concept of hell remains prominent in the Christian religion.

In the night of drinking, the bill has mounted. Understandably, George is dismayed to hear the second soldier's "Put it on the bill." There is, of course, that literal bill, but there is also a moral reckoning. In *The Sun Also Rises* Hemingway paid great attention to who pays reckonings and how much. In a memorable line, Lady Brett Ashley asks Jake Barnes, "Don't we pay for all the things we do, though?" (26). Sometimes the price is steep. A substantial number of characters in *Men Without Women* have confronted or will soon confront the necessity to pay the price. The third Roman soldier is paying a price as "Today Is Friday" begins. The sustaining core of the Christian faith has been the theme that Jesus paid the supreme price for humanity at the Crucifixion.

273:31–34 **"Good-night, gentlemen"** . . . **"Good-night, gentlemen."** It is the literal bill that George has in mind when he asks for something on account, and the second soldier appears oblivious to the larger consequences of the day, certainly to any price he might have to pay for his part in it. Jewish people will, however, have a huge price to pay. Reminding attentive readers of that history, Hemingway creates a large measure of empathy for George at the story's end. George bows low, his nouns of address telling. The second soldier completes the trio of George's "Lootenants," and in short space he twice calls the soldiers "gentlemen." They, too, have a price to pay. "Good-nights" play a similar role as the pub closes at the end of "A Game of Chess" in Eliot's *The Waste Land*. There "ladies" rather than "gentlemen" receive the greeting (ll. 170–72).

273:35–44 *The three Roman* . . . **"That's all."**
The final scene of the drama takes place outside in the street. But stasis rather than movement prevails. The Crucifixion is not an event one can simply walk away from. The dialogue in front of the wineshop neatly captures the essence of the three soldiers. The overconfident second soldier gets the most lines. He again produces

one of his "dirty labels" and stereotypes. His "kike" would be a maiden use of the derogatory noun commonly given Jews. His "just like the rest of them" was familiar by Hemingway's time as a stereotype for Jews as well as African Americans and other minorities. The first soldier has a single line, one showing his ability to get beyond stereotypes. His "George is a nice fella" reminds us—and the second soldier—of his companion's favorable impression of Jesus. Without having to repeat that judgment, Hemingway reminds his readers of it.

Having begun with the emotional and physical state of the third soldier, the narrative ends with that focus. The third soldier is the one who has been most deeply affected by what he has seen at Calvary and what he has been part of. He has felt the Crucifixion, literally, at the gut level. He wants to go to the barracks, a place where soldiers sleep. Since the Sabbath has begun in Jerusalem, the coming day should provide the best opportunity for uninterrupted sleep, if he can manage it. But for the guilty (and the third soldier—like several other characters in *Men Without Women*—feels a heavy burden of guilt), sleep is a boon hard to obtain. Twice he affirms that he "feels like hell." Hemingway takes the third soldier to the emotional place where we find Jake Barnes in *The Sun Also Rises* as the fiesta comes to its disastrous end. Twice Jake declares, "I feel like hell" (222, 223). According to tradition (based on 1 Peter 3.18–20), Jesus descended into hell following his burial. For Jesus, the next step was resurrection. What the next step for the third soldier might be is not promised, though it is from such that the church grew. If the second soldier seems the total cynic and realist, the first soldier observes events with intellectual detachment. He casts a caring but realistic eye on events. Hemingway considered for the story's title "Today Is Friday, or The Seed of the Church" as well as "One More for the Nazarene." The latter option reflects the metaphor of Jesus as boxer, losing but giving a good account of himself. But it may also suggest the future of the third soldier; he is the one most likely to become part of the church of the Nazarene. Some readers will be reminded of the centuries-old tradition of selling and sharing hot cross buns on Good Friday and of the children's song "Hot Cross Buns": "If you have no daughters, / give them to your sons."

Against the feeling of the third soldier, the second soldier affirms what the first soldier had posited at the beginning of the story: that the despondent soldier had been out here "too long." The first soldier no longer offers so easy a verdict. Having accepted that reading, the second soldier ends the story by repeating it yet again: "You been out here too long. That's all." His adding "That's all" makes the explanation far too restrictive. Ironically, it stresses just how wrong he is—about the third soldier and about Jesus.

If we read "Today Is Friday" on a biographical level, we intuit that the conversation about Jesus and his meaning will be a continuing one for Ernest Hemingway. If after his divorce from Pauline the church had a diminished place in Hemingway's thoughts, Christianity and its imagery continued to surface. Mark Spilka was on target when he observed that Hemingway's "religious feelings were never wholly quiescent" (183). None of the three soldiers would disappear. In *By Force of Will: The Life and Art of Ernest Hemingway*, Scott Donaldson probes the religious dimension in Hemingway's life and its reflection in his work. In the years when Hemingway wrote the stories that became *Men Without Women*, Christianity was often on his mind. The careful reader of "Today Is Friday" will not be surprised to discover it at play in the struggles of characters in subsequent works.

BANAL STORY

"Banal Story" has never been a favorite of critics or students. Nor did Hemingway rank it high in his oeuvre. First published in the *Little Review* (over a year before publication in book form), the story (*vignette* might be a more accurate designation) may succeed too well in realizing its title. Of all the stories in *Men Without Women,* it demands the least from its readers. In his first listing of stories for the collection, Hemingway made no mention of the story. But he came to sense that the piece could be more than filler for the book, and he recognized where it would contribute most to the impact of the whole.

As the penultimate story, it contrasts with the masterful final story, a story no critic has ever judged banal. And it plays against the preceding story, a story based on four narratives that profoundly affected the world and still challenge the careful reader—a sharp contrast to the stories in the now defunct *Forum* that Hemingway savages in "Banal Story." Placed where it is, "Banal Story" accents the metafictional emphasis of *Men Without Women.* For the book, Hemingway made only modest changes, but they helped clarify the story's concern with writing.

That Hemingway in 1925 would take the *Forum* as a worthy target for satire is understandable. It counted as one of the "serious" monthlies of the time, and it had recently attempted to broaden its goals and increase its circulation. In 1923 H. G. Leach assumed the editorship. The magazine, which had been concerned with contemporary problems since its inception in 1886, began to include fiction in its offerings, even as Leach sought to accent debate and controversy in its essays.

274:1–4 **So he ate . . . was life.** The opening "So" implies hunger. In *A Moveable Feast* Hemingway famously declared that for a young writer, "hunger is good discipline" (75). The opening paragraph establishes that the unnamed character of the piece is a writer—a young writer, circumstances suggest, learning his trade. His writing room is spare and none too comfortable. The electric stove provides no noticeable heat, but perhaps some, since it feels good when the writer sits on it. The opening sentence conveys ingestion and rejection. Eating an orange involves some involvement; providing pungency, the orange is typically juicy, and its seeds are not part of the eating pleasure. The image of spitting conveys evacuation (like eating, a necessary human activity). In the manuscript version, Hemingway had included several incidents of literal flatulence, and the *banal* of the title catches a visual pun with *anal*; one of the three acceptable pronunciations of *banal* would provide an exact rhyme. The writer learns from other writers what to reject as well as what is valuable.

The inside-outside contrast emphasized in the passage is a contrast that plays throughout *Men Without Women*. In inclement weather, reading can be an ideal activity. But inside, it can also be a temptation: "How good it felt!" Books, Ralph Waldo Emerson had declared, "are for the scholar's idle times" ("The American Scholar" 58). Life is in the world. A writer loses contact with actual life at his peril.

274:5–8 **He reached . . . *There* was Romance.** A second orange suggests both a good orange and a substantial appetite. Although George Monteiro thinks that the narrator has been perusing a newspaper (the *New York Times*, he suggests), he may well be looking at an issue of the *Forum* (142). He is drawn to items that provide gist for a writer seeking the dramatic: Edouard Mascart's boxing match in Paris with Danny Frush on 27 January 1925, the extraordinarily heavy snow in Mesopotamia, an impending cricket match in Australia that involves English players. The attraction of these items is the romance that they provide—not what they might tell us about life. There had been no romance in "Fifty Grand" or in "The Battler" from *In Our Time*, and the reader will discover that "Romance" is not what the narrator seeks.

274:9–14 **Patrons . . . undercurrent of humor.** The narrator has found a brochure promoting the well-established American magazine the *Forum*. Magazines frequently contain inserts promoting the magazine in hopes of securing subscriptions. Although the vast majority of the stories in *Men Without Women* are set "in another country," America remains an important subtext throughout the book. "Banal Story" addresses American tastes. Claiming to reach "the thinking minority," the magazine knows the uses of flattery. The writer who turns to the *Forum* models aims at writing one of the "best-sellers" of tomorrow. The magazine offers "prize short stories." With *In Our Time*, Hemingway challenged standard notions of the prize short story, and "Banal Story" is another such challenge: it could never be a commercially viable story. Grace Hall Hemingway, let it be recalled, was dismayed at her son's subject matter and had encouraged him to write stories that could "guide" readers by depicting wholesome characters. Detailing just those ingredients his mother had espoused, Hemingway's summary presents a wry humor. The homespun tales in the *Forum* could scarcely reveal a very large bit "of real life" on the open ranch or anywhere else. The tension between the crowded tenement (the setting for harsh naturalistic fiction) and "comfortable" homes is laughable.

274:15–21 **I must read . . . older orders of things?** The writer's thought that he "must" read them is tongue-in-cheek. He is reading the promotional literature with Mencken-like amusement.

Although they have not been able to locate any promotional flyer, the critics Philip R. Yannella, Wayne E. Kvam, and George Monteiro have perused issues of the *Forum* that Hemingway used as sources for his satire. The catalogs in "Banal Story" mock the magazine's attempts to instruct (its concerns with the issues of the day) as well as its attempts to delight (its fiction). The author of *In Our Time* had long since put aside any interest in popular fiction as a guide. The unnamed narrator of "Banal Story" has also outgrown any flirtation with such models.

Serious matters take on a ridiculous slant in the rhetorical question that the *Forum* flyer uses to whet the appetites of prospective subscribers. The question of living space, what Hitler would identify as lebensraum, would unsettle the world in the next decade—a reality already signaled in "Che Ti Dice la Patria?" to readers of *Men Without Women*. As readers of the *Forum* were informed, the Japanese were also seeking living space. Increasingly, the question would indeed become war or peace? But the broaching of the possibility of another war in the tired language of the *Forum* reveals how unaware the writer of that language must be about the Great War, not yet a decade in the past.

Flight to Canada? The American reader recognizes a long-standing joke. If matters do not go well in the United States, the disgruntled have often made this quip (usually in jest) about moving to Canada. Following the Revolutionary War, many colonists unhappy with the result of that war did just that. American slaves also fled to Canada. Later, the Vietnam War sent disapproving Americans to Canada. In 1927 the inner circle of Hemingway's acquaintants would find another joke. Canada was not a place to which Hemingway would wish to emigrate. From January to May 1920 he had lived in Toronto, where he freelanced for the *Star* and bristled under his treatment from the city editor, Harry Hindmarsh. Furthermore, Toronto was too much like Oak Park for Hemingway's taste.

With the Scopes trial (1925) still rankling conservative forces in the United States, science indeed seemed to threaten the orthodoxies. Like the *Forum,* American pulpits and politicians often decried "our civilization" and touted the "older orders of things." Literary modernism—in which Hemingway played so large a part—had at its core a mistrust of the "older orders of things." The methods of the modernists were quite different from those of the *Forum.*

274:22–27 **And meanwhile, in the far-off . . . Young Stribling.** The "And meanwhile" is an obvious transition of popular literature. Here it takes the reader to a setting made for "Romance," the jungles of Yucatan, but in its serious mode, the *Forum* might address the destruction of the rain forest there, clearly a threat to the old order. That destruction might also provide living space.

As Monteiro suggests, Hemingway uses an article by a Yale undergraduate, "Big Men—or Cultured?" for humor that anticipated developing complexities in Hemingway's friendship with F. Scott Fitzgerald. The Yale student argued for culture for its own sake rather than to facilitate one's emergence as a big man on campus. Hemingway had elected not to attend college, in part because he was driven by a very different concept of big man than that espoused by the college student. The idea of manhood becomes more central in the concluding section of "Banal Story." The theme has been before the reader of *Men Without Women* from the opening story. Driven by his concept of manhood, Hemingway was also intent on being cultured—his way. His "Take Joyce" brings to the table the writer whose culture Hemingway never challenged and whose writing he continued to admire. James Joyce was, indeed, college educated, but a "big man" only in the world of letters. Juxtaposing Joyce, who was a wordsmith extraordinaire, and President Calvin Coolidge (known as Silent Cal) would have been even funnier in 1927, when readers encountered it in *Men Without Women,* than it was in 1925, when Hemingway first drafted "Banal Story." The thirtieth president may well have been a "big man" to the average American (thrust into the presidency after Harding's death, he won the election on his own in 1924 and would have been reelected had he chosen to run again in 1928), but he was hardly a hero of the intellectuals. When he died in 1930, Dorothy Parker quipped, "How do they know?" The impact is much reduced for contemporary readers.

Young Americans, especially those in college, have long been admonished to aim for the stars. Jack Britton was a star of the boxing world, and Hemingway had just used him as a source in his creation of Jack Brennan in "Fifty Grand." Jack, we recall, "could say what he wanted" (232). But someone else had to tell his story. Dr. Henry Van Dyke, by contrast, was a prolific and popular writer in several genres, including the short story and the romance. In his boyhood, Hemingway likely encountered Van Dyke's essays on outdoor life. A Presbyterian minister before becoming a professor at Princeton, Van Dyke wrote travel sketches, fiction, poems, and criticism that would suit the *Forum*'s attempt to capture the "warm, homespun, American" essence. No, this star could not be easily "reconcile[d]" with Jack Britton's.

If Van Dyke's stardom was on the decline when Hemingway wrote, that of T. S. Stribling was decidedly on the rise. Hemingway was almost certainly aware of its arc. During the 1920s Stribling, sometimes counted a forerunner of William Faulkner, was writing realistic novels set in the American South. Stribling's star would peak in 1932, when his novel *The Store* received the Pulitzer Prize. By calling the author "Young Stribling," Hemingway mocks him. In point of fact, Stribling was eighteen years older than Hemingway. His was not a star that inspired Hemingway.

274:28–30 **And what of . . . girl of eighteen.** Seeking some balance, the *Forum* turns from the notion of the big man to ask about "our daughters." The pamphlet comes, after all, in the decade of the flapper. But the promise of any serious attention to the changing status of women is undermined by the flippancy of the paragraph. It mocks the English heroine of A. Hamilton Gibbs's novel *Soundings*, which was being serialized in the *Forum*. In the October 1924 issue, Gibbs provided the epigraph of the novel: "Life is an uncharted ocean. The cautious mariner must needs take many soundings 'ere he conduct his barque to port in safety." The banal novel will, the narrator is confident, provide him no insight about women of eighteen years old or of any age.

275:1–3 **It was a splendid . . . Betsy Ross.** A judgment of "splendid" would please the booklet's creators—were it not given in mockery. The series in the succeeding paragraph is a study in the absurd. The girl of eighteen is presumably making soundings, and the *Forum* has three "stars" to guide her. Joan of Arc is there because Mark Twain's novel about Joan had received a large advertisement in the magazine. Twain considered it the greatest of his novels, though posterity thinks otherwise. Called *Personal Recollections of Joan of Arc*, the novel was first published in 1896. Its revival in 1925 was occasioned by George Bernard Shaw, who had made Joan an inspiring figure in his play *Saint Joan*, which was first performed in 1923, then published the next year. (The *Forum*, desirous of being up to date, had published an interview with Shaw and the University of North Carolina mathematics professor Archibald Henderson, who studied and wrote about the drama; Henderson later published a biography of Shaw.) Betsy Ross remains an American icon as the legendary maker of the American flag and courageous defender of the young republic, but she hardly seems in Joan's class. Noticeably, the catalog has no contemporary woman to serve as model for the young woman of eighteen.

275:4–8 **Think of . . . adventuring.** Mention of the specific year places the present moment of the story even as it calls attention to how quickly the controversial issues of any moment become dated. Although the catalog of questions and issues is founded in specific pages of the *Forum*, few readers much care that there is a source in the pages of the magazine. Fortunately, the story is not dependent on that knowledge; the catalog amuses as it mocks attempts by the magazine to flaunt its flexibility, its willingness to see "two sides to Pocahontas" as well as to question Picasso's artistry. Not many Americans in 1925 had seen art by Picasso, but Hemingway certainly had. The notion of "a risqué page in Puritan history" might get a chuckle from an American reader in 1925, and though standards were changing, Hemingway reminds readers that the Puritan code was still strong in his country. That code had, in fact, necessitated deletion of the scatological humor found in the manuscript version of the story, and his early story "Up in Michigan" remained too risqué to take a place in *Men Without Women*. A reader unaware that the *Forum* had printed an article about the life of tramps might instead set the mind wandering to the "codes" operating in the lives of the tramps found in Hemingway's "The Battler," the story that is part of *In Our Time*. The tenor of all that the writer has surveyed mocks the *Forum*'s invitation to send the mind adventuring. With *The Sun Also Rises* doing so well, Hemingway's readers were already equating Hemingway with adventure; in the coming decade, adventure would become a hallmark of the life and work of Ernest Hemingway.

275:9–13 **There is Romance . . . laid down the booklet.** The magazine's platform buckles against itself. Embracing the ordinary ("Romance [is] everywhere"), it lauds the unusual. The "full life of the mind" jars against the "life . . . intoxicated" with "Romance." The lauded "brevity" and the life of the mind might be at odds. Brevity is, as Shakespeare's Polonius remarked, the soul of wit—and the spirit of Polonius hovers over this catalog. A little can go a long way, and so the writer puts the promotional booklet aside.

275:14–16 **And meanwhile, stretched flat . . . drowning with the pneumonia.** The last paragraph of the "brief" and "witty"—but probably "smart"—"Banal Story" is also the longest. It is also the paragraph that will linger longest in the reader's mind. In technique, the paragraph resembles the interchapters of *In Our Time*— statements are brief, but not witty and smart. Specifically, it recasts chapter 14 of that work, the interchapter in which the torero Maera is dying from the thrust of the bull. That chapter is prelude to the Nick Adams story that concludes *In Our Time*. The paragraph on Maera dying from pneumonia in "Banal Story" is prelude to the Nick Adams story that concludes *Men Without Women*.

The narrative now honors "Manuel Garcia Maera." (A comma after *Garcia* would make clear that *Maera* is a nickname.) Hemingway had seen and admired Maera in July 1923 during his immersion into the world of the bullfight, the contest in the arena that is about death. In his report for the *Toronto Star Weekly*, he described Maera as "dark, spare and deadly looking, one of the very greatest toreros of all time" (*Dateline* 351). Two years after his triumphs with the bulls, Maera lies on his deathbed, inside a darkened room of his house, not in the sunshine of the arena. The description of the death accents the tube in each lung and does not shield the reader from the "drowning" that pneumonia entails.

275:16–19 **All the papers . . . lithographs.** The dead hero belongs to the ages. By not breaking the paragraph, Hemingway creates a sense of the flow of the process. Because Maera's death was expected, the papers had ample time to prepare supplements on the dead torero. Andalusia (Andalucía in Spanish) is Maera's home province, so the press there has made much of Maera's end. The death occasions commercial opportunity, and the full-length colored pictures sell well. But since the pictures do not also show the bull, the men and boys receive a stylized, romantic image of Maera. The narrator reports an immediate loss beyond the death: the men and boys lose their memories of Maera and replace them with the images on the lithographs. In the book, the line evokes the advice of the major in "In Another Country": a man ought to find those things that he cannot lose. For Hemingway, that ideal comes closer to realization through careful prose than it can through lithographs.

275:20–24 **Bull-fighters were . . . next to Joselito.** Hemingway was very attuned to the presence of the competition, no matter the art. Noting the response to Maera's death, the narrator pays the ultimate compliment to Maera: "He did always in the bull-ring the things they could only do sometimes." The placement of "always" after the verb gives more prominence to the word than the conversational placement before the verb does. The attention to Maera's art supports the metafictional spine of the story, the more so in the context of the supplements just mentioned. Relieved to have the great one gone, "one hundred and forty-seven bull-fighters" nevertheless give him due honors. As was customary in European cultures, the mourners walk behind the coffin to the cemetery. The rain hints at the pathetic fallacy. Maera's burial spot is not with his family, but with the fellowship of great bullfighters. He is buried next to Joselito, the great bullfighter, who, like Maera, died young (at the age of twenty-five). Since that death came in 1920, Hemingway did not see Joselito perform. But he was aware that Joselito met his death in the arena.

275:24–26 **After the funeral . . . in their pockets.** The final sentence of the story enlarges the perspective to include the other mourners at what was an exceptionally large procession. Repairing to the cafés, mourners are able to purchase "many colored pictures." The final image being that of the pictures folded up and put in the men's pockets, we know that already Maera's presence is fading. What Maera did in the ring, he did, ultimately, for himself.

Especially given the metafictional theme of the story, the reader may consider the story from the biographical perspective. If Hemingway identified with the aspiring writer at the fore through most of the story, did he also ponder his own death in Maera's? We might find a number of parallels in the two deaths and in the two funerals. When Hemingway wrote "Banal Story," he was close to the ages of Maera and Joselito when they died, their brilliant work in the arena abruptly ended. Hemingway was drawn to the bullfight because he thought it touched the core of the human story—death and how one meets it. His own death, of course, would be among the best known of his century.

Recognizing that the banal dominates the penultimate story of *Men Without Women*, Wirt Williams had some basis for declaring the dramatic skeleton of tragedy to be present in it. The story mocks "the life of the mind" and portrays an awareness of death and the consciousness of death—"life's most profound realities" (94). The awareness would be for the reader, not for Maera as we experience him in the story—but that awareness was likely central to Maera's life as a matador.

Had Maera died in the bullring, his ending would have been considered heroic. In *Death and the Sun,* after surveying the deaths of matadors, Edward Lewine summarizes: "it is a tradition in bullfighting that it is right and proper for a matador to die in the ring; that is the matador's destiny and his calling. So when it happens, it is as though all fairy tales were coming true" (178). Lewine's words "right and proper" can serve to remind us that the juxtaposition of death in the bullfighting arena and death in war plays an important part in *Men Without Women.* The article of faith that most Americans held as they sent their sons off to fight in the Great War is caught in the Latin words from an ode by Horace containing the line *dulce et decorum est pro patria mori* ("It is sweet and glorious to die for fatherland," *Odes,* 3.2. 13). In 1920 the English poet Wilfred Owen used that Latin to title his poem that blasted the maxim as "[t]he old lie" (l. 27). The informal Maera, we recall, derives from *madera* (wood), the essential matter or strength.

Had Hemingway recounted a death in the ring, he would have given his reader a more romantic story, a more uplifting story. Instead, Maera's death (as was the case with the historic Manuel López Garcia known as Maera) demonstrates one of the cruel ironies of life as the brilliant fighter dies drowning from pneumonia. Because Joselito died in the arena, his death had a heroic dimension absent in Maera's. And though Maera would be buried next to Joselito in the cemetery in Seville, his tomb is much smaller. (Both Maera and Joselito are important toreros in *Death in the Afternoon,* and Hemingway provided several photographs of each.)

Ending "Banal Story" with the death of Maera, Hemingway affirms his artistic creed: truth, however grim, claims his artistic allegiance. And by making "Banal Story" the penultimate story of *Men Without Women,* Hemingway was able to make the story do much more than it could by itself. The reader moves from the account of a young torero suffering the prolonged death from pneumonia to contemplation of a young American lying on a makeshift pallet in a wartime hospital in Milan, bent on keeping the scepter of death at bay. In "Now I Lay Me," Hemingway would also affirm that he was in no way interested in stories in which "all fairy tales were coming true."

NOW I LAY ME

Hemingway concludes *Men Without Women* with a story that powerfully accents the unities of the book. Having ended *In Our Time* with a Nick Adams story that readers had not encountered in any previous publication, he reminded readers of that structure by again ending with an unpublished Nick story, thus affirming the importance of Nick to the collection. "Now I Lay Me" demands to be read against "In Another Country"; indeed, Hemingway had once called it "In Another Country—Two." Life-altering crises for Nick Adams occur in two stories in which he is named; he is also present in first-person stories in which the protagonist is not named, "In Another Country" among them.

"Now I Lay Me" highlights the theme caught in the book's title. There are, in fact, three men in the final story who are without a woman. The orderly, John, has a wife in Chicago, but he had removed himself from that family context to visit his relatives in Italy, was conscripted into the Italian Army, and now lies wounded in a makeshift hospital. Nick Adams, who also lies wounded in that hospital, has no wife and no clear intention to obtain one. Nick's father, a remembered presence in the story, though legally married, appears decidedly "without" the helpmeet of the prescription that Nick Adams knew well: "It is not good that man should be alone; I will make a help meet for him"—so the Creator declares in Genesis 2.18.

The emotional link from the paragraph about Maera's death and burial in "Banal Story" to Nick Adams, the "I" of "Now I Lay Me," is substantial. Evoking "The Undefeated" and the bullfighter Manuel "alone" in the arena, Maera reminds us of the many men of *Men Without Women* who lie damaged or in despair.

The title "Now I Lay Me" is among Hemingway's more obvious allusions, the still familiar childhood prayer from the eighteenth century that ends "If I should die before I wake, / I pray the Lord my soul to take." In part it suggests that the narrator sees something of his childlike mind in the narrative he is about to share; near the story's end Nick describes a haunting memory from his childhood. The story about to unfold, like the opening story of *Men Without Women*, foregrounds the idea of death and the concept of prayer and an afterlife. The childhood prayer is ego centered and abounds with first-person pronouns: *I, me, my.*

276:1–12 **That night we lay . . . make the experiment.** The final story is set in the darkness of night. Readers of *Men Without Women* are accustomed to encountering pronouns with vague antecedents that become clear later in the story. Almost immediately the narrative turns to an "I" who does not share even his first name until well into the story. The story is at midpoint before the "we" is identified or becomes important. It is the "I" who most matters. The characters are lying on the floor, far removed from the comfortable world where children recite "Now I Lay Me" beside or in comfortable beds. The lying is a passive activity, but the narrator's listening is decidedly active, listening tuned to a high degree. The regular sound of the munching of the silkworms suggests the process of a relentless life force. The "I myself" sets the narrator, Nick Adams, apart from the rest of the "we." Sleeping is the expected activity of night. As in the childhood prayer, the narrator associates sleep with death—though he eschews that word. In the false start to "Indian Camp," the first story in *In Our Time*, Hemingway had portrayed the young boy Nick Adams lying on a cot at night, fearing that he might die. Nick's remembrance of the Protestant hymn that begins "Some day the silver cord will break" incites an extreme anxiety. The false start was published as "Three Shots" in the posthumously published *The Nick Adams Stories*.

As "Now I Lay Me" begins, the narrator acknowledges a condition that he can now recognize as irrational—though such responses are not uncommon for soldiers who have seen combat. The narrator is such a one and remembers being "blown up" at night. The verb has a grim finality. The damage quickly reveals itself as more psychic than physical. The narrator wishes to remain awake because he fears a repetition of that experience, one in which there is now some component of will: "let myself go." The experience that he dreads and does not want to repeat is known clinically as an out-of-body experience: he feels his soul leave the body. (As much as 15–20 percent of the population has had an out-of-body experience [Blackmore 472].) For the narrator, stopping the experience as he is about to fall asleep is possible "only . . . by a very great effort." At the moment of the writing of the narrative, the narrator knows that the soul would not really have left him, but during the summer he describes, his condition was such that he "was unwilling to make the experiment"—a choice of words that indicates how far he has come at the moment of the telling.

276:13–27 **I had different ways . . . use him for bait.** Nick quickly becomes specific about the "very great effort" that keeps him from falling asleep. The trout streams of his boyhood now become streams of redemption as he "very carefully" fishes them from end to end. Iterating the "very carefully" of the process, Nick enumerates the complexities and then the result: "sometimes catching trout and sometimes losing them." Nick is also describing the process of his writing, the form of redemption that is the subtext of the story and the book.

When Nick recounts a noon pause for lunch, Hemingway (and possibly Nick the writer) makes allusion to "Big Two-Hearted River" in *In Our Time*. In part I and part

II, his careful detailing of preparation for eating and the eating itself emphasizes the psychological play involved, a ritualistic quality. After his traumatic encounter with the big trout in part II, Nick leaves the "deepening water" and sits on the bank to eat his sandwiches (which have been dipped in cold water). He remains there, smoking "and watching the river," recalling Nick's lengthy pause on the bridge in Seney, Michigan, to watch the trout holding steady in the stream (179). "Now I Lay Me" can usefully be read as the deep memory that Nick in "Big Two-Hearted River" holds back, the dark swamp that he later promises that he will fish.

The challenge of securing bait is integral to Nick's fishing these streams of the mind. Specific rules for the search suggest the quests of legend. Nick takes only ten worms; when those are gone he must improvise. He is severely tested: digging is difficult where the cedars keep out the sun so that no grass grows and he finds only bare moist earth. Nick's mention of the time he "could find no bait at all" creates an alarming moment—a moment of panic—as when the Knight Perilous in *The Waste Land* finds the empty chapel. Nick's improvisation with the trout he has had to cut up suggests nightmare more than triumph.

276:28–277:9 **Sometimes I found . . . acted about the hook.** The enumeration of life in the swampy meadows affirms Nick's familiarity with the natural world. The catalog of creatures creates a kind of poetry, enhanced by the repetition of the word *sometimes*. The word is used twice in the paragraph, as it had been used twice in the preceding paragraph. The search for bait is marked by failure as much as success: grubs will not stay on the hook, and angleworms are adept at slipping into the ground as soon as the log is raised. From the sense of repetition carried by "sometimes," the paragraph moves to a vivid particular when Nick recounts finding a salamander under an old log, a lovely creature—"very small and neat and agile and a lovely color." Nick's attention to securing bait climaxes with his experiments with the salamander that becomes nearly human as it tries "to hold on to the hook," causing Nick to choose never again to use salamander as bait. It is the same with crickets "because of the way they acted about the hook." The swamp meadow where Nick seeks bait takes him even closer to bad dreams. In the dry meadow, the grasshoppers are abundant. The passage contains a sense of joyousness that is also part of Nick's collecting and observation of the hoppers in "Big Two-Hearted River." In both stories, the hoppers please Nick for their own sake as well as for their usefulness as bait. Swimming in the stream but eventually "taken" by a trout, the hoppers mirror the rhythm of life. In "Big Two-Hearted River" an entire paragraph details a grasshopper that evokes the human as it "took hold of the hook with his front feet, spitting tobacco juice on it" (175). But a stronger Nick can there use the grasshopper. In "Big Two-Hearted River" Nick discovers an abundance of grasshoppers. Chronologically in the Nick saga, that good fishing is in the future; the events recounted here are among those Nick at the Big Two-Hearted wants to keep at bay.

277:10–24 **Sometimes the stream . . . miles to get to them.** The fourth paragraph continues to evoke ritual and a prose poetry. The word *sometimes* occurs three times, echoed in "some nights" and "some of those streams." The paragraph progresses from the reassurance of an open meadow and the leisure created by the sight of swimming grasshoppers to mounting anxiety in Nick's efforts to stay awake—to keep death at bay. Fishing that will get Nick through the night becomes repetition that entails revision. The process is much like that of the writer. Starting at the lake and reversing the course, Nick seeks all the trout he had missed coming down. The contrast with "Big Two-Hearted River" is pronounced; there a stronger Nick "did not care about getting many trout" (178). On his pallet in Milan, Nick does experience the pleasure in the invention of his own streams. Some of them were "very exciting," giving him the sensation of "being awake and dreaming"—as in John Keats's "Ode to a Nightingale," a poem concerned with the creation of the work of art that defies death. "Do I wake—or sleep?" the poet asks as he concludes his encounter with his lethe-wards instincts (l. 80). The ode would almost certainly have been among those Hemingway encountered in high school (Reynolds, *Hemingway's Reading* 41). Reynolds lists *The Poetical Works of John Keats* in the Key West inventory of Hemingway's books.

The streams that Nick remembers inventing have marked specificity and are placed precisely in a geography. So vivid are his imaginings that later he often fuses the real and the imaginary streams. The lines caution about anyone's reliance on memory. More important, they bear strongly on the metafictional quality of "Now I Lay Me." A reader should beware of reading this story—or any Hemingway story—as autobiography, though there are biographical details given to Nick that can be corroborated in Hemingway's life. Paul Smith thought that Hemingway may have kept "Now I Lay Me" from magazine publication because he feared it would be read simply as autobiographical record (173). Stories in a book read differently.

277:25–38 **But some nights . . . sleep in the daylight.** Nick's narration has moved toward the increasingly complicated: now he must describe those nights when he lies "cold awake," unable to fish either real or imagined streams. Creativity failing him, he resorts to the ritual of prayer. As the title of the story suggests, Nick is no stranger to prayer. Here the praying becomes Roman Catholic (Hail Mary; Our Father) as well as Protestant (Our Father). The emphasis of the praying is different from that evoked by the ego-centered prayer from childhood "Now I Lay Me." These prayers begin with concentration on the divine, its majesty and grace, before humble supplication from the self. Nick's praying is unusual, if not bizarre, as he tries to pray for everyone he has ever known, though the reader who knows *The Sun Also Rises* will recall Jake Barnes's similar effort during the Fiesta of San Fermín. Recalling everyone he has ever known is a challenge to the mind, doubtless a good exercise for a writer, especially one who goes back to his earliest memories. A reader would recognize—as Hemingway surely did—that he was practicing good Freudian psychology. Nick knows that the parents who gave him life have shaped his course in crucial ways. His earliest memory would delight any Freudian. He remembers, in the attic of the house where he was born, hanging from the rafters a tin box (female genitals) that holds a slice of his parents' wedding cake. The attic also contains jars of snakes (male genitals) and other specimens that his father gathered as a boy, though the backs of some of the specimens have turned a charnel white since some of the alcohol has evaporated. Nick does not interpret but rushes from the images to recalling and praying for the many people he has met. If each gets an Our Father and a Hail Mary, he can get through the night and then, perhaps, go to sleep. The theme of sleep and sleeplessness, important throughout *Men Without Women,* gets its most forceful statement in its concluding story.

277:39–43 **On those nights . . . reached the war.** The mental exercise that Nick engages in during "those nights" is considerably more demanding than the fishing exercises. The spiral of time reverses the order that controlled the fishing process (which originated at the river's source); now Nick begins his recollections just before the war and moves back to that attic and then works back to the war. On the hard nights, both the starting junctures and the concluding juncture involve trauma. "Those nights" are much like the condition Keats describes in "Ode to a Nightingale": "Where but to think is to be full of sorrow. / And leaden-eyed despairs" (ll. 27–28).

277:44–278:6 **I remember, after my grandfather . . . pray for them.** Nick's memory here does parallel a verifiable event in Hemingway's life. Ernest Hall, his mother's father, died on 10 May 1905, some two months before Ernest turned six. By October, Grace Hemingway had sold his house, which had also been home to Grace and Clarence Hemingway and their young family. The family moved to a rented house while the new house (designed by Grace and made possible through her inheritance) was being built. Doubtless, there were discards with the moves, but there is no record of that process.

Important to the story, however, is the juxtaposition of the move "to a new house built by my mother" and the story's first explicit mention of war in the preceding paragraph. The events from Nick's early memory entail similar terror: fire, flames, and the popping of jars in the heat. The war and the move involve a testing of manhood: "I remember the snakes burning in the fire in the back-yard." The demon that memory can be is accented in this short paragraph by the rapid staccato of three repetitions of "I remember" and one "I could not remember."

278:7–14 **About the new house . . . "What's this?" he asked.** As in a prolonged war, Nick remembers repetitions of "good cleanings" planned and executed by his mother. Surprise is a crucial element in battle strategy, and the memory that gnaws at Nick here involved that tactic. While his father was out hunting, his mother "made a good thorough cleaning." As the doctor surveys the fire "still burning in the road," he may reflect that the action is meant in part to punish him for his absence, for his engagement in the primal male role as hunter. The "good thorough cleaning" is a strong statement that the new house is indeed hers; the "good" of the phrase is double edged. The doctor may well ask, "What's this?" as he gazes into the fire. For the reader of *Men Without Women,* the image suggests the domestic burning that the narrator of "A Canary for One" views as his train approaches Paris.

278:15–25 **"I've been cleaning out"** . . . **the buggy.** We encounter here the single sentence that Mrs. Adams speaks in *Men Without Women*. It is enough, a ringing measure of her power. Her use of "dear" alludes to "The Doctor and the Doctor's Wife," where the word accented her ability to manipulate her husband, to demean him, to unman him. She makes her pronouncement from the porch, portal of her domain. Her smile is as chilling to the older Nick as are her words. Nick's perspective here is much like that of Shakespeare's Hamlet, who declares that "one may smile, and smile, and [yet] be a villain" (*Hamlet* 1.5.108). Hamlet is not thinking of his mother when he speaks the line, but the prince does have a huge problem with his mother and her cheerfulness, especially since he judges that she has betrayed his father. Pondering "The undiscover'd country from whose bourn / No traveller returns" (*Hamlet* 3.1.79–80), Nick's mind-set at the opening of the story is much like the Dane's. Similarities mount as the story progresses.

The rest of the paragraph describes the reaction of the vanquished, a memory etched deeply in Nick's mind. The doctor responds to his wife's words exclusively by his actions, his kick of protest aimed to retrieve whatever of value might have survived the flames. He is content, as it were, to leave his wife to heaven—as the king's ghost admonished Hamlet to do. The doctor (again like Hamlet's father) looks to his son to aid him in the recovery. Raking "very carefully in the ashes," he creates a teaching moment that is not lost on Nick. The objects that he retrieves all come from the primal world of the Indians, the world that will always hold appeal for Nick. The objects are all blackened and chipped by the fire, their condition corresponding to the exposed foundations that mark where the town of Seney, Michigan, once stood and the burnt countryside around it that Nick encounters in "Big Two-Hearted River." A second mention that the doctor travels by horse and buggy puts him at great remove from the mechanized order that led to the Great War and Nick's lonely presence in an Italian hospital.

278:26–37 **"Take the gun"** . . . **pray for them both.** Mrs. Adams having quickly read the doctor's body language and retreated to her domain, the doctor continues his effort to salvage his possessions, careful to involve Nick in the process. He addresses Nick four times in the paragraph. The first three continue in the imperative mode.

The first is a command to carry his gun and game bags (no mention is made of the contents of the game bags, but they are not likely empty) into the house. (In "The Doctor and the Doctor's Wife" the doctor's gun inside the cottage underscored his frustration.) Though there is no clear indication of how long the Adams family has been in their new home when the great cleaning occurs, the event probably precedes the time of "The Doctor and the Doctor's Wife," when Nick invites his father to join him in hunting black squirrels. Nick seems quite young here, since the gun is heavy and bangs against his legs and the doctor must give his son advice on good procedure. After the gun is inside, and the paper ready for the doctor, Nick observes the doctor's careful attention to the rescued objects. The doctor's fourth sentence in the paragraph is haunting Nick years later: "The best arrow-heads went all to pieces." Nick then watches his father carry them into the house, returning the remnants to his space, a small counteroffensive. Though the father has a remnant only, he has taught his son well. Hunting will forever be an activity that links father and son. As young Nick stays outside on the grass with the two game bags for some time, we may recall his preference to be outside when he knows that his mother wishes him inside. And so the mother creeps into the paragraph again at its conclusion, and Nick returns us to the time in Milan and the demands of his prayer for both parents.

278:38–279:9 **Some nights, though . . . and listened to them.** The story takes seriously its depiction of Nick's agonies with prayer. For Nick, prayer stems from a desire to understand his life and the forces that made it. It tests his endurance and his memory. Prayer (and memory) fails him when it moves from the transcendent perspective to the verbalizing of inadequacy. It is noteworthy that the memory circuit breaks at the point when he must petition personally: at "Give" and "forgive." Short as the Lord's Prayer is, failure to be able to remember it all accents the high level of stress Nick feels on some nights. This is trauma of high magnitude.

Nick's agony reflects his wavering religious faith. The prayers that he cannot remember begin with a centering of the self in God before petitions for self or others. None of Nick's praying emerges as an act of contrition. He would like for Christian faith to sustain him. But at no time does the story suggest that Nick believes that God has heard his prayers.

When attempts at prayer fail, Nick turns to recalling names of animals and then—moving back to the human—names of food and streets and the like. In all these lists he creates, Nick recalls names, reversing Adam's task in Genesis of providing names. Clearly, Nick's is a fallen world. Adam, on the other side of Eden, never experienced the isolation Nick recalls, when he "could not remember anything at all." On those nights he just listens, and the narrative takes us back to the act of listening with which the story began.

As powerful as Nick's evocation of the nights that tested him most is, the same words convey to us the strength that Nick has since gained to be able to share such intimate thoughts. The lines we read are in confessional mode, the very mode that had proved most difficult to Nick in his praying. Even as the title of the story comes from a child's prayer, the need for a night-light also reflects the world of childhood. Nick's reliance on a night-light when he can get it recalls Mr. Campbell's being able to sleep at noon, but not at night, in "A Pursuit Race." From the strength of his condition as he looks back at that particular night, Nick can acknowledge that he likely slept on some of those nights without knowing it. Careful writer that he is, Nick senses that he can now relate what transpired on that night when he lay with his eyes wide open, listening to the silkworms eating.

279:10–22 **There was only one . . . in the blankets.** For essentially half of the story, only Nick's psyche has been before the reader, a pattern similar to that in the preceding "Banal Story." Nick's condition will now be sharpened by juxtaposition against another person with whom he shares the room. In addition to listening to the worms eating the leaves, Nick listens to his orderly, who also lies awake, perhaps disturbed by the discomfort of the accommodations of blankets on straw, but there is a good deal more to keep him from resting well. Nick suggests that his companion has not had "as much practice being awake" as he himself has had. Whatever the level of noise from tossing and turning—and later conversation—the worms go about their process of eating, indifferent to human existence. Midstory references to World War I become more pronounced. The guns of war have almost become white noise for Nick, whose engagement has been with the sound of the worms. Possibly the noise of the guns is more disturbing to the orderly than to Nick. The war has had a high cost for him: though he emigrated to the United States, while visiting relatives in 1914 he was conscripted into the Italian Army. That history and the fact that he is a father may have led to his assignment as Nick's orderly, saving him from the trauma of the front. With the wounded Nick, he has time to think of the life he had in the States, to regret becoming a man without a woman for extended duration. Aware of the orderly's restlessness, Nick lets him know through reciprocal motion that he is also awake. He is willing to talk if the orderly wishes but does not himself initiate it.

279:23–33 **"Can't you sleep" . . . "It's all right."** The format of the story changes dramatically. Dialogue becomes paramount, as in "The Killers," "Hills Like White Elephants," and "Today Is Friday." Rank is scrupulously maintained in any well-disciplined army. Because Nick and the orderly have adjoining pallets, they have known something of each other as individuals, but the orderly always addresses Nick by his rank. The orderly's initiating question not only relates to the moment but is the haunting question of the entire story. Nick's simple "No" far exceeds the orderly's ability to understand its implications. The sleeplessness that the orderly admits to is of a very different order. Recognizing that sleeplessness of any magnitude bespeaks of anxieties and uncertainties, Nick assumes the role of therapist, asking the orderly if he would like to talk for awhile. Quickly assenting, the orderly shows his primary frustration: being where he doesn't want to be. Nick, however, takes some satisfaction in the separate peace occasioned by his wounding. He is grateful to be alive—away from the "noises of the night" only a few miles away and away from the scene of the great cleanings of his boyhood that sometimes haunt his night thoughts.

279:34–42 **"Tell me about"** . . . **"a lot of money."** Nick continues in the role of the therapist, suggesting that the orderly talk about the home place (where Nick has recently wandered in his nighttime exploration). The attentive reader will recognize that Chicago is also familiar terrain for Nick (in "The Battler" he had identified it as his hometown; in "The Killers" Nick is in Summit, a Chicago suburb). There is, however, no indication that the two men share Chicago; the orderly comes from a different culture. The orderly is less inclined than Nick to make repetition a part of his method of dealing with the past. But Nick as therapist is less disinterested than it at first appears. Why should he be so curious about the orderly's marriage? The interest at once harkens back to the depiction of Nick's parents (as well as to "A Canary for One") and forward to later reflections on Nick's view of marriage for himself. The orderly not wishing to rehash the story of his courtship and marriage, Nick keeps that marriage to the fore. His question contains a striking pause that highlights the wife, the wife Nick does not have. The orderly takes the wife's loyalty for granted: "She writes me all the time." The wife's faithfulness a given, he is impressed with his wife's business acumen: the wife is making "good money."

279:43–45 **"Don't you think"** . . . **"I'm nervous."** Nick's question confirms that the two men are in a makeshift ward: there are others sleeping nearby, men at least for now exempt from the battles at the front. These others "sleep like pigs," the orderly says. He claims to be "different" because he is "nervous." By the end of the story, he will not seem so very different, nor his nervousness nearly as pronounced as Nick's.

280:1–10 **"Talk quiet"** . . . **"how you hear things."** Nor is the orderly's concern for others a match for Nick's. Nick desires quiet: gentle voices allow others to sustain the boon of sleep and further the calm that prayer seeks to gain. He offers John a cigarette to foster that atmosphere. Although there is considerable attention to drinking in the stories of *Men Without Women* (as in *In Our Time*), there is much less emphasis on smoking. But the instances of it are memorable and connected with nervousness. In "Big Two-Hearted River," Nick smokes after his remembrance of Hopkins, when his mind was starting to work. In part II of the story, after the climactic moment when the big trout gets away, Nick takes out a cigarette—just after we are told that "he did not want to rush his sensations any" (177). And so here two men with starkly different degrees of nervousness sit smoking in the dark. The orderly has noticed that Nick does not smoke very often. He uses smoking as a measure of his success in conquering nerves. The orderly, by contrast, mainly has a habit—one he might like to break, but not very strongly: "I suppose you get so you don't miss it." More prone to the glib, he resurrects a folk myth that "a blind man won't smoke because he can't see the smoke come out." (Blind people sometimes do smoke, but those blind from birth are less likely to do so because of the danger from fire and the difficulty of lighting a cigarette or pipe.)

280:11–22 **We were both quiet . . . "will get better."** The smoking does promote calm, and the two men are able merely to listen. As if to reestablish similarity, the orderly asks if Nick can hear the "damn" silkworms chewing, though his adjective accents difference. With the image of the worms again central, the orderly senses trust strong enough on the part of the lieutenant to ask about the habitual sleeplessness at night that he has observed. At this moment of comradeship, Nick addresses the orderly by name for the first time. Since much of Nick's effort toward recovery takes place only in the private rituals of his own mind, it is surely a positive sign that he can say to another that he had got "in pretty bad shape" and "at night it bothers me." Though John claims to be "just like" Nick in this regard, the evidence is to the contrary.

280:23–25 **"Say, Signor Tenente" . . . "hell of a reason."** Realizing that Nick as an American need not have become part of the war, John logically asks, "Why?" Nick doesn't offer a very concrete reason, as John has. "I wanted to, then" strikes John as not well thought out. Nick's reasons for going to war are complex. On his hospital bed in Milan, he was trying to discover himself what the answer to John's question was—and before John ever asked it. In part, he was eager to put even more distance between himself and his mother's house. But he was also drawn to the war as the ultimate test of manhood. Like Ernest Hemingway, Nick had matured at a time when Theodore Roosevelt's belief that manhood had to test itself was dominant. Roosevelt had helped rally American support for entering World War I, but the death of his son in the war would alter profoundly his confidence that it was noble and fitting to die for one's country. Nick's views about death in battle—especially his own death in battle—are markedly different from those that Hemingway offered his family from his Milan hospital bed in a letter of 18 October 1918. He tells them that he is determined to stay until the war has ended. "Dying," he declared, "is a very simple thing. I've looked at death and I really know." As if he had just read Horace's famous ode with the line *dulce et decorum est pro patria mori* ("'Tis sweet and glorious to die for fatherland," Bk. 3.2, line 13), he declares that "the mother of a man that has died for his country should be the proudest woman in the world and the happiest" (*Letters* 19). There was more than a little bravado in his letter and something of a cruel game with his mother. Nick's thoughts and words in "Now I Lay Me" indicate that Hemingway reflected on his war experience more deeply and more honestly in the story than he had in the letter. In 1920 Hemingway wrote "The Tale of Orpen," an apprentice fantasy in which a wounded British soldier in the war dreams first that he is in Valhalla, where the heroes are bored by the constant fighting they are supposed to enjoy, then proceeds to heaven, where (like Lord Nelson and other legendary heroes) he can acknowledge his love of garden and home, not battlefield. The legendary heroes crave the arms of their wives, not the arms of war. Matters are not so simple in "Now I Lay Me," but the arms of wives (John's wife and the wife that Nick does not have but John thinks he should get) and the arms of war provide an important tension—one that Hemingway would continue to treat. (See Bickford Sylvester's "The Sexual Impasse to Romantic Order in Hemingway's Fiction.") In 1922 Hemingway wrote his satirical poem "Roosevelt," exposing his boyhood hero for his military bravado. The reader of "Now I Lay Me" knows that Nick becomes a writer and that the effects of war—much more than the battles of war—are major topics of Nick's art.

280:26–40 **"We oughtn't to talk"** . . . **"sends them to me."** John's amazement at Nick's proffered reason for being in uniform has caused him to raise his speaking voice. Nick again cautions him to lower the volume, in part out of the wish to change the focus of the conversation from the sensitive area where it has gone. As he had before, John likens the sleeping Italian soldiers to pigs: they wouldn't understand what was being said, and so, John argues, Nick need not fear that his inner life is the focus of a large audience.

It is a happy irony of the narrative that Nick the writer is sharing his inner life with a large audience. Nick is grateful that John switches the topic to Nick's plans once he is back in the States. The plan is minimal: a job at a newspaper. While making clear that Nick is not returning to a woman (as John will), Nick's answer also makes overt the centrality of the metafictional core of the book. The work that the reader has in hand represents a kind of writing very different from journalism. But Nick is not sure that Chicago will be the place where he will return. John touts the writing of Arthur Brisbane (1864–1936), a name that in the 1920s would have resonated with most American readers of *Men Without Women*. Brisbane's career was unparalleled in American journalism. William Randolph Hearst had hired him away from Joseph Pulitzer; in 1900 he began editing Hearst's Chicago newspaper, the *American*, and did so until his death. He was most famous for his syndicated column "Today," the column that John's wife clips and sends him. Even more than John's wife, Brisbane was "making good money." That John finds him a "great writer" indicates John's inadequacy as a critic. The more knowing saw numerous faults and mocked the "Brisbanalities." Some of those individuals may have recognized an amused link to "Banal Story." Nick will aim at a very different kind of writing.

280:41–281:2 **"How are your kids?" . . . "hell of a note."** Neither Brisbane nor Chicago sports pages much interest Nick. Family is the concept that has held his attention—as he looks back and as he looks forward. So he asks about John's children. Ever practical, John counts the children as the bonus that kept him from having to stay on the front lines. Traditionalist that he is, as the father of three daughters, he wants a son. It is not surprising that in a collection called *Men Without Women* we would encounter few children, but this story (like "Ten Indians") contains poignant moments about the frailty of childhood. Nick's "I'm glad you've got them" provides a wistful note that contrasts with the attitude of the American man in "Hills Like White Elephants," who wants his girl to have an abortion.

281:3–11 **"Why don't you try" . . . "don't think so."** The conversation has progressed to its most intimate. John senses that there is indeed a difference between their situations: "Imagine a young fellow like you not to sleep." All in all, John is feeling quite fortunate. And he attempts to play healer: "You got anything on your mind?" Though Nick denies that he has, the reader has felt the weight of that burden.

281:12–35 **"You ought to get married" . . . "sleep, Signor Tenente."** The emotional progression of the exchange between the two men and the advice that John now gives Nick parallel the conversation between Nick and Bill in "The Three-Day Blow" in *In Our Time*. Bill, however, had shared a good deal more with Nick than John has, and he knows in fact a good deal of Nick's complicated feelings about his family (Nick's attitude toward his father surfaced in that conversation in front of the fireplace) and about his recent courtship with Marge, a relationship that Bill had encouraged Nick to end. Touting the preferred state of male friendship, Bill had declared: "Once a man's married he's absolutely bitched" (90). Here, John gives the opposite advice. If Nick were to marry, he "wouldn't worry." Like Bill, John tries to give advice practical application, though he sounds as callow as Bill in doing so. Marry for money, he advises. He argues that Nick has all the right credentials: he is good looking, has been wounded "a couple of times," and has been decorated for valor. John recommends an Italian girl with money. His case for an Italian ("the way they're brought up") parallels the too confident lady of "A Canary for One" and her confidence in the superiority of American husbands. John's chauvinistic declaration that Nick doesn't need to talk to them, needs only to marry them, invites a crass substitute for "marry." The attentive reader will recall the failure of the husband in "Canary" to talk to his wife—and perhaps the failure of husbands to talk with wives in "Cat in the Rain" and "Out of Season" in *In Our Time*.

Nick is polite, but he has abundant reason to be skeptical of John's declaration: "A man ought to be married. You'll never regret it. Every man ought to be married." As he gently brings their conversation to an end, Nick promises to remember John's advice, and that remembrance provides an ominous aspect of the remembering that is at the core of the story. John's admonition that Nick get some sleep is not a wish that Nick seeks—not on this anxious night.

281:36–40 I heard him . . . in the leaves. Whereas in "The Three-Day Blow" Nick and George can set the Marge business aside (at least temporarily) by going outside, armed like hunters, into the bracing wind, Nick here returns to his mental exercises. Those exercises in careful listening recapture the rhythms that opened the story. Nick's mental discipline is striking as he eventually ceases to listen to John's snoring ("like pigs," in John's lexicon) and turns instead to the gnawing of the silkworms and to their droppings.

281:40–43 I had a new thing . . . with my prayers. Against the relentless natural process of living and dying that the worms represent, Nick keeps his promise to John by contemplating all the girls he has ever known and what kind of wives they would make. The theoretical exercise leads to no preference but eventually seems like a distraction from the greater pleasure of fishing and the more noble enterprise of prayer.

281:44–282:4 Finally, though, I went back . . . almost altogether. Because the streams remain ever new while the girls of Nick's remembering soon lose their distinctiveness, Nick in the final story of the collection almost seems destined to remain one of the men without women. He confesses to giving up thinking about them "almost altogether."

282:4–11 But I kept on . . . fix up everything. St. Paul admonishes believers to pray without ceasing (1 Thess. 5.17), and Nick in the hospital continues in that mode. The modernist tension is nicely captured in the concluding lines of the story. Modernism is skeptical of the received wisdom of preceding centuries, certainly belief in prayer. Nick, skeptical about John's belief that marriage "would fix up everything," is of his time; there are no certitudes. He may even doubt the efficacy of prayer, though he holds to it as a useful exercise.

Whether as answer to Nick's prayer or otherwise, John is exempt from the October offensive, a relief to Nick. For others sleeping near them, the October offensive of 1917 would lead to calamitous defeat at Caporetto. (That retreat would be of crucial importance in Hemingway's *A Farewell to Arms*.)

For Nick, as the story ends, John's welfare remains a concern. There has apparently been no change in his relationships with the others for whom he has been praying. The bond in the foreground of this story is the one created by the reality of war. The twice wounded Nick, in the hospital in Milan, continues his slow recovery several months later. John's visit is in keeping with his sympathy for Nick on those nights with the silkworms. He is sorry that Nick has made no progress toward marriage—and would be even sorrier if he could visit Nick the writer of "Now I Lay Me," still unable to commit to marriage.

The affirmation at the end of the story comes from our sense of the success of Nick's being able to share with his readers the inner turmoil of that earlier time—but not in any affirmation of earlier formulas for a satisfactory life. "So far," he confesses, he has never married. It is Nick the artist who triumphs in "Now I Lay Me."

Where, then, does "Now I Lay Me" leave the reader who considers the fourteen stories of *Men Without Women* as a work with a modernist unity, a work similar to *In Our Time* in its collective force? Having begun with a long story that makes no mention of female presence and portrays a male defining himself through his art in the corrida, the arena where man tests his courage against powerful beast, *Men Without Women* ends with a story where the protagonist is haunted by memories of a destructive female power. On his hospital pallet, Nick Adams must confront not only his brush with death on an Italian battlefield but the memories of his mother's challenges to his father's masculinity. In "In Another Country," an Italian major had warned of another kind of threat to a man who aligns himself to a woman: he puts himself in a position with the potential for severe emotional trauma should the woman die. Is a man's life better without commitment to a woman, a life such as the bullfighter Manuel appears to have chosen? Can fulfillment as an artist be enough?

Several of the men in the book are without commitment to a woman. The major in "A Simple Enquiry" is frankly homosexual, but the rules of the military culture and his national culture are such that he is doomed to sexual frustration. William Campbell in "A Pursuit Race" runs his race alone, plagued by demons sometimes starkly sexual and misogynistic. Al and Max in "The Killers" have defined themselves outside all norms of conventional life, choosing to be "killers." In "Today Is Friday," Jesus of Nazareth, whose commitment is to a cause rather than to a woman is the victim of a brutal and undeserved killing and dies with a valor that validates his life. But "his girl" (we are meant to think Mary Magdalene) had remained at the cross with the other women, who then observed Jesus' burial and on the third day went to annoint his body, discovering that it was gone. In Mark's Gospel (16.9) and John's (20.11–17), Jesus appears first to Mary Magdalene. She then conveys the news to the disciples. Hemingway's "the women stuck by him" points to this dimension of the biblical narrative.

Other men in *Men Without Women* have found happiness with a woman, but that happiness did not last. Besides the major in "In Another Country," who lost his wife when pneumonia ended their brief marriage, there is the American man of "Hills Like White Elephants," who judges fatherhood incompatible with the life he wishes to lead, creating a defining separation between himself and his partner. With sorrow, the narrator of "A Canary for One" and his wife are separating, no longer able to communicate or even talk to each other. In "Ten Indians" Dr. Adams sleeps alone, legally married for many years, but as "Now I Lay Me" clearly enunciates, now a man essentially alone and lonely.

Men Without Women, however, provides a more complex picture. Against the Adams marriage, "Ten Indians" places Mr. and Mrs. Garner, happily traveling together, emotionally together. The narrator's wife in "A Canary for One" accepts that her marriage has ended, but she can revisit its early joys, and whatever her present bitterness, she does not deny what she had. And though Jack Brennan in "Fifty Grand" focuses his energy on defending his honor and manhood in the boxing ring, he is fully committed to his wife and daughters. Jack is a man absolutely dependent on his wife: he is needy of female presence. (Readers familiar with Hemingway's biography know that he shared this need with Brennan: Hemingway married young and never divorced a wife until the replacement was waiting.) The reader of *Men Without Women* who has also read *In Our Time* already knows from "Cross Country Snow" what Nick's orderly of "Now I Lay Me" does not: Nick indeed marries and comes to accept fatherhood as compatible with his marriage. With the challenge of his art, he is willing to accept the risks of marriage, risks that the stories indicate are many. Symbolically, we find them in "An Alpine Idyll," where the Swiss peasant unthinkingly places the lantern in the jaw of his dead wife. Though he loves her, he has forgotten her personhood, suggesting that in death as in life he had taken her role as server for granted. The narrator of the story has needed the reminder as he and his companion return from mountain skiing, pleased with a season of male camaraderie, ready to return to obligations and possibilities. They are like the male travelers of "Che Ti Dice la Patria?" who are happy to be back in France where men can still find love and where artists can freely practice their craft.

Although the final story of *Men Without Women* ends with Nick mocking his orderly's belief that marriage "would fix up everything," the book as a whole cautions us against seeing him as a confirmed misogynist. Still unmarried, Nick is in the world beyond the hospital and practicing the craft of writing. In his writing, he is probing his own fears about his masculinity, probing the complexities of the human heart, seeking to understand men who shun commitment to women, and men who have made such commitments. He knows that there are no simple answers. Now metaphorically fishing the swamps that he eschewed in "Big Two-Hearted River," the final story of *In Our Time,* Nick will be able to take further risks in art and in love.

WORKS CITED

Anderson, Sherwood. *Winesburg, Ohio.* 1919. New York: Penguin Books, 1996.

Aristotle. *Poetics.* Tr. Gerald F. Else. Ann Arbor: University of Michigan Press, 1960.

Arnold, Matthew. "Dover Beach." *Poetical Works.* New York: Oxford University Press, 1950.

Baker, Carlos. *Ernest Hemingway: A Life Story.* New York: Charles Scribner's Sons, 1969.

Beegel, Susan F. "The Death of El Espartero: An Historic Matador Links 'The Undefeated' and *Death in the Afternoon.*" *Hemingway Review* 5.2 (Spring 1986): 12–23.

Bender, Bert. *The Descent of Love.* Philadelphia: University of Pennsylvania Press, 1996.

Blackmore, Susan. "Out-of-Body Experiences." *The Encyclopedia of the Paranormal.* Amherst, NY: Prometheus Books, 1996. 471–83.

Bloom, Harold, ed. *Ernest Hemingway.* New York: Chelsea House, 2005.

Brontë, Emily. *Wuthering Heights.* 1847. New York: W. W. Norton, 1963.

Brooks, Cleanth, and Robert Penn Warren. *Understanding Fiction.* New York: Appleton-Century-Crofts, 1943.

Browne, Thomas. *The Garden of Cyrus.* 1642. In *Religio Medici and Other Writings.* New York: E. P. Dutton & Co., 1951. 185–260.

Chaucer, Geoffrey. *The Poetical Works of Chaucer.* Ed. F. N. Robinson. Boston: Houghton Mifflin Company, 1933.

Comley, Nancy R., and Robert Scholes. *Hemingway's Genders.* New Haven, CT: Yale University Press, 1994.

Connolly, Cyril. Review of *Men Without Women. New Statesman,* 26 November 1927: 208.

Crane, Stephen. "The Blue Hotel." 1899. *The Red Badge of Courage and Other Writings.* Boston: Houghton-Mifflin, 1960. 251–78.

Dalzell, Tom, and Terry Victor, eds. *The New Partridge Dictionary of Slang and Unconventional English.* Vol. 2. London and New York: Routledge, 2006.

Darwin, Charles. *The Descent of Man and Selection in Relation to Sex.* 1871. Princeton, NJ: Princeton University Press, 1981.

Dodd, Lee Wilson. Review of *Men Without Women. Saturday Review of Literature,* 19 November 1927: 322–23.

Dolch, Martin, and John V. Hagopian. "The Killers." *Insight I: Analyses of American Literature.* Ed. John V. Hagopian and Martin Dolch. Frankfurt-am-Main: Hirschgraben, 1962. 99–103.

Dolch, Martin, John V. Hagopian, and W. Gordon Cunliffe. "A Canary for One." *Insight I: Analyses of American Literature.* Ed. John V. Hagopian and Martin Dolch. Frankfurt-am-Main: Hirschgraben, 1962. 96–99.

Donaldson, Scott. *By Force of Will: The Life and Art of Ernest Hemingway.* New York: Viking Press, 1977.

———. "Preparing for the End: Hemingway's Revisions of 'A Canary for One.'" *Studies in American Fiction* 6 (Autumn 1978): 203–11.

Donne, John. "Problem XL, Why Doth the Poxe Soe Much Affect to Undermine the Nose?" 1633. *The Complete Poems and Selected Prose.* Ed. Charles M. Coffin. New York: Modern Library, 1952. 295–96.

Dubus, Andre. *Meditations from a Movable Chair.* New York: Knopf, 1998.

Dunbar, Paul Laurence. "Sympathy." *The American Tradition in Literature* II. 11th ed. Ed. George B. Perkins and Barbara Perkins. Boston: McGraw Hill, 2007. 859–60.

Eliot, T. S. *The Love Song of J. Alfred Prufrock.* 1917. *Collected Poems, 1909–1962.* New York: Harcourt, Brace, 1963. 3–7.

———. *The Waste Land.* 1922. *Collected Poems, 1909–1962.* New York: Harcourt, Brace, 1963. 37–55.

Emerson, Ralph Waldo. "The American Scholar." *Essays and Lectures.* New York: The Library of America, 1983. 51–71.

Fontana, Ernest. "A Pursuit Race." *Explicator* 42 (1984): 43–45.

Frost, Robert. "After Apple-Picking." *The Poetry of Robert Frost: The Collected Poems.* Ed. Edward Lathen. New York: Henry Holt and Company, 1969. 68–69.

———. "Birches." *The Poetry of Robert Frost: The Collected Poems.* Ed. Edward Lathen. New York: Henry Holt and Company, 1969. 121–22.

———. "Home Burial." *The Poetry of Robert Frost: The Collected Poems.* Ed. Edward Lathen. New York: Henry Holt and Company, 1969. 51–55.

———. "Mending Wall." *The Poetry of Robert Frost: The Collected Poems.* Ed. Edward Lathen. New York: Henry Holt and Company, 1969. 33–34.

———. "Once by the Pacific." *The Poetry of Robert Frost: The Collected Poems.* Ed. Edward Lathen. New York: Henry Holt and Company, 1969. 250.

Gibbs, A. Hamilton. *Soundings.* Boston: Little, Brown, and Company. 1925.

Green, Jonathon, ed. *Cassell's Dictionary of Slang.* 2nd ed. London: Weidenfeld & Nicholson, 2005.

Hardy, Thomas. *Tess of the D'Urbervilles.* 1891. Boston: Houghton, Mifflin, 1960.

Hemingway, Ernest. "The Capital of the World." 1936. *The Complete Short Stories of Ernest Hemingway.* The Finca Vigía Edition. New York: Charles Scribner's Sons, 1987. 29–38.

———. *Dateline: Toronto: The Complete "Toronto Star" Dispatches, 1920–24.* Ed. William White. New York: Charles Scribner's Sons, 1985.

———. *Death in the Afternoon.* 1932. New York: Charles Scribner's Sons, 1960.

———. *A Farewell to Arms.* 1929. New York: Charles Scribner's Sons, 1949.

———. *For Whom the Bell Tolls.* 1940. New York: Charles Scribner's Sons, 1960.

———. *Green Hills of Africa.* 1935. New York: Charles Scribner's Sons, 1935.

———. *In Our Time.* 1925. *The Complete Short Stories of Ernest Hemingway.* The Finca Vigía Edition. New York: Charles Scribner's Sons, 1987. 63–181.

———. "Italy, 1927." *New Republic* 50 (18 May 1927): 350–53.

———. *Men Without Women.* 1927. *The Complete Short Stories of Ernest Hemingway.* The Finca Vigía Edition. New York: Charles Scribner's Sons, 1987. 183–282.

———. *A Moveable Feast.* 1964. New York: Charles Scribner's Sons, 1964.

———. *The Old Man and the Sea.* New York: Charles Scribner's Sons, 1952.

———. "Roosevelt." *Complete Poems.* Ed. Nicholas Gerogiannis. Lincoln: University of Nebraska Press, 1979. 45.

————. *Selected Letters, 1917–1961.* Ed. Carlos Baker. New York: Charles Scribner's Sons, 1981.

————. "The Short Happy Life of Francis Macomber." 1938. *The Complete Short Stories of Ernest Hemingway.* The Finca Vigía Edition. New York: Charles Scribner's Sons, 1987. 5–28.

————. "The Snows of Kilimanjaro." 1938. *The Complete Short Stories of Ernest Hemingway.* The Finca Vigía Edition. New York: Charles Scribner's Sons, 1987. 39–56.

————. *The Sun Also Rises.* 1926. New York: Charles Scribner's Sons, 1954.

————. "The Tale of Orpen." John F. Kennedy Library Hemingway Collection, Item # 445. 17.

————. "Three Shots." *The Nick Adams Stories.* New York: Charles Scribner's Sons, 1972. 3–6.

————. *The Torrents of Spring.* New York: Charles Scribner's Sons, 1926.

————. "Up in Michigan." 1923. *The Complete Short Stories of Ernest Hemingway.* The Finca Vigía Edition. New York: Charles Scribner's Sons, 1987. 59–62.

————. *Winner Take Nothing.* 1933. *The Complete Short Stories of Ernest Hemingway.* The Finca Vigía Edition. New York: Charles Scribner's Sons, 1987. 283–377.

The Holy Bible, King James Version. New York: Oxford University Press, 1945.

Horace. *The Odes and Epodes,* with English translation by C. E. Bennett. Cambridge: Harvard University Press, 1968.

James, Henry. *Daisy Miller.* New York: Harper and Brothers, 1904.

————. *Washington Square.* 1880. New York: Thomas Y. Crowell, 1970.

Joyce, James. *Dubliners.* 1914. New York: Modern Library, 1969.

Judson, J. Richard. *Rubens: The Passion of the Christ,* Part VI, Corpus Rubenianum Ludwig Burchard. Turnhout, Belgium: Harvey Miller, 2000.

Keats, John. "Ode to a Nightingale." 1819. *The Complete Poetry and Selected Prose of John Keats.* Ed. Harold Edgar Briggs. New York: Modern Library, 1951.

Kert, Bernice. *The Hemingway Women.* New York: W. W. Norton, 1983.

Krutch, Joseph Wood. Review of *Men Without Women. Nation,* 16 November 1927: 548.

Kvam, Wayne E. "Hemingway's Banal Story." *Fitzgerald/Hemingway Annual* 1974. Ed. Matthew J. Bruccoli and C. E. Frazer Clark Jr. 181–91.

Lawrence, D. H. *The Prussian Officer and Other Stories.* London: Duckworth & Co., 1914. 1–33.

Lewine, Edward. *Death and the Sun: A Matador's Season in the Heart of Spain.* London: Black Swan, 2005.

Lewis, Robert W. "Hemingway in Italy: Making It Up." *Journal of Modern Literature* 9 (1981–82): 209–36.

Lowerson, John. "Bowls and Bowling." *Encyclopedia of World Sport: From Ancient Times to the Present.* Ed. David Levinson and Karen Christiansen. Santa Barbara, CA: ABC-CLIO, Inc., 1996. 139–47.

Lynn, Kenneth. *Hemingway.* New York: Simon and Schuster, 1987.

Marlowe, Christopher. *The Jew of Malta.* 1589. Baltimore, MD: Johns Hopkins University Press, 1978.

Mellow, James R. *Hemingway: A Life Without Consequences.* Boston: Houghton Mifflin, 1992.

Melville, Herman. 1853. "Bartleby, the Scrivener." *Billy Budd and Other Tales.* New York: New American Library, 1961. 103–40.

————. *Billy Budd.* 1924. *Billy Budd and Other Tales.* New York: New American Library, 1961. 7–88.

————. *The Confidence Man: His Masquerade.* 1857. Indianapolis, IN: Bobbs-Merrill, 1967.

Mencken, H. L. Review of *Men Without Women. American Mercury,* 28 May 1928: 127.

————. Review of *Men Without Women. Time* 10, 24 October, 1927: 38.

Monteiro, George. "The Writer on Vocation: Hemingway's 'Banal Story.'" *Hemingway's Neglected Short Fiction*. Ed. Susan F. Beegel. Ann Arbor: UMI Research Press, 1989. 141–48.

Montgomery, Constance Cappel. *Hemingway in Michigan*. New York: Fleet, 1966.

Montgomery, Paul. "Hemingway and Guy Hickok in Italy: *The Brooklyn Eagle* Articles." *Hemingway Review* 25.1 (2005): 112–18.

Noyes, Alfred. "The Barrel-Organ." *Collected Poems*. London: John Murray, 1966. 22–24.

Oliver, Charles M. *Ernest Hemingway A to Z: The Essential Reference to the Life and Work*. New York: Facts on File, 1999.

O'Neill, Eugene. *Ah, Wilderness!* 1933. *The Plays of Eugene O'Neill*. Vol. 2. New York: Random House, 1955. 158–298.

Owen, Wilfrid. "Dulce Et Decorum Est." *Modern British Poetry*. Ed. Louis Untermeyer. New York: Harcourt, Brace, 1950. 359–60.

Perkins, George, Barbara Perkins, and Phillip Leininger, eds. *Benét's Reader's Encyclopedia of American Literature*. New York: Harper Collins, 1991.

Pound, Ezra. "Ballad of the Goodly Fere." 1909. *Poems and Translations*. New York: The Library of America, 2003. 109–11.

Rascoe, Burton. Review of *Men Without Women*. *Bookman*, September 1927: 90.

Reynolds, Michael. *Hemingway: The American Homecoming*. Cambridge: Blackwell, 1992.

———. *Hemingway: The Paris Years*. Cambridge: Blackwell, 1989.

———. *Hemingway's Reading, 1910–1940: An Inventory*. Princeton, NJ: Princeton University Press, 1981.

Sartre, Jean-Paul. *No Exit and Three Other Plays*. New York: Vintage, 1955.

Schulberg, Budd. *The Harder They Fall*. New York: Random House, 1947.

———. *Sparring with Hemingway and Other Legends of the Fight Game*. New York: Random House, 1995.

Shakespeare, William. *Hamlet. The Complete Works*. Ed. G. B. Harrison. New York: Harcourt, Brace, 1952. 885–934.

———. *King Lear. The Complete Works*. Ed. G. B. Harrison. New York: Harcourt, Brace, 1952.

———. *Macbeth. The Complete Works*. Ed. G. B. Harrison. New York: Harcourt, Brace, 1952.

Smith, Julian. "Hemingway and the Thing Left Out." *Journal of Modern Literature I* (1970): 169–72; rpt. in *The Short Stories of Ernest Hemingway: Critical Essays*. Ed. Jackson J. Benson. Durham, NC: Duke University Press, 1975. 135–47.

Smith, Paul. *A Reader's Guide to the Short Stories of Ernest Hemingway*. Boston: G. K. Hall, 1989.

Spilka, Mark. *Hemingway's Quarrel with Androgyny*. Lincoln: University of Nebraska Press, 1990.

Sterne, Laurence. *Tristram Shandy*. 1759. Rutland, VT: C. E. Tuttle, 2000.

Stevens, Wallace. "Sunday Morning." 1923. *The Collected Poems of Wallace Stevens*. New York: Alfred A. Knopf, 1974. 66–70.

Sylvester, Bickford. "The Sexual Impasse to Romantic Order in Hemingway's Fiction: *A Farewell to Arms, Othello*, 'Orpen,' and the Hemingway Canon." *Hemingway: Up in Michigan Perspectives*. Ed. Frederic J. Svoboda and Joseph J. Waldmeir. East Lansing: Michigan State University Press, 1995. 177–87.

Twain, Mark. 1884. *Adventures of Huckleberry Finn*. Cambridge: Riverside Press, 1958.

Warsh, Cheryl Krasnick. "Keeley, Leslie Enrought, 1832–1910." *Alcohol and Temperance in Modern History: An International Encyclopedia*. Vol. I. Ed. Jack S. Blocker, Daniel M. Fahey, and Ian R. Tyrrell. Santa Barbara, CA: ABC-CLIO, Inc., 2003. 346–47.

————. "Keeley Institutes." *Alcohol and Temperance in Modern History: An International Encyclopedia.* Vol. I. Ed. Jack S. Blocker, Daniel M. Fahey, and Ian R. Tyrrell. Santa Barbara, CA: ABC-CLIO, Inc., 2003. 347–49.

Williams, Wirt. *The Tragic Art of Ernest Hemingway.* Baton Rouge: Louisiana State University Press, 1981.

Wilson, Edmund. "The Sportsman's Tragedy." *New Republic,* 14 December 1927: 102–3.

Woolf, Virginia. "An Essay in Criticism." Review of *Men Without Women. New York Herald Tribune Books,* 9 October 1927: 1, 8.

Yanella, Philip R. "Notes on the Manuscript, Date, and Sources of Hemingway's 'Banal Story.'" *Fitzgerald/Hemingway Annual* 1974. Ed. Matthew J. Bruccoli and C. E. Frazer Clark Jr. 176.

ADDITIONAL RELATED READINGS

Beegel, Susan F. *Hemingway's Craft of Omission: Four Manuscript Examples.* Ann Arbor: UMI Research Press, 1988.

Benson, Jackson J., ed. *New Critical Approaches to the Short Stories of Ernest Hemingway.* Durham, NC: Duke University Press, 1990.

————. *The Short Stories of Ernest Hemingway.* Durham, NC: Duke University Press, 1975.

DeFalco, Joseph. *The Hero in Hemingway's Short Stories.* Pittsburgh, PA: University of Pittsburgh Press, 1968.

Flora, Joseph M. *Ernest Hemingway: A Study of the Short Fiction.* Boston: Twayne, 1989.

————. *Hemingway's Nick Adams.* Baton Rouge: Louisiana State University Press, 1982.

Jain, S. P. *Hemingway: A Study of His Short Stories.* New Delhi: Gulab Zazirani for Arnold-Heinemann, 1985.

Johnson, Kenneth G. *The Tip of the Iceberg: Hemingway and the Short Story.* Greenwood, FL: Penkeville, 1987.

Waldhorn, Arthur. *A Reader's Guide to Ernest Hemingway.* New York: Farrar, Straus and Giroux, 1972.

INDEX

Locators in **bold** indicate chapter span of each story. Names of fictional characters are alphabetized by first name.

Cappel, Constance Montgomery, xiv

Cassell's Dictionary of Slang (Green, ed.), 47

"Cat in the Rain" (Hemingway), 174

"Che Ti Dice La Patria?" (Hemingway), **70–80**; ending of, 78; *Men Without Women,* placement in, 73; stylistic devices in, 78, 80; themes and images in, 72, 73–74, 75, 77, 78–79, 157; weather in, 78

Chicago Tribune, 88

children, 174

Christianity, 154

cigarettes, 7, 12, 18, 19, 171, 172

"Clean, Well-Lighted Place, A" (Hemingway), 23, 128, 137, 152

Cohn, Irving, 76

coleta (pigtail), 7, 10, 13, 14, 28, 29

colors: in "Che Ti Dice La Patria?", 73; in "Today is Friday," 146; in "The Undefeated," 17, 18, 20, 23, 24

combat theme, 147

confession, 87

confidence, 34

Confidence Man, The (Melville), 34

Connolly, Cyril, x

Coolidge, Calvin, 158

Corbett, Jim, 89

Crane, Stephen, 5, 61

"Cross-Country Snow" (Hemingway), 7, 33, 105, 133, 177

Crucifixion, 28, 145, 148, 150, 152, 153

cuadrilla, 9

"Daisy Miller" (James), 128

Dalzell, Tom, 47

D'Annunzio, Gabriele, 70

darkness, 3, 14, 116

Darwin, Charles, 114

"Day's Wait, A" (Hemingway), 116

death, 162

Death in the Afternoon (Hemingway), xii; banderilleros in, 21; bull ranch role in, 7; bullfights in, 8, 9, 17; homosexuality in, 110; matadors in, 11, 13; picadors and, 9; *varra* (pic) in, 19

Death and the Sun (Lewine), 10, 162

deception, 119

delirium tremens, 112, 141, 142, 143

Dempsey, Jack, 88

Descent of Love, The (Bender), 114

Descent of Man and Selection in Relation to Sex (Darwin), 114

desire, 42, 104, 109, 110

dialogue, 78, 82, 83, 170

division, 52

"Doctor and the Doctor's Wife, The" (Hemingway), xiii, 96, 115, 116, 117, 168

doctors, 33–34

Dodd, Lee Wilson, x

Dolch, Martin, 54

Donaldson, Scott, 81, 128, 154

Donne, John, 35–36

Douglas, Alfred, 108

"Dover Beach" (Arnold), 32

drinking: alcoholism, 112, 141, 143; attention to in *Men Without Women,* 171; in "A Canary for One," 133; in "Fifty Grand," 95, 139; in "Hills Like White Elephants," 43, 45–46; in *In Our Time,* 171; in "Now I Lay Me," 171; in "A Pursuit Race," 139; in "Ten Indians," 95; in "Today is Friday," 146, 149, 150, 152. *See also* delirium tremens

Dubliners (Joyce), 111, 120

Dubus, Andre, 32, 40–41, 111

Dunbar, Paul Laurence, 123

dust, 72, 73, 77, 79

dying, 172–73

eating, 73–74, 78–79, 164–65

Ebro Valley (Spain), 43

electric lights, 32, 116, 140

Elevation of the Cross, The (Rubens), 150

Eliot, T. S., xiii; epigraph for "A Portrait of a Lady," 31; portrayal of Jesus in *The Waste Land,* 145; *The Waste Land* in *Men Without Women,* 38, 47, 66, 139, 152, 165

Ellison, Ralph, 32

Emerson, Ralph Waldo, 156

"End of Something, The" (Hemingway), 47

Eucharist, 146

Farewell to Arms, A (Hemingway): ending of, 41, 50; Frederic Henry in, 6, 33, 37, 39, 41, 64; *Jew of Malta* and, 31; stylistic devices in, 50; themes and images in, 6, 33, 37, 64, 79–80; women's sacrifice in, 49

Fascism, 70

Fauré, Gabriel, 144

feminine perspectives, 42

"Fifty Grand" (Hemingway), **81–103**; anti-Semitism in, 82, 89, 93, 100; critics and, 88; drinking in, 95; ending of, 103; Jack Brennan in,

80, 82, 90, 158; marriage in, 176–77; sleep in, 87, 89, 92, 95, 96; stylistic devices of, 81, 82, 83, 84–85, 86, 87; themes and images in, 81, 82, 83, 86, 91, 100; weather in, 98–99

First Forty-Nine Stories, The (Hemingway), 146

Fitzgerald, F. Scott, ix, 31, 158

Fontana, Ernest, 140

Forum (magazine), 155, 156, 157, 158–60

Frederic Henry *(A Farewell to Arms)*, 6, 33, 37, 39, 41, 64

Frost, Robert, 77, 128, 132, 135

Fuentes ("The Undefeated"), 16, 22

"Gambler, the Nun, and the Radio, The" (Hemingway), 40

"Game of Chess, A" (Eliot), 152

ganaderia (bull ranch), 7

Garcia, Antonio, 6

Garcia, Manuel "Maera," xii, 4, 160, 162

Garden of Eden, 50

Gardner, Ava, 54

gender roles, 51

genre, 146

Gibbs, A. Hamilton, 159

Gospels, 49, 50, 146, 147, 148–49

Green, Jonathon, 47

Green Hills of Africa (Hemingway), 34

guilt, 153

Gulagar, Clu, 54

Haba, Antonio de la "Zurito," 10, 12

Hagopian, John, 54

Hall, Ernest, 167

Hamlet (Shakespeare), 168

hands, 12, 14, 34, 107, 109

"Hands" (Anderson), 104

happiness, 140

Harder They Fall, The (Schulberg), 88

Hardy, Thomas, 22

Harold Krebs ("Soldier's Home"), 67

Harry ("Snows of Kilimanjaro"), 33

Hearst, William Randolph, 173

heartbreak, 120–21, 122, 126. *See also* beloved (during war)

Heliogabalus, 35

hell, 69, 152, 153

Hemingway, Clarence E., xiii, 116, 167

Hemingway, Ernest: bullfights and, 3, 9, 16, 161; in Canada, 157; on dying, 172–73; "In Another Country," writing of, 39; family home,

xiii–xiv; journeys and, 70; loneliness and self-doubt of, 95; marriages of, 177; paintings and, 4; racism and, 59–60, 153–54; religion and, 145–46, 154; themes and images in his writing, 33, 50, 140; view of his own writing, 25; works as embodiment of, 4; writing styles and methods of, 23, 33, 132, 146. *See also* individual works by

Hemingway, Grace Hall, xiii, 113, 126, 128, 156, 167

Hemingway, Hadley (was Richardson), xiii, 42, 87, 95, 126–27, 129, 146

Hemingway, John "Bumby," 95

Hemingway, Marcelline (later Sanford), 128–29

"Hemingway and Guy Hickok in Italy" (Montgomery), 70

Hemingway in Michigan (Montgomery), 113

Hemingway (Reynolds), 42, 70

Hemingway Society, 129

Henderson, Archibald, 159

Henry, O., 54

Henry's (lunchroom in "The Killers"), 54–55, 61, 68

Hickok, Guy, 70, 75

hills imagery, 44, 46

"Hills Like White Elephants" (Hemingway), xii, 42–53; abortion discussed in, 44, 46–49, 50; comparisons to other stories, 73, 123, 140, 143, 174; drinking in, 43, 44–46, 52; ending of, 110; gender roles in, 51; genre and, 146; images in, 43, 44, 46, 48, 52, 53, 73, 74; Jig in, 47; pregnancy in, 44, 48, 49, 52, 53; stylistic devices in, 47, 50, 51, 52, 53, 84–85, 170; themes in, 43, 52, 54, 56, 176; *The Waste Land* in, 47

Hindmarsh, Harry, 157

"Home Burial" (Frost), 135

homosexuality, 60, 62, 108–10, 176

Hotchner, A. E., 54

huckleberries, 117

Huckleberry Finn (Twain), 112

humor, 138, 147

Hunt, Holman, 4

"In Another Country" (Hemingway), 31–41; comparisons to other stories, 161; Dubus and, 40–41; medical experiments in, 38–39; stylistic devices in, 32; themes and images in, 33–34, 35–36, 65, 147, 176; *The Waste Land* in, 38; women in, 31, 37, 49; World War I in, 31; writing of, 39

In Our Time (Hemingway), xiii; bullfights in, 3; drinking in, 171; ending of, 163; Hemingway's life and, 4; interchapters of, 160; Manuel Garcia in, 4; Nick Adams in, 55, 67

"Indian Camp" (Hemingway), 16, 40, 67, 120, 164

innocence, 65, 111

insomnia. *See* sleep, sleeplessness

"Italy 1927" (Hemingway), 70, 75

Jack Brennan ("Fifty Grand"), 80, 82, 90, 158

Jake Barnes (*The Sun Also Rises*), x, 4, 42

James, Henry, xii, 127, 128

Jesus of Nazareth, 145, 148–49, 152, 176

Jew of Malta, The (Marlowe), 31

Jewish heritage, 56, 62

Jig ("Hills Like White Elephants"), 47

Joe Garner ("Ten Indians"), 111

Johnson, Jack, 88

Joselito, 161, 162

Joyce, James, xi, 111, 120, 158

Judas Iscariot, 145

Keats, John, 166, 167

Keeley, Leslie, 141

Keeley Institute, 141

Kert, Bernice, 42

"Killers, The" (Hemingway), **54–69**; Al in, 60; comparisons to other stories, 61, 138, 143, 149; ending of, 68–69; Henry's, 54–55, 61, 68; homosexual innuendos in, 60, 62; images in, 61, 63, 64, 69; Jewish heritage in, 56, 62; Nick Adams in, 65; Ole Andreson in, 61; placement in *Men Without Women,* 54; as a prototype Hemingway story, 54; stylistic devices in, 60, 65, 66, 67, 69, 170; themes in, 54, 56, 65, 81, 140, 176; title of, 147; waiting in, 54, 61, 63, 64, 69; *The Waste Land* in, 66; women in, 66

Killers, The (movie), 54

King Lear (Shakespeare), 69

Krutch, Joseph Wood, x

Kvam, Wayne, 157

Lancaster, Burt, 54

Lardner, Ring, 88

"Last Good Country, The" (Hemingway), 116

Lawrence, D. H., 104, 110

Leach, H. G., 155

lebensraum. *See* living spaces

Lewine, Edward, 10, 162

Lewis, Kid, 89

light images, 116. *See also* electric lights

"Light of the World, The" (Hemingway), 104

Light of the World, The (Hunt), 4

liquor. *See* drinking

listening, 82, 130, 134, 135–36

Little Review, 155

Liveright, Horace, 93

living spaces, 157

Liz Coates ("Up in Michigan"), 47

Lowerson, John, 71

luck, 5–6

Lynn, Kenneth, xi, 93

Macbeth (Shakespeare), 66, 68

Maera (Manuel Garcia), xii, 4, 160, 162

"Maison Tellier, La" (Maupassant), 104

Man Nobody Knows, The (B. Barton), 149

manhood, 158

Manuel Garcia (*In Our Time*), 4

Manuel Garcia ("The Undefeated"): *coleta* and, 7, 10, 13, 14, 28, 29; enduring and, 82; face of, 13; historical reference for, 4; sleep and, 12; stance in the ring, 22–23; wound of, 7

Mariposa (bull) ("The Undefeated"), 6–7

Marlowe, Christopher, 31

marriage, 176–77

Marvin, Lee, 54

masculine perspectives, 42

matadors, xii, 11, 12, 13, 18

Maupassant, Guy de, 104

meals, 62, 63, 73–74, 78–79

medical experiments, 38–39

Melville, Herman, 34, 39, 66, 81, 140

Mencken, H. L., x

Men Without Women (Hemingway), ix–xi; America as subtext in, 156; children in, 174; death in, 162; drinking in, 171; foreign locales in, 31; gender perspective in, 42; reckonings in, 152; redemption in, 164; sleep and sleeplessness in, 89, 140, 171; story placement in, 3, 54, 73, 111, 138, 155, 162; stylistic devices of, 71, 74, 163, 176; suffering and, 136; themes and images in, 87, 104, 153, 155, 156, 158, 173; *The Waste Land* in, 38, 47, 66, 139, 152, 165; women in, 31, 37, 68; World War I in, 33, 162

men without women (theme): in "A Canary for One," 176, 177; in "Hills Like White Elephants," 176; in "In Another Country," 176; in "The Killers," 176; in "Now I Lay Me," 163, 170, 175, 176, 177; in "A Pursuit Race," 138, 142, 176; in "A Simple Enquiry," 176; in "Ten Indians," 114, 120, 176, 177; in "Today is Friday," 176; in "The Undefeated," 3

"Mending Wall" (Frost), 128

metafiction, 155, 161, 173

Miguel Retana ("The Undefeated"), 4–5, 60

Mike Campbell *(The Sun Also Rises),* 139

money, 81, 83, 86

Monteiro, George, 156, 157, 158

Montgomery, Constance Cappel, 111, 113

Montgomery, Paul, 70

Moveable Feast, A (Hemingway), 7, 32, 155

muleta, 23

Mussolini, Benito, 77

New Partridge Dictionary of Slang and Unconventional English (Dalzell and Victor, eds.), 47

New Republic, 70

Nicene Creed, 152

Nick Adams, x; in "The Battler," 7, 33, 65; in *In Our Time,* 55, 67; in "The Killers," 65; in "Ten Indians," 112

No Exit (Sartre), 69

noses, 35–36, 105, 143

Nouvelle Revue français, La, 81

novilladas, 8, 9

"Now I Lay Me" (Hemingway), xiii–xiv, 163–77; cigarettes in, 171, 172; comparisons to other stories, 148, 166, 168, 170, 171, 173, 174; drinking in, 171; ending of, 163, 177; prayer in, 166, 169–70; redemption in, 164; sleeplessness in, 89, 140, 144, 166–67, 170–71, 172; stylistic devices in, 111, 163, 165, 166, 170, 177; themes and images in, 3, 163, 164, 170, 172, 173, 175, 176, 177; *The Waste Land* in, 165; World War I in, 170, 172, 175

Noyes, Alfred, 141

October offensive of 1917, 175

"Ode to a Nightingale" (Keats), 166, 167

Old Man and the Sea, The (Hemingway), 6, 150

Ole Andreson ("The Killers"), 61

Oliver, Charles, xiii

"Once by the Pacific" (Frost), 77

O'Neill, Eugene, 112

"Out of Season" (Hemingway), 174

Owen, Wilfred, 162

Parker, Dorothy, 158

Passion story, 91, 146

patriotism, 37

Perkins, Maxwell, ix–x, xi

Personal Recollections of Joan of Arc (Twain), 159

Petoskey (MI), 117

Pfeiffer, Pauline, 42, 87, 95, 146, 153

picadors, xii, 9, 17, 19

Picasso, Pablo, 159

Pie Jesu (Fauré), 144

Pinin ("A Simple Enquiry"), 106, 107

Poetical Works of John Keats, The (Keats), 166

politics, 75

"Portrait of a Lady, A" (Eliot), 31

Pound, Ezra, 145

prayer, 166, 169–70

pregnancy, 44, 48, 49, 52, 53

prose poetry, 132, 166

Prudence Mitchell ("Ten Indians"), 111

"Prussian Officer, The" (Lawrence), 104, 110

Puerta del Sol (Madrid), xii, 9

Pulitzer, Joseph, 173

"Pursuit Race, A" (Hemingway), 138–44, 146, 170, 176

racism, racial epithets: in "Fifty Grand," 82, 89, 93, 100; in "The Killers," 59–60; in "Today is Friday," 148, 153

rain, 98–99, 161

"Ransom of the Red Chief, The" (Henry), 54

Rascoe, Burton, x

Reagan, Ronald, 54

reckonings, 152

redemption, 164

religion, 145–46, 154

repetition: in "An Alpine Idyll," 132; in "A Canary for One," 130; in "Fifty Grand," 84–85; Hemingway's use of, 23; in "Hills Like White Elephants," 47, 51, 52, 53, 84–85; in "The Killers," 60, 69; in "Now I Lay Me," 165; in "A Pursuit Race," 140, 143; in "A Simple Enquiry," 105, 109; in "The Undefeated," 5, 18, 19, 23, 27, 28

resignation, 90

resurrection, 40

Reynolds, Michael S., 42, 70, 93, 123, 130, 166

Tristam Shandy (Sterne), 35–36
Twain, Mark, 112, 159
Typee (Melville), 34

"Undefeated, The" (Hemingway), xii, 3–30, 78; banderilleros in, 20–21; cigarettes in, 19; comparisons to other stories, 3–4; confession in, 87; critics and, 88; Fuentes in, 16, 22; images in, 17, 18, 20, 23, 24, 26; Manuel Garcia in. *See* Manuel Garcia ("The Undefeated"); Mariposa (bull), 6–7; *Men Without Women,* placement in, 3; Miguel Retana in, 4–5, 60; picadors in, 9; stylistic devices of, 5, 18, 19, 23, 27, 28, 29–30, 32; themes in, 3, 5, 14, 20, 25, 27, 29, 82; as tragedy, 30, 103; waiters in, 11–12; Zurito's hands and, 34, 112
undefeated theme, 20, 25, 27, 29, 102, 151
Understanding Fiction (Brooks & Warren), 65
"Up in Michigan" (Hemingway), 47, 159

Van Dyke, Henry, 158
vara, 19
verb tense, 66
"Very Short Story, A" (Hemingway), 78
Victor, Terry, 47

waiting, 54, 61, 63, 64, 69, 87
Walcott, Joe, 100
Walsh, Ernest, 7
war, xiv, 32, 35–36, 39, 40, 173. *See also* World War I
Warren, Robert Penn, 65, 68
Warsh, Cheryl Krasnick, 141
Washington Square (James), 127
Waste Land, The (Eliot), xiii; in "Hills Like White Elephants," 47; in "In Another Country," 38;

in "The Killers," 66; in *Men Without Women,* 38, 47, 66, 139, 152, 165; in "Now I Lay Me," 165; portrayal of Jesus in, 145; in "A Pursuit Race," 139; in "Today is Friday," 152
weather, 77, 78, 98–99, 105. *See also* rain; snow
white elephants, 44, 49
Wilde, Oscar, 108
Willard, Jess, 88, 89
Willard-Dempsey fight, 88
William Campbell ("A Pursuit Race"), 139
Williams, Wirt, 30, 161
Wilson, Edmund, x
Windemere cottage, xiii, 113, 116, 126
Winesburg, Ohio (Anderson), 104
Winner Take Nothing (Hemingway), 23, 40
women: in "Cross-Country Snow," 133; in *A Farewell to Arms,* 49; feminine perspectives and, 42; in "In Another Country," 31, 37, 49; in "The Killers," 66; in *Men Without Women,* 31, 37, 68; sacrifice and, 49
World War I: in "In Another Country," 31; mechanized warfare and, 33; in *Men Without Women,* 33, 162; in "Now I Lay Me," 170, 172, 175; in "A Simple Enquiry," 104, 105; trench warfare and, 105
Woolf, Virginia, x, xii
wounds, 7, 27, 29, 32–33, 35
Wuthering Heights (Brontë), 49

Yannella, Philip, 157
"Yes, We Have No Bananas" (Silver & Cohn), 76
Youmans, Vincent, 122

Zurito (Antonio de la Haba), 10, 12
Zurito ("The Undefeated"), xii, 10, 12–17, 18–20, 30, 34, 112